Also AVAILABLE IN THE *GENTLE ART* SERIES

BOOKS

The Gentle Art of Verbal Self-Defense
More on the Gentle Art of Verbal Self-Defense
The Last Word on the Gentle Art of Verbal Self-Defense
Success with the Gentle Art of Verbal Self-Defense
Staying Well with the Gentle Art of Verbal Self-Defense
Genderspeak: Men, Women, and the Gentle Art of Verbal Self-Defense

AUDIO PROGRAMS

Mastering the Gentle Art of Verbal Self-Defense
Success with the Gentle Art of Verbal Self-Defense
The Gentle Art of Verbal Self-Defense for Parents and Kids
The Gentle Art of Verbal Self-Defense for Parents and Teenagers

The Gentle Art of
WRITTEN
SELF-DEFENSE

Suzette Haden Elgin

MJF BOOKS

NEW YORK

Published by MJF Books
Fine Communications
Two Lincoln Square
60 West 66th Street
New York, NY 10023

Library of Congress Catalogue Card # 95-82179
ISBN 1-56731-113-X

This edition is reprinted by arrangement with Prentice-Hall Inc./Career & Personal
Development.

Manufactured in the United States of America

MJF Books and the MJF colophon are trademarks of Fine Creative Media, Inc.

10 9 8 7 6 5 4 3 2 1

Preface

The book you're about to read is part of a series devoted to the *Gentle Art of Verbal Self-Defense*, a system for improving communication. If you already know the *Gentle Art* system well, the book will show you new ways to use your knowledge. If you're new to the *Gentle Art*, that's not a problem; you'll find everything you need, including an overview of the system, provided for you here.

- There are times when you need to transmit a particular message in an effort to set things right—but you know that a face-to-face (or phone-to-phone) encounter would be a truly negative experience for everyone involved.

- There are times when the <u>last</u> thing you want and the thing you most dread is a live interaction with someone—but you really want to communicate with that person all the same, and you want more control over your message than you can get from sending a greeting card or a potted plant.

- There are times when things have gone so badly that you're afraid there <u>are</u> no words that can make them better, but the alternative—just giving up—is unacceptable (or unbearable) or is ruled out by factors beyond your control.

For all those times, the best solution is usually a <u>letter</u>, whether it serves as the final step you take or only prepares the way for a spoken exchange later on.

This book is written for everyone who has ever had to write a difficult letter, and for everyone who has wished they could but has had to settle instead for the sorry consequences of silence. It will show you how to use the *Gentle Art of Verbal Self-Defense* when you write—so that although there will still be difficult situations, there will no longer be any difficult letters.

My grateful thanks go to Virginia Satir, to John Grinder, to Thomas Gordon, to Leonard Newmark, and to the many other scholars and researchers whose work laid the foundation on which mine is based. I am especially grateful to my editors, Ellen Schneid Coleman and Barbara O'Brien, who have been an unfailing source of help and encouragement. Thanks are due as always to my students, my clients, my readers (especially those who write me letters!), and to my long-suffering household. The responsibility for mistakes and omissions is mine and mine alone.

Suzette Haden Elgin, Ph.D.
Ozark Center for Language Studies
P.O. Box 1137
Huntsville, Arkansas 72740-1137

About This Book

Everybody does something regrettable once in a while, or inadvertently becomes involved when somebody <u>else</u> does something regretable. Maybe you *flubbed:* You thought you knew what to do and you did it, but you were wrong. Maybe you *floundered:* You didn't know what to do but you did something anyway, hoping for the best, and you were wrong. Maybe it wasn't your fault—maybe you became tangled in the effects of your own *frailties* or those of others. Maybe, as is usually true, the mess you face is a little bit of flubbing, a little bit of floundering, and a dash of frailty thrown in to top it off. Whatever the exact circumstances, *flubs* and *flounderings* and *frailties* add up to TRIPLE-F SITUATIONS.

And there you are. Wondering. What can you <u>do</u>? How can you <u>explain</u>? How can you make things right? What can you <u>say</u>? How do you even <u>begin</u>?

Begin with this book, which was written for just such dismaying situations, and follow the instructions it provides.

WHAT YOU'LL FIND IN THIS BOOK

- Fifty model letters to be used in Triple-F situations...when the flubs, flounderings, and frailties that plague every human life threaten to become overwhelming

- Instructions for adapting any of the model letters to your own personal Triple-F situations

- A simple and effective TRIPLE-F <u>pattern</u>, to help you write your own original Triple-F letters with ease

- A careful analysis of each model letter that makes clear why and how it works as it does

- A <u>fifty-first</u> letter, as a bonus, that you can send as a <u>gift</u>

- A brief punctuation guide, written by a linguist, that will put an end to punctuation errors in your letters <u>forever</u>

- A brief guide to <u>formatting</u> your letters

- A glossary that explains every word or phrase in the book that might be unfamiliar to you

- A list of Triple-F letter topics, to help you choose the letter you need

- An index, to help you when you're not <u>sure</u> what you need, or can't remember where in the book you saw it.

- An overview of the system (the *Gentle Art of Verbal Self-Defense*) on which the book is based.

And that's not all . . .

You'll also find more than one hundred model letters for <u>routine</u> business situations, included here for your convenience—plus a pattern for generating original business letters of your own.

How to Use This Book

Use it as a reference, as you would any letter book. Read it quickly, to become familiar with what it offers you. Put it on your bookshelf, ready and waiting for the day you find yourself in a Triple-F situation. Then take it down and use its handy features to locate the letter you want to send.

Use it as a guide to developing superb letter-writing skills—and letter-writing strategies—that will give you a substantial advantage in both your professional and your personal life. Read through it quickly to get an idea of its contents and approach. Then go back and work through each chapter in detail, at your own speed.

Use it (and give a copy to others to use) as you would a good novel—for the simple pleasure of reading it!

How This Book Is Different from Other Letter Books

1. The situations for which Triple-F Letters are written rarely appear in letter books; this book is written for human beings.

2. The letter-generating patterns in this book represent high technology, the technology of contemporary linguistic science. This book is written for <u>twenty-first</u> <u>century</u> human beings.

3. The foundation of this book is the *Gentle Art of Verbal Self-Defense*, a scientifically based system for improved communications.

The *Gentle Art* has been tested for more than a quarter of a century and has helped hundreds of thousands of people to achieve their full communication potential.

Welcome to *The Gentle Art of Written Self-Defense Letter Book . . .*

Contents

Preface v

About This Book vii

Triple-F Letter Topics xx

CHAPTER ONE

Beyond the Basket of Fruit: When You Should Write a Letter Instead, 1

Life's Little Catastrophes 2

What Do You Do Now?: Why You Need This Letter Book 3

Welcome to the Real World! 6

CHAPTER TWO

"I Didn't Mean to Do It . . .": Triple-F Scenario One, 9

Letter 1—Flub: You Closed Someone Else's Deal, 10

Analysis of Letter 1 11

Using the Power of Presuppositions, 13 / Presuppositions and Possessives, 14 / Presuppositions and Nominalization, 15 / Presuppositions and Factives, 17 / To Apologize or Not to Apologize, 18 / What Letter 1 Does for You, 20

Supplementary Letters 22

Letter 2—Flub: You've Announced Someone Else's Plan, 22

Letter 3—Flub: You've Announced Someone Else's News, 22

CHAPTER THREE

"I'm Not the Kind of Person Who Does That Kind of Thing!": Triple-F Scenario Two, 24

Letter 4—Flub: You've Mistreated Someone's Heirloom, 25

Analysis of Letter 4 26

> *Hedges—and Hedge-Clipping, 27 | Shifting Sentence Focus, 28 | "As You Know" Strategy, 33*

The Triple-F Letter Pattern 34
Custom-Tailoring Your Letters 36
Supplementary Letters 39

Letter 5—Flub: You've Exposed Someone's Past—In Front of Her Inlaws, 39

Letter 6—Flub: You've Damaged Someone's Prized Possession, 40

CHAPTER FOUR

"If I'd Only Known . . .": Triple-F Scenario Three, 41

Letter 7—Flub: You've Ranted About the Unemployed—In Front of Your Unemployed Brother-in-Law, 43

Analysis of Letter 7 44

> *Using the Satir Modes, 45 | Making Exceptions, 49*

Letter 8—Flub: You've Griped About the Disabled—In Front of a Client with a Disabled Child, 49

Getting to Computer Mode: Three Resources 50

> *Resource #1—Use the "Third Person," 51 | Resource #2— Use the Focus Shift, 51 | Resource #3—Use Indefinites and Generics, 53*

Supplementary Letters 53

*Letter 9—Flub: You've Cut Down the Wrong Three Acres
of Trees, 53*

*Letter 10—Flounder: You Said You'd Show Them 'Round Your
Town—But You Didn't Mean It, 54*

CHAPTER FIVE

"I'm Only Human . . . ":
Triple-F Scenario Four, 56

*Letter 11—Flub and Frailty: You Forgot—and Broke—Your
Promise to a Valued Customer; Version 1: Neutral Mode, 57*

Analysis of Letter 11, Version 1 58

Letter 11, Version 2: Touch Mode, 60

Analysis of Letter 11, Version 2 61

> *Using the Sensory Modes, 62*

Letter 11, Version 3: Sight Mode, 67

Letter 11, Version 4: Hearing Mode, 68

Supplementary Letters 69

*Letter 12—Flub and Frailty: You've Given Away the Job You
Promised to a Friend, 69*

*Letter 13—Flub and Frailty: You've Spent the Money You
Owe a Friend, 70*

CHAPTER SIX

"It's Out of My Hands . . . ":
Triple-F Scenario Five, 72

Letter 14—Frailty: There Will Be a Dress Code After All, 73

Analysis of Letter 14 74

Using Parallelism, 77 | Warning: Allow for Dominance Displays!, 80 | Providing an Illusion of Choice, 81

Letter 15—Frailty: The Training Sessions Won't Be Optional After All, 82

Analysis of Letter 15 82

Supplementary Letters 85

Letter 16—Frailty: The Health Insurance Deductible Will Go Up After All, 85

Letter 17—Frailty: You Have to Sell the Family Farm After All, 86

CHAPTER SEVEN

"I Got Part of It Right . . . ":
Triple-F Scenario Six, 87

Letter 18—You Need to Write a Cover Letter, 88

Letter 19—Flub: You've Been Quoted—But the Words Weren't Your Own, 88

Analysis of Letter 18 89

Analysis of Letter 19 90

Metaphors and How to Use Them, 93 | Using Quotations Safely and Effectively, 96

Letter 20—Flub: You've Quoted Somebody—Incorrectly, 97

Letter 21—Flub: You've Quoted Lincoln—But the Words Are Jefferson's, 98

CHAPTER EIGHT

"It Just Slipped My Mind . . . ":
Triple-F Scenario Seven, 100

Letter 22—Flub and Flounder: You Took All the Credit—for a Team Effort; Version 1: Informal, 101

Analysis of Letter 22, Version 1 102

Writing in Code, 103 | More About Metaphors and How to Use Them, 105 | The Formality Continuum, 108

Letter 22, Version 2: Formal, 109

Supplementary Letters 110

Letter 23—Flub and Flounder: You Failed to Give Credit Where Credit Was Due, 110

Letter 24—Flub and Frailty: You've Failed to Acknowledge Help With Your Research, 111

CHAPTER NINE

"I Can't Imagine How This Happened!": Triple-F Scenario Eight, 113

Letter 25—Flub and Frailty: You've Left a Colleague's Work Out of Your Bibliography; Version 1: Informal, 114

Analysis of Letter 25, Version 1 115

Writing Carefully Crafted Truths, 117

Letter 25, Version 2: Formal, 120

Analysis of Letter 25, Version 2 121

What "Awkward" Really Means, 125

Supplementary Letters 126

Letter 26—Flub and Frailty: You've Left a Committee Member Out of Your Press Release, 126

Letter 27—Flub and Frailty: You've Left the Local Expert Off Your Panel, 127

CHAPTER TEN

"I Could Cut My Tongue Out": Triple-F Scenario Nine, 129

Letter 28—Flub and Frailty: You've Made a Sexist Remark to a Visiting V.I.P., 130

Analysis of Letter 28 131

> *English Verbal Attack Patterns (VAPs), 133 | Using the Personal Anecdote, 136 | Using the "Group" Compliment, 137 | A Warning About VAPs in Written Language, 138 | Writing Responses to Verbal Attacks, 139*

Letter 29—Let's Talk This Over, 139

Supplementary Letters 141

Letter 30—Flub: You've Called Your Doctor a Quack—in Front of the Staff, 139

Letter 31 (to a mother-in-law)—Flub: You've Said Terrible Things About Her—and She Knows, 142

CHAPTER ELEVEN

"But I Never Dreamed You Were Serious!": Triple-F Scenario Ten, 144

Letter 32—Flub and Frailty: You've Got to Cancel—Much Too Late, 145

Analysis of Letter 32 146

> *Presuppositions and Time Words, 148 | Laying Paper Trails, 150*

Letter 33—Flub: You've Got to Cancel—Immediately!, 150

Letter 34—You've Got to Lay a Paper Trail: Letter, 151

Letter 35—You've Got to Lay a Paper Trail: Memo, 153

Letter 36—Flub and Frailty: You Can't Make That Speech After All, 154

Letter 37—Flub: You Shouldn't Have Volunteered Your Spouse, 155

CHAPTER TWELVE

"It's Not My Fault!": Triple-F Scenario Eleven, 156

Letter 38—Flub and Frailty: You've Got to Correct a Colleague's Foolish Mistake, 157

Analysis of Letter 38 158

Using and Avoiding Trojan Horses, 158

Triple-F Scenario, Continued 160

Analysis, Continued 161

Writing Disclaimers, 162

Letter 39—Answering the Furious Response to Letter 38, 163

Analysis of Letter 39 164

Supplementary Letters 166

Letter 40—Flub and Frailty: You've Got to Overrule a Colleague's Offer to a Customer, 166

Letter 41—Flub and Frailty: You've Got to Take Back a Job Offer, 167

CHAPTER THIRTEEN

"Somebody Was Supposed to Tell You . . . ": Triple-F Scenario Twelve, 169

Letter 42—Frailty: She Won't Be Getting the Award After All— and You've Got to Tell Her; Version 1: Leveler Mode, 171

Analysis of Letter 42, Version 1 171

Letter 42, Version 2: Computer Mode, 175

The Man/Woman Communication Problem—Overview . . . 176

Supplementary Letters 178

*Letter 43—Frailty: He Won't Be Getting the Promotion After
All—and You Have to Tell Him, 178*

*Letter 44—Frailty: She Won't Be Giving the Speech After All—
and You Have to Tell Her, 179*

CHAPTER FOURTEEN

"I'd Give My Right Arm Not to Have to Tell You This": Triple-F Scenario Thirteen, 180

*Letter 45—Frailty: You've Got to Tell a Respected Colleague
that He Must Retire, 182*

Analysis of Letter 45 183

Using Punctuation to Achieve Effects, 186

*Letter 46—Frailty: You've Got to Tell a Colleague to Shape Up—
or Else, 188*

Triple-F Scenario Fourteen 189

*Letter 47—Frailty: You've Got to Tell a Colleague to Shape Up—
Please, 190*

Using Three-Part Messages to Express Complaints 191

Supplementary Letters 193

*Letter 48—Frailty: His Speech Was Full of Errors—and You
Have to Tell Him, 193*

*Letter 49—Frailty: She Can't Sing the Solo Any More—and You
Have to Tell Her, 194*

Letter 50—Flub and Frailty: You Said "I Love You," But You Don't, 195

CHAPTER FIFTEEN

Beyond the Small Appliance: The Letter as Gift, 197
Bonus Chapter

Letter 51—The Gentle Art of Crafting a Gift, 198

Analysis of Letter 51 200

Appendix A: More Than One Hundred Routine Letters, 205

Appendix B: A Brief Guide to Punctuation, 245

Appendix C: Glossary, 249

Appendix D: The Gentle Art of Verbal Self-Defense—
    an Overview, 254

Index, 262

TRIPLE-F LETTER TOPICS

IN THIS SITUATION . . .	TURN TO MODEL LETTER . . .

**When you have been,
or appear to be**

callous and uncaring	5, 7, 8, 28, 31
careless or forgetful	4, 6, 4, 11, 25, 26, 27
discourteous	10, 30, 31
prejudiced and elitist	7, 8, 28
selfish and arrogant	7, 8, 22, 23
sexist	28, 42, 31
untrustworthy	1, 6, 9, 11, 12, 13, 14, 15, 16, 17
weak and spineless	13, 32, 42

**When you have embarassed
or hurt or insulted**

a colleague	25, 8
your company, university, organization, etc.	19, 20, 21, 24
your doctor, lawyer, etc.	30
a family member	7, 31
a friend	5, 12, 13
your boss or other superior	28
your host or hostess	4

When you need to

lay a paper trail	34, 35
respond to someone's verbal abuse	29
write a cover letter	18
write "in code"	22

When you have been

careless with someone's property	4, 6, 9

IN THIS SITUATION . . .   **TURN TO MODEL LETTER . . .**

careless with the facts   19, 20, 21, 26, 27

When you have said

something abusive or cruel   28, 30, 31

something you're
ashamed of   28, 31

something that was an
error of fact   19, 20, 21

"I love you"—but you
don't love him or her   50

When you have failed

to keep a promise   10, 11, 12, 14, 15, 16, 17, 36
to pay a debt   13
to put safeguards in place   11, 12, 45, 46
to foresee a serious problem   14, 15, 16, 17
to be a team player   22, 23
to remember something
important   11, 12, 24, 25, 26, 27

When you have

made a careless commitment
you can't follow through on   10, 32, 33, 36, 37

committed someone else to
something, unwisely   37

given away information
others wanted kept
confidential   2, 3, 5

given in to a foolish
impulse   13

made a foolish public
"speech"   7, 8, 28

offended your community's
pride   27

spoiled someone's plans   1, 2, 3

IN THIS SITUATION . . .	**TURN TO MODEL LETTER . . .**
used something for the wrong purpose	4
made a serious real-world error	4, 9, 1
violated your own principles	13
let down a valued customer	11
said yes when you should have said no	32, 33, 36
procrastinated too long	32, 44, 45
violated customs in your field	24, 25, 26, 27
When you want to write a routine business letter	More than one hundred routine letters, pages 209–244

Chapter One

Beyond the Basket of Fruit

When You Should Write a Letter Instead

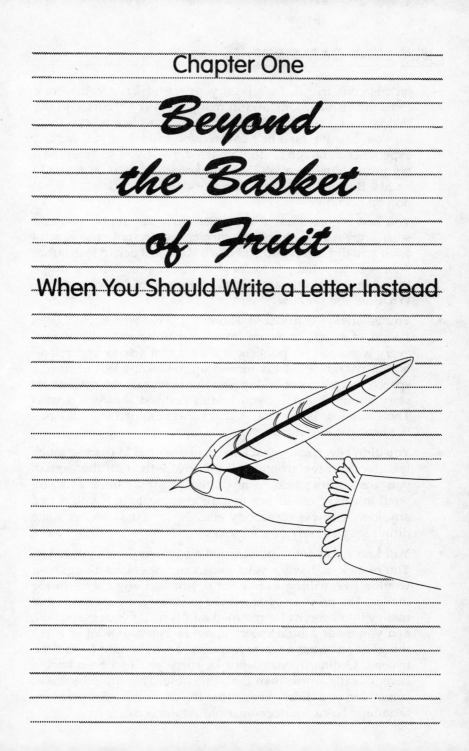

LIFE'S LITTLE CATASTROPHES

- Jack is your friend. He's been your friend since you were a clerk in the mailroom, and in many ways it's accurate to say that he took you <u>out</u> of the mailroom. He's always been there for you. Many a time he's covered for you when you weren't experienced enough to do it yourself. Now you've accepted a big promotion—to a job that you know Jack was sure would be his. But you have to go on working with Jack . . . . What do you do now?

- You had a great time at the office party last night. You had such a great time that this morning you're not sure exactly what you <u>did</u> last night. Still, it's a bit of a shock to learn from your secretary that you told a visiting vice-president she ought to be at home taking care of her kids instead of "playing office." What do you do now?

- You've always considered Thoreau a great writer. He's been a kind of hobby of yours for a long time, and you've read every word he ever published. It's easy for you to understand how a paragraph of his turned up, unacknowledged, in the speech you gave last Friday. But until you saw the newspaper story about your talk, you hadn't realized that you'd used Thoreau's words. Naturally, <u>that</u> paragraph had to be the one the newspaper quoted . . . .

- You didn't even know that Larry had divorced Marianne, much less that he'd remarried. And you really thought the woman you were sitting next to at dinner <u>was</u> Marianne. . . . you wouldn't have called her that all evening long if you'd had any idea she was somebody else. Now you know why she didn't laugh at any of your jokes . . . .

- You know you got a little carried away over lunch yesterday. You're sick of having your tax money spent on things you wouldn't be willing to pay for if you had any choice in the matter. The news story about the government putting all that money into benefits for retarded adults made your blood boil, and you made a little speech about it. You said a lot of harsh things about what a waste it was, and what ought to be done instead. Ordinarily you'd just be sorry you had been such a bore. But it's worse than that, this time. This time there was something you didn't know: that the client your firm was entertaining has a fourteen-year-old retarded daughter. . . .

- It's true that your mother-in-law weighs more than the current cultural ideal. It's true that she spends more time at the doctor's office than is reasonable for a woman as healthy as she is. It's even true that she has a tendency to whine. But you never dreamed she'd hear about your saying any of those things! The idea that your sister would go straight home, call her up, and tell her what you'd said never entered your head. You thought you could <u>trust</u> your sister, but you were very wrong. . . .

- It never occurred to you—when you told the couple you met at the convention that you could get them an appointment with your CEO—that they'd take you up on it. It was just idle conversation; you never expected to hear from them again. And now you've got this card from them saying they'll be in town next week and want to talk to your boss, and you can't possibly deliver. He'd have your head on a platter if you even <u>suggested</u> that he talk to them about their fundraising project. . . .

WHAT DO YOU DO NOW?

Why You Need This Letter Book

In all of these examples and the thousands more like them that clutter up real life, the "What do I do now?" question has to be answered. Talking to the other person face to face, or even on the phone, would be a hellish ordeal; you want to avoid that if it's humanly possible. But you want to do <u>something</u>. You could send a card . . . one of those new "sensitive" ones. You could send flowers. You could send one of those wicker platters of dried fruit. Or a nice basket of fancy pears. Or a couple of tickets to a show. . . .

You could do those things. That's true. But here's a much better answer. YOU COULD WRITE A LETTER. Anybody can send a basket of pears—all you have to do is pick up the phone and order it done. It's not as if you grew them yourself and made the basket with your own two hands. Letters are different. Letters are special. For at least the following five reasons:

- So few people write personal letters today, let alone <u>good</u> ones, that they provide a genuine "touch of class." Like a brief, snappy, to-the-point speech, letters make you stand out as someone who is exceptional and deserving of unusual respect.

- Letters are <u>truly</u> personal. Writing a letter yourself demonstrates clearly that you're willing to invest some of your own resources of time and energy.

- Letters completely eliminate the problem of Loss Of Face. People who would feel forced to respond to you angrily or defensively in person or on the phone—to preserve their image, or for other reasons—can read a letter, react naturally in privacy, and recover their composure without embarrassment.

- Letters don't require you to think on your feet, the way you'd have to in a conversation. You can make a letter perfect before you send it. And with today's computers—even if you write the final version by hand—making it perfect doesn't mean you have to copy it over and over and over again.

- Letters are forever. They don't have to be thrown out in a couple of days, the way flowers do; they don't get eaten the way fruit does. They can't be distorted, or forgotten, the way spoken words can. A letter can be taken out and read again; a letter can be put away and treasured. When you care enough to <u>write</u> "the very best," and write it yourself, that means something. That's not trivial, or temporary.

There's just one problem: Writing letters tends to be as foreign an action for people today as driving to town in a horse-drawn buggy. And for many of the same reasons. Once upon a time every educated adult knew how to hitch horses to a buggy. Then modern technology came along with much faster methods for moving people and things from place to place. Once upon a time every educated adult knew how to write graceful and effective letters—and then modern technology came along with much faster methods for moving messages from person to person. But the two situations have important differences. Getting out on the freeway with a buggy and team would certainly make you late for your meeting, would probably get you arrested, and might very well get you killed. Writing a letter, on the other hand, is dangerous only if you do it badly. This book will make it possible for you to do it <u>well</u>.

Scores of letter books are available today, and many of them are best-sellers. They cover a huge set of standard (and stodgy) business scenarios, plus the occasional personal letter to be written at the office. They contain letters to say you're opening a business, promoting somebody, changing your prices, hiring or firing somebody, offering a new product, demanding payment for the first (or the fourth and last) time, congratulating a colleague on an award, and so on. All those useful things and hundreds more like them. Because people today get no training in writing any letters except the ones counselors make them write home from camp, they *need* these letter books.

But what about all the nonstandard (and nonstodgy) situations? What about all the times when you've done something awful in your professional or your personal life, or become tangled in the awful doings of someone else? Where are the letter books to help you when something dreadful has <u>happened</u> and everybody around you is too embarrassed to mention it, but nobody is able to forget it? Where are the letter books you can turn to when you've made one of the multitude of errors that are part of everybody's life, even with all of us doing our best to avoid them?

People need a book for <u>those</u> situations . . . a book of letters that can be written and sent when things have gone terribly wrong. A book of letters for personal and professional flubs, flounderings, and frailties: what we might call "Triple-F" situations. People do blunder . . . it's the nature of human beings to blunder. And then, not knowing what to do, they tend to adopt one of three very counterproductive strategic positions:

The Magic Ostrich Strategy

"I couldn't have done that. . . . I'm not that kind of person. Let's just all pretend I <u>didn't</u> do it."

The Outraged Lamb Strategy

"I did that, yeah. But I'm not that kind of person. I could only have done that if people suckered me into it or forced me to do it. And they have a lot of <u>nerve</u>, getting me into a mess like this!"

The Worthless Worm Strategy

"I did that. I can't believe it, but I did it. It's awful. And <u>I'm</u> awful. And I can never look anybody in the eye again as long as I live."

(The indirect variations on these strategies are "I couldn't have gotten involved in that," "I did get involved in that, yeah, <u>but</u> . . ."

and "I got involved in that. I can't believe it, and I'll never be able to forgive myself for it, but I did get involved.")

When people take the role of the Magic Ostrich, the Outraged Lamb, or the Worthless Worm, things don't get better. What happens instead is communication breakdown and massive pollution of their language environment. And years later when somebody asks why they and Joe (or Jane) don't get along, they may not even remember that it all started when somebody goofed and nobody knew how to set things right with Jane (or Joe) afterward.

WELCOME TO THE REAL WORLD!

Flubs—when you thought you knew what to do and you did it, but you were wrong—<u>will</u> happen. Flounderings—when you knew you didn't know what to do, but you did something anyway, and it was wrong—<u>will</u> take place. For example:

- when you fired Joe, and you realize you shouldn't have done it, and you need to get him back;

- when you quoted your customer a price for your product that you can't possibly deliver on;

- when you lost the file and you hadn't made a backup;

- when you said "I love you," but you don't;

- when you sent letters to two people, with information that should have been confidential—but you put the letters in the wrong envelopes;

- when you used a doodad on your hosts' coffee table for an ashtray, and then learned that it was a valuable antique intended only to be <u>looked</u> at;

- when you said the story was off the record, but somehow it got published anyway;

- when you had forgotten that your partner's pregnancy was supposed to be a secret, and you announced it in a meeting;

- when you found yourself backed into a corner and—in simple panic—you lied and claimed the problem was Jane's fault;

- when you promised Joe a job because you couldn't think of any way to refuse him, and now you can't follow through on it;

- when your brother showed you his new baby and the child was so ugly that you were caught off guard, and you laughed;

- when you borrowed Jack's copier because yours was broken, and then you broke that one, too;

- when you told your doctor you would never be back, and then realized you wanted an appointment.

Frailties—when you become involved in a foul-up, even though you didn't do anything wrong yourself—will be part of people's lives and the lives of those around them. For example:

- when you won the award Joe was absolutely sure he would be winning . . . or got the promotion Jane was absolutely sure would be hers;

- when you promised you'd bring the lobster, and then there wasn't any lobster to be had anywhere, and you had to arrive without it;

- when you were given a bad investment tip and you passed it on to your uncle, and now he's lost several thousand dollars;

- when the young man you invited to your dinner party as a table partner for your sister turned out to be a total loss, and had roving hands to boot;

- when you planned a big surprise party for Joe and Jane and invited all your mutual friends, and then you learned that they're getting a divorce;

- when your boss has ordered you to write a particular letter, and you've got to do it, but you'd rather be deep-fried.

This is the real world; this is the way it is. But the situation isn't hopeless. This book presents a system for writing letters in response to your own Triple-F situations. Letters that let you handle those situations efficiently, effectively, and with no loss of face on either side. No more trying to paint goofs over or paint them another color; no more dragging them around forever as part of life's baggage. No more cards and plants that provoke only "Well, that was the least you could do, and I'll bet you didn't even pick it out yourself!!" reactions. No more Magic Ostrich or Outraged Lamb. No more Worthless Worm.

What people want to do when something goes wrong in a human relationship is fix it. Set it right. Put it behind them forever and get on with their lives. This book makes that possible.

It's not just another collection of motivational platitudes. It's not just another collection of boilerplate pages. This book provides you with model letters, but it also teaches you how to change those letters to make them truly your own. And it shows you how to expand on the letters and tailor them to the multitude of Triple-F situations that don't appear in these pages because they come straight from <u>your</u> life.

This book is based on the proven concepts and strategies of the *Gentle Art of Verbal Self-Defense* system that has helped hundreds of thousands of people handle <u>spoken</u> confrontations successfully and confidently and with ease.[1] It can be trusted to get you through the day . . .

and through the night . . .

and through the Morning After.

---

[1] Readers who are unfamiliar with the *Gentle Art* system, or who need a quick review, will find an overview on page 254 at the end of this book.

Chapter Two

"I Didn't Mean to Do It..."

Triple-F Scenario One

Dear Professor Einstein:

If our promotions department had envisioned the effect of our product on your hair, I assure you we would never have sent a complimentary lifetime supply to your home. I will arrange to have the remaining one hundred twenty-six cases picked up immediat...

Regr...

P.J.F...

*L*ast night, you closed a terrific deal with Metamega Corporation. You went home delighted with yourself and amazed at how fast the transaction went from casual discussion to firm close. When you told your boss about it this morning, however, you learned that one of your colleagues had been working with the Metamega official for weeks and had considered the deal a sure thing—with his name on it. You're not willing to give up the new account and the benefits that go with it; after all, you're the one who actually made the sale. For all you know, your colleague was mistaken, and he would have lost the account to another firm if you hadn't stepped in.

But you know how Jack is going to perceive the situation. He's going to feel that you've stolen his account, even if he's a good sport about it on the surface. You have to go on working with him, and you'd rather not have him holding a grudge against you. WHAT DO YOU SAY IN YOUR LETTER?

You could do it this way . . .

Dear Jack,

I want you to hear this from me first: Last night I closed a terrific deal with Metamega Corporation. Carl tells me you've been working on that deal for weeks. That's a shock to me, and I'm sorry.

If I'd known the deal was one of your projects, I would have left it alone, but I didn't know. And now, unfortunately, it's too late to do anything about it. I hope you won't hold this against me, and that we can continue to be good friends as we have been in the past.

Sincerely,

You could do it that way—but I don't recommend it. You can do a lot better than that. Please look at Letter 1, below.

LETTER 1
Flub: You've Closed Someone Else's Deal

Dear Jack,

Last night at a civic meeting I ran into Joe Trino, from Metamega. We got to talking about Metamega's current needs, and before I went home we had closed a deal. We've got the Metamega account now for a two-year period, with an option to renew if all goes well.

My discovery this morning that the Metamega deal was something you'd been working on for weeks was a shock. I want you to know that I'm sorry. And I'm sure you know that if I'd had any idea the deal was a project of yours I would have left it strictly alone; I didn't know.

Jack, this is one of those things that just happens sometimes. It's clear that you and I need to find more time to sit down and discuss what we're doing, so we don't get our lines crossed like this in the future. In the meantime, we both know that what made it possible for me to close the deal so quickly and easily wasn't my superb salesmanship—it was the groundwork that you had already done. You have my thanks, and my apologies.

Sincerely,

Letter One is far more likely to achieve the results you want: giving Jack the facts; offering him your apology; and letting him know that you don't intend to give the account—or any part of the action—back to him. You can do this without turning Jack into a personal enemy, and without making him feel that he <u>has</u> to challenge you in order to save face. He may still be angry, but your letter will have made it possible for the two of you to go on working together until time can heal the wounds. The analysis below will explain how this was done, one paragraph at a time.

ANALYSIS OF LETTER 1

First Paragraph

Last night at a civic meeting I ran into Joe Trino, from Metamega. We got to talking about Metamega's current needs, and before I went home we had closed a deal. We've got the Metamega account now for a two-year period, with an option to renew if all goes well.

You've opened your letter with an immediate clear statement of the facts. Jack will learn what happened directly from you, instead of hearing about it through the company grapevine; that's important. But it doesn't say "I want you to hear this from me first," and that's important too. There are many situations when "I want you to hear this from me first" is a good idea. (See Letters 18 and 19, on page 88, for two examples.) But in this particular case you don't want to give Jack the impression that you've done something people would feel obligated to run tell him about. Your position is that you have nothing to hide and no reason to feel guilty.

We have a tendency to confuse the emotion of *regret* with the emotion of *guilt*, and it's a dangerous confusion. It's appropriate to regret that something has happened to cause another person distress, and to say you feel that way, but it's appropriate to feel guilt only when you are in fact directly or indirectly responsible for what happened. It's unfortunate that English uses the words "I'm sorry" to express both emotions. "I'm sorry it's raining" is one thing; "I'm sorry I broke your chainsaw" is quite another.

The paragraph above tells Jack that your meeting with Trino, and the discussion that followed, were <u>accidental</u>. "I ran into Joe Trino" and "we got to talking" accomplish that for you, making it clear that both were chance events rather than things you had planned. And finishing with "an option to renew if all goes well" points out to Jack, tactfully, that things <u>won't</u> go well if Metamega gets the impression that there's conflict in your firm over the deal. It lets you remind Jack that he's expected to function as a team player and help you keep the customer happy, without any need for you to challenge him by saying so directly.

Second Paragraph

My discovery this morning that the Metamega deal was something you'd been working on for weeks was a shock. I want you to know that I'm sorry. And I'm sure you know that if I'd had any idea the deal was a project of yours I would have left it strictly alone; I didn't know.

Take a close look at the first sentence in this section of the letter. It's a carefully structured sentence, and every part of it does double and triple work for you. And it brings us to the first *Gentle Art* technique to be discussed in this book.

USING THE POWER OF PRESUPPOSITIONS

Suppose I ask you if you cheat on your income taxes. That's a rude question, and it's wide open for either a yes or no answer. On the other hand, suppose I ask you if you've <u>stopped</u> cheating on your income taxes. That's equally rude, and again you can answer either yes or no, but there's a significant difference: the question is anything <u>but</u> wide open. You can say "Yes, I've stopped cheating" or "No, I haven't stopped cheating"; it makes no difference. Either way, you're admitting that you did cheat. Inescapably, to *stop* doing something means that at some point you *started* doing it. Chunks of meaning like that, understood by every native speaker but not present in the surface words of the sentence, are <u>presupposed</u>. That is: they are assumed to be true in advance and are taken as givens. The word "stop" presupposes the word "start," making "start" an inseparable part of its meaning.

In the same way, "Even <u>Bill</u> could close this deal" has as part of its meaning a presupposed sentence saying that Bill is no great shakes as a closer of deals. And if you add extra emphatic stress to the word "this"—"Even <u>Bill</u> could close <u>this</u> deal"—yet another presupposed statement is added to the meaning of the sentence. Every native speaker of English knows that "Even <u>Bill</u> could close <u>this</u> deal" says negative things about both Bill and the deal in question.

Presuppositions can be contradicted, sure, just as open claims can. You can respond to someone's "It's too hot in here" with "No, it's not," and you can challenge "Even <u>Bill</u> could close this deal" with "Wait a minute, Bill's not as bad as all that!" but it's <u>harder</u> to argue about things that are presupposed. Presupposed information will often sail right on by your reader when openly claimed information would be challenged. To use the power of presuppositions in your letters, follow this basic rule:

> ### ANYTHING YOU PREFER NOT TO ARGUE ABOUT SHOULD BE PRESUPPOSED.

For example: "You failed" is an open claim, and openly insulting; so is "You're careless." But suppose you write a letter that contains one of these two sentences. . . .

1. "Your failure surprised everyone in the office."
2. "Your carelessness was a surprise to all of us."

These examples <u>presuppose</u> "you failed" or "you're careless," as if it were something everyone knows and takes for granted. However, they're structured as mild compliments. Your only <u>claim</u> is that people were surprised. This doesn't change the fact that you're saying something negative to your reader, but it makes it much less confrontational and reduces the loss of face for the person you're criticizing.

Now look again at the first sentence in the paragraph we've been analyzing:

"My discovery this morning that the Metamega deal was something you'd been working on for weeks was a shock."

You could have said "I discovered this morning that the Metamega deal was something you'd been working on for weeks." But that would be an open claim, and a target for argument. Turning the claim—"I discovered"—into "my discovery" allows you to take its truth for granted. You are claiming only that the discovery was a shock to you.

Two language patterns are interacting here to let you construct this kind of presuppositional sequence. Both are very familiar to you as a speaker of English; you undoubtedly use them often without being conscious of what you're doing. You can get more mileage from them in your written language, however, by using them as conscious and deliberate communication strategies. Let's look at them both carefully.

Presuppositions and Possessives

It's a grammatical fact about English that anything marked as owned, or otherwise possessed, is automatically presupposed to <u>exist</u>. There are languages (Navajo, for example) in which "My beautiful white horse does not exist" is a perfectly good sentence; English isn't one of them. When you say "I have a new car" you are making an open claim, but when you say "My new car is pale Williamsburg blue" you are <u>presupposing</u> "I have a new car" by using the possessive word "my" before "new car." Your only claim is that your car is a particular color. The more details you put in your description, the stronger the presupposition of existence becomes.

Suppose you say "My new foreign car with the mag wheels that I bought in Atlanta has given me nothing but trouble." Your listeners are unlikely to come back at you with "You don't own a car" unless they have special information about you or know you to be a pathological liar. Companies use this strategy when they say "Our revolutionary new product is now available" instead of "We have a revolutionary new product." Politicians say "My plan for lowering taxes is unique" and "My opponent's determination to keep taxes high will surprise no one" instead of "I have a plan for lowering taxes" and "My opponent is determined to keep taxes high, which will surprise no one."

You already know how to mark a sequence of English as something possessed with one of the possessive words (*my, our, your, their, etc.*) or a possessive phrase with "apostrophes," as in "Jack's plan" or "the Metamega Corporation's headquarters." That information, along with the rules about what kind of language chunk you can do that to, is filed in the flawless English grammar that is part of your mental equipment. You know, for example, that you can't do this to a verb or an adjective. You can only do it to nominals: chunks of language that are functioning as nouns. Even if you can't define any of these grammar terms, you nonetheless have all this information already available, and you are an expert in its use.

Presuppositions and Nominalization

The problem is that often the item you need to presuppose is not a nominal, and therefore can't be "possessed." Suppose Joe's secretary has destroyed one of your computer files, and you decide that a letter of complaint is in order. You can write "Your secretary destroyed one of my files." But that's an open claim, and it's openly confrontational. What you want to do instead is presuppose that it happened—but you know you can't put a possessive in front of "destroyed." "You're careless" is a similar example; you know you can't put a possessive in front of "careless," either. You need a way to use verbs and adjectives like "destroy" and "careless" as if they were nouns. You can do this easily. Because English has a specific language process used for that purpose, called, logically enough, nominalization.

Some English verbs and adjectives have special nominalizing endings, and that information is also stored in your internal grammar. You will know all about changes like these:

you destroyed		your destruction
she resigns		her resignation
he abandoned	BECOMES	his abandonment
we refuse		our refusal
Jack departs		Jack's departure

I am careless		my carelessness
they were lazy	BECOMES	their laziness
Jack was reluctant		Jack's reluctance

But <u>any</u> English verb can be nominalized by adding "-ing" to it, and any English adjective can be nominalized by putting "be" in front of it. Like this . . . .

"You destroyed the file" BECOMES "Your destroying the file . . ."

"He abandoned the child" BECOMES "His abandoning the child . . ."

"They were lazy" BECOMES "Their being lazy . . ."

Usually, when a special nominalizing form is available it's a bit more elegant. If elegance is appropriate for the letter you're writing and is one of your goals, you would use that form. However, the form with "-ing" (or "be" plus "-ing") will always be <u>correct</u>.

Here are the steps you follow:

1. Select the sequence you want to presuppose.
2. a. If it's a nominal, put a possessive word or phrase in front of it. ["my car"; "the company's stock"]

    b. If it's a verb, add "-ing" or a nominalizing ending like "-tion" to it; then put a possessive word or phrase in front of it. ["Her destroying the file . . ."; "The auditor's rejection of our plan . . ."]

    c. If it's an adjective that has a nominalizing ending like "-ness," and you want to use that form, add the ending; then put a possessive in front of it. ["Her carelessness . . ."; "The Senate's unwillingness or inability . . ."]

    d. For any other adjective, add a possessive word or phrase, followed by "being." ["Their being angry . . ."; "The Senate's being unwilling or unable . . ."]
3. Add whatever you need to finish your sentence. ["Their being angry was anticipated by our negotiators."]

Let's get right down to the bare, brutal facts here for a moment; let's talk <u>grammar</u>. Some readers may feel uneasy about carrying out those three steps, because they suspect that they couldn't accurately sort a list of words into verbs and adjectives. If you feel that way, you're not alone; language courses leave many people with that kind of insecurity. Everywhere I go, I meet successful and accomplished people who tell me "I don't understand grammar" and go on to explain that when they took English classes in school they did very badly.

Don't <u>worry</u> about it. Put an "-ing" on the word and ask yourself: Is this an acceptable English word? If it's not a verb, you will reject the result instantly—you will know immediately and without hesitation that "carelessing" or "reluctanting" aren't English. Or put "being" in front of the word and ask yourself: "Is this an acceptable chunk of English?" You will, with equal speed and confidence, reject "being destroy" or "being lose."

This is important. It proves that you <u>do</u> know whether you're looking at a verb or an adjective, no matter what you may have been led to believe. Think about it: If you didn't know, you wouldn't be able to discard those incorrect forms. I've met many people who couldn't define the grammatical terms "subject" and "predicate" and were unable to identify subjects and predicates on tests. I've never met anyone in normal health whose sentences were not <u>composed</u> of subjects and predicates. Trust your internal grammar; it won't mislead you.

Presuppositions and Factives

One additional source of English presupposition power is used in Paragraph Two: the set of words that are called <u>factives</u> because statements that follow them in a sentence are presupposed to be true. "Know" is a factive; therefore, "I want you to know that I'm sorry" <u>presupposes</u> that the embedded sentence "I'm sorry" is a true statement. The sentence in the model letter beginning with "I'm sure you know" presupposes "if I'd had any idea the deal was a project of yours I would have left it strictly alone."

Here are a few more factives you can use to presuppose that what you're about to write is a fact and not subject to argument, with example sentences.

FACTIVE	EXAMPLE
regret	"We regret that you are unwilling to comply with the terms of our contract."
be sorry	"We are sorry that you are unable to understand Clause 11, Section B."

forget   "I had forgotten that your prices are completely out
              of line."

be aware   "Our lawyers are aware that your firm is guilty of
              altering test data."

realize   "We realize that you cannot meet your deadline."

understand   "I understand that you are unable to carry your
              share of the workload at this time."

Notice that whether a factive is used positively or negatively doesn't change the effect. "I knew that you were late" and "I didn't know that you were late" both presuppose that the embedded sentence—"You were late"—is true.

Don't be concerned abut the rules determining whether these presupposed statements begin with the word "that" or not. (As in "We know that you are a suspect" versus "We know you are a suspect.") You will apply those rules automatically, just because you are a fluent speaker of English. Like many such rules, you know them below the level of your conscious awareness, and you apply them with ease even though you couldn't explain them on an essay test. It's not something you have to worry about.

Now, back to the analysis.

To Apologize or Not to Apologize

Another thing worth remarking on in this paragraph is something that you didn't do. You said you were sorry, and then you left that *statement* alone. You didn't tack something onto the apology to cancel it out or weaken it. Far too often people make apologies because they feel they must, and then take them back or water them down to nothing or otherwise mutilate them. For example, you could have written this:

"... Carl tells me you thought this deal was yours, because
you've been working on it for a while. I hope he's wrong;
but if he's not, I want you to know I'm sorry you feel
that way. ..."

Any time you write "I'm sorry you feel that [X]," you're not saying you're sorry for what you did or for what happened. You're just sorry that your reader perceives the situation negatively, and you're adding a strong hint that the perception is an error. This is always a temptation; nine times out of ten it's a temptation you should resist. It pretends to be an apology at the same time that it challenges your reader's judgment, and it only provokes hostility.

Recently I wrote a letter of complaint, and said I felt that I deserved an apology; if the apology had been forthcoming, the incident would have been closed. Instead, I got a reply containing a sentence like this one:

> "I'm sorry that what I did (in your opinion) didn't meet current business standards (as you perceive them.)"

That's not an apology. It's an insolent thumbing of the writer's nose. It made me furious, and I won't forget it. It would have been much better, and would have made me far less angry, if the writer had just leveled with me and said, "I don't think I did anything wrong, and I refuse to apologize." We would still have been in disagreement on the issue, certainly. But I wouldn't have felt that I'd been deliberately and obnoxiously insulted, and it would still have been possible to negotiate toward compromise.

The rule is simple:

IF YOU CAN'T APOLOGIZE SINCERELY, DON'T APOLOGIZE AT ALL.

When you're talking to someone face to face, you can use body language—especially the intonation of your voice—to take back the surface message carried by your words. You can say "Of course I'm sorry!" in a tone of voice and with a facial expression that makes it unmistakably clear that you're not sorry at all. And your listener, who is right there with you, can come back at you with "Well, thank you very much!" in a way that can only be understood as meaning "You don't sound one bit sorry to me—I don't believe you. And I resent your phony apology." With written language, those body language resources aren't available, and other devices have to be substituted for them. One possibility is the device used by my correspondent above: the comment in parentheses. As in . . .

"When I (in your opinion) made a mistake . . ."

"When (according to you) I failed to follow through . . ."

This is a direct challenge to your reader; don't do it unless you have excellent reasons. For instance, suppose you need a way to let the reader know that what you're writing is something you are obligated to write but don't necessarily believe. You might get that across with "When I learned that (according to the personnel office) you've been coming in late every day. . . ." Even then, think three times before you do it.

If what you did, or what you were involved in, is serious enough to make writing a letter necessary, the person you're writing to probably expects an apology. Leaving the apology out, or making an apology that you proceed to cancel with other words, is a strategic error. If you're not sorry, regardless of expectations, say so—but put that message inside a sincere statement of regret, as in these two examples.

"I'm not sorry for what I did—but I'm very sorry that it caused you distress."

"I'm not sorry for what I did—but I'm deeply sorry about the consequences for you."

Now we can move on to . . .

PARAGRAPH THREE

Jack, this is one of those things that just happens sometimes. It's clear that you and I need to find more time to sit down and discuss what we're doing, so that we don't get our lines crossed like this in the future. In the meantime, we both know that what made it possible for me to close the deal so quickly and easily wasn't my superb salesmanship—it was the groundwork you had already done. You have my thanks, and my apologies.

Having told Jack what has happened and apologized for it, you use this final paragraph to fasten down your message in a way that will make him feel like a dog in a manger if he complains. With this paragraph, you accomplish a long list of good things.

WHAT LETTER 1 DOES FOR YOU

1. You point out that this kind of thing happens once in a while, which is certainly true and reinforces once again your claim that it was an accident.

2. You tell Jack that you expect the two of you not only to refrain from becoming enemies over this incident but actually to work together more closely because of it.

3. Although you freely admit that you're sorry (and repeat that you're apologizing), you are careful here to bring Jack into the

situation with at least some of the responsibility for the flub. You suggest that you and Jack will work more closely "so we don't get our lines crossed like this in the future." The words "we" and "our" let Jack know that he had a part in this foul-up, too, without making any open claim to that effect.

4. You nail the paragraph down with a <u>compliment</u>—saying <u>for</u> Jack what he's sure to be thinking anyway, which is that you couldn't have closed the deal so swiftly if he hadn't taken care of the preliminary work. And you use "we both know" to presuppose that this is true, for you and for Jack. When you say this yourself, you keep Jack from feeling obligated to say it.

5. You use the power of presupposition to let you say to Jack, unambiguously: "I am a superb salesman." That is the statement presupposed by "my superb salesmanship." But you do it in a way that can't be faulted. You do it in passing, in the course of saying that you realize it isn't the only reason the deal was closed, and you do it indirectly.

With "you have my thanks and my apologies," the case for a positive relationship without a lingering grudge has been well and thoroughly made. You've done it without groveling, and without sacrificing any of your own dignity; you've done it with absolutely no loss of face for Jack. And you've done it in a way that spares your company the tension and stress that goes with any chronic hostility between colleagues. Success, all around. Congratulations.

It isn't "evasive" or "manipulative" to put items you know are likely to provoke argument into a structure that presupposes their validity. On the contrary. It's simple courtesy. Many people in our culture believe that when they hear something that <u>might</u> be the source of an argument they are <u>obligated</u> to argue about it. They will follow that rule and argue even when an argument is the last thing they want—even when they don't actually care about the issue one way or another. They've always been told that if you don't stick up for yourself people will walk all over you, and an open "You failed" or "You're careless" brings them bolt upright and ready for combat. Structuring your language in such a way that the other person is not put into this "Defend your honor or look like a wimp" position is a <u>positive</u> strategy for everyone involved, and a demonstration of your skill as an effective communicator.

SUPPLEMENTARY LETTERS

LETTER 2
Flub: You've Announced Someone Else's Plan

Dear Angela,

Yesterday I ran into Tom Baker at the airport, where we were both waiting for delayed flights, and we got to talking. To pass the time, I told him about the plan our division has for setting up a new E-mail system. I'm happy to be able to report that he thought it was a great idea and was ready to approve it on the spot.

My discovery this morning that you had set up a meeting on the 14th, specifically to present the E-mail plan to Baker, was a shock. I want you to know that I'm sorry. And I'm sure you know that if I'd had any idea you wanted to do a formal presentation, I wouldn't have mentioned the plan; I didn't know.

Angela, this is one of those things that just happens now and then. It makes it very clear that you and I need to find more time to sit down together and discuss what we're doing, so we don't get our wires crossed like this in the future. In the meantime, we both know that the reason Baker liked the plan so much wasn't my superb persuasive skills—it was the careful work you put into getting it <u>right</u>. You have my thanks, and my apologies.

Sincerely,

LETTER 3
Flub: You've Announced Someone Else's News

Dear Phil,

This morning I ran into Dorothy Jones in the cafeteria, and we got to talking. She told me she was worried about her status here, and I went out of my way to reassure her. I told her she had no need to worry, and that I knew for a fact that you intended to promote her to administrative assistant. She was absolutely delighted.

A few minutes ago, to my complete surprise, your secretary told me how much you were looking forward to giving Dorothy the news about the promotion. I want you to know I'm sorry. And I'm sure you know that if I'd had any idea you wanted to tell her yourself I wouldn't have said a word; I didn't know.

Phil, this is just one of those things that happens from time to time. It should make us realize that we need to find more time to sit down together and discuss personnel matters, so that this kind of mix-up doesn't happen again. In the meantime, we both know that what really matters is not the messenger, but the message. You've made an excellent choice in Mrs. Jones, and she's going to be extremely valuable to the firm in her new position. You have my congratulations and my apologies.

Sincerely,

Chapter Three

"I'm Not the Kind of Person Who Does That Kind of Thing!"

Triple-F Scenario Two

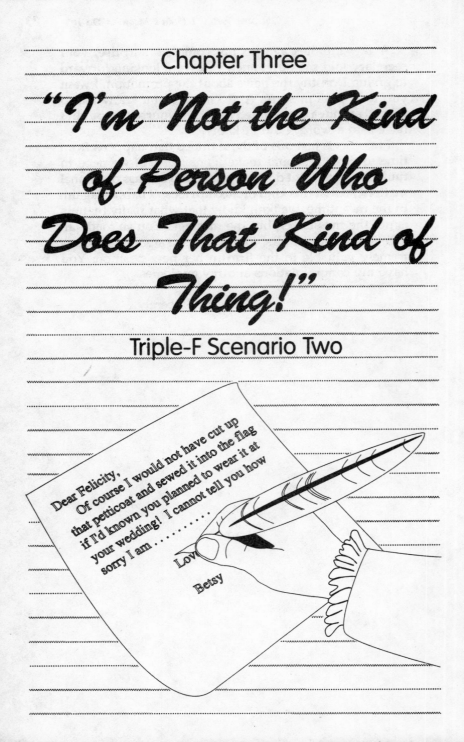

Dear Felicity,
Of course I would not have cut up that petticoat and sewed it into the flag if I'd known you planned to wear it at your wedding! I cannot tell you how sorry I am . . . .

Lov
Betsy

*L*ast night you were a dinner party guest at the home of a couple you know only slightly. They're business connections—people you regularly run into at business functions—but not personal friends. You enjoyed the dinner and the living room conversation that followed; apparently you enjoyed both so much that you didn't pay nearly enough attention to your surroundings. It seemed to you that your hostess was a little chilly when you took your leave last night; you assumed she was just tired. But this morning someone who is a personal friend called you at the office to tell you a couple of things. First: The little dish you used for an ashtray over coffee was an heirloom that had belonged to Jennifer Kensington's great grandmother. And second: Your cigarettes left a mark on the dish that won't come off. Your friend says Mrs. Kensington is heartsick about this.

It seems to you that your hostess could have simply said a word or two to caution you when you picked up the dish, instead of suffering in silence while you made a fool of yourself. It seems to you that that would have been both good sense and courtesy on her part. But she didn't, and now you have this mess on your hands. You don't want her to think you're the kind of clod who doesn't understand or care about the damage done. You know smoking isn't exactly looked upon as a social plus these days, and it occurs to you now—too late—that the reason you picked up the dish was because nothing that was obviously an ashtray had been provided. No doubt that should have told you something at the time. You don't want this incident to be a source of problems in your business relationships, which will continue to involve the Kensingtons. WHAT DO YOU SAY IN YOUR LETTER?

LETTER 4
Flub: You've Mistreated Someone's Heirloom

Dear Mrs. Kensington,

This letter won't be the letter you deserve to receive; I'm not eloquent enough, or skilled enough, to write that letter. It represents the best efforts of a man who is deeply ashamed to have repaid your gracious hospitality by clumsily damaging a treasured heirloom.

A mutual friend called me this morning, to tell me that the little dish I mistook for an ashtray at your home last night belonged to your great-grandmother, and that it may have been permanently stained by my cigarettes. I am so very sorry.

In future I will pay more attention to what I am doing and I will be more careful. I hope that you, in future, will not hesitate to tell me at once if I'm about to make a mistake of this kind again. I will be grateful if you will allow me to have the dish sent to someone who is an expert in repairing the sort of damage I did, at my expense. Perhaps we can remove the <u>evidence</u> of my carelessness; I know there's no way I can remove the memory. I should have realized that someone with your good taste would not furnish her home with anything that is ordinary.

Sincerely,

Let's take a good look at this letter to see how it's put together, what strategies it uses, and why it works as it does.

ANALYSIS OF LETTER 4

First Paragraph

This letter won't be the letter you deserve to receive; I'm not eloquent enough, or skilled enough, to write <u>that</u> letter. It represents the best efforts of a man who is deeply ashamed to have repaid your gracious hospitality by clumsily damaging a treasured heirloom.

This is humble pie, most assuredly, but it's elegant humble pie. You've let Jennifer Kensington know that an apology is coming, and you've stated the facts without any hesitation. Mrs. Kensington probably had a lot to say after you went home last night about how clumsy you were, about how much the little dish meant to her, and about how ashamed you should be for repaying her hospitality in the clutzy way you did. Your second sentence acknowledges your awareness of all that and says it all for her in black and white so there can be no possible misunderstanding: You do know how she feels, and you have accepted the responsibility for your actions without argument.

HEDGES—AND HEDGE-CLIPPING

This is a wise move, and is unusual enough to make a lasting impression on your reader. It's a tremendous improvement over the usual practice, which is to send messages we could summarize as "I know I did something wrong, but it wasn't my fault" or worse, "I know you believe I did something wrong, but you're mistaken." Those messages are like "I'll say I'm sorry because I have to, but I don't think I have anything to apologize for"—they are insults added to injury. And they have something else in common. They are all examples of what linguists call <u>Hedges</u>: a way of saying something and at the same time fending off the natural response to your utterance. The two classic Hedges we encounter most frequently in our daily lives are:

1. "I know this is a stupid question, but . . ."
2. "I know you don't want to hear this, but . . ."

<u>Annoying</u>, right? No question about it! Hedges are cowardly. People who use them assume in advance that what they are about to say or write is going to get a negative reaction. Every Hedge has behind it a metamessage (a message <u>about</u> the message) that goes like this: "After I say this you're going to want to say [X];I'm going to say [X] first, however, so that if you come at me with it I can say, 'Look, I already <u>said</u> that!'" Hedges are without exception infuriating and confrontational.

If you find yourself forced to convey a Hedged message, in speech or in writing, <u>clip that Hedge</u>. By deleting the word "but," which triggers most of the negative reaction, and adding a sentence of mild regret. Like this:

1a. "I know this is a stupid question. It's unfortunate that I have to ask it." (Followed by the question.)
2a. "I know you don't want to hear this. I regret that it has to be said." (Followed by the statement.)

It's better to use no Hedges at all, not even little inconspicuous ones. Unless you absolutely cannot avoid them, leave them out.

Second Paragraph

A mutual friend called me this morning to tell me that the little dish I mistook for an ashtray at your home last night belonged to your great-grandmother, and that it may have been permanently stained by my cigarettes. I am so very sorry.

The first sentence in this paragraph tells Mrs. Kensington—twice—that what you did was an accident. The word "mistook," and the information that you knew nothing about what had happened until the friend called you, carry that message. Saying that the dish "may have been" permanently stained is a good strategic move, and one that will be supported in your next paragraph when you offer to pay for letting an antiques expert try to remove the stain. And the wording of the sentence is not in any way accidental. Please compare it with the version below:

> A mutual friend called me this morning. She says that last night I mistook a dish that had been your great grandmother's for an ashtray, and that I may have stained it permanently with my cigarettes.

Notice the difference? In the version you used in your letter, the attention is firmly focused on the physical <u>objects</u> involved—the dish, the nonexistent ashtray, and the cigarettes—rather than on your actions and shortcomings. The sentence isn't about you—it's about that <u>dish</u>. This linguistic process—the shifting of focus—is one of the most valuable resources English offers. It will be worth our while to give it some careful attention.

SHIFTING SENTENCE FOCUS

The part of the sentence that the writer wants to mark as most deserving of attention is called its <u>focus</u>. In speech you can mark focus with the rough and ready mechanism of giving it emphatic stress, as in "I am interested in the <u>price</u> of the service." In written English, as shown in the example, you can indicate emphatic stress by underlining. But that sort of emphasis should be used rarely. There are more graceful, and less distracting, ways to accomplish the same goal. Very roughly, the rule goes like this:

MOVE THE NOMINALS IN YOUR SENTENCE AROUND IN ORDER TO DRAW DELIBERATE ATTENTION TO SOME AND DOWNPLAY ATTENTION TO OTHERS, ADDING EXTRA ONES WHEN YOU NEED THEM.

This isn't a completely free process, because there are grammar rules that interfere. In English, "man bites dog" means one thing and "dog bites man" means another, and there are constraints on word order that have to be respected. But within those constraints you can do amazing things.

Suppose you are Multimajor Oil Company, and one of your captains has had a serious oil spill in the Mediterranean Sea. You'd like to keep the attention anywhere but on your company, obviously, but you have to issue some kind of letter announcing what has happened. You know you can't say "Spilled oil in the Mediterranean." English is so adamant about requiring nominals that you often have to put one in even when it makes no sense, as in "It is raining." There is no "it" that rains; English requires you to put it there all the same. This isn't true of all languages; Spanish and Navajo speakers are content with subjectless sentences when the subject would be a word like "it" or "he." But except in advertisements ("Kills germs! Makes floors shine!") written English requires a nominal in subject position. It has nothing at all to do with <u>logic</u>. What are your options, then? You certainly don't want to write "Spills oil! Kills marine life! Pollutes shorelines!"

When people report their experiences and their ideas, they have a long list of possible slots they could fill with nominals. Most of the time they leave a lot of the slots empty because they don't feel any need to fill them. Which slots are available usually depends on what other words are used—it's okay to say just "Helen ate," but "Helen shut" won't do. You have to at least put the word "something" after "shut," even if you don't particularly care what was shut. For the sentence about the oil spill, the possibilities look like this, with the nominals slots numbered for your reference:

SOMEONE	SPILLED	SOMETHING	IN SOME QUANTITY	IN SOME PLACE
1		2	3	4

AT SOME TIME	WITH SOMETHING	IN SOME WAY	FOR SOME REASON
5	6	7	8

Your mental grammar will tell you that the only slots you <u>have</u> to fill are #1 and #2, as in "Multimajor spilled oil." Then you can decide which of the others are appropriate and necessary. Your critics might very well want to fill slots #7 and #8 with "in a totally careless manner and for no conceivable reason other than gross negligence," but you're not likely to do that. Nor are you likely to want to add exactly how <u>much</u> oil was involved (slot #3) unless it was so small an amount that it's in your interest to do so. Finally, everybody knows that what goes in #6 is "with an oil tanker"; that doesn't have to be mentioned. This leaves you with:

"Multimajor spilled oil in the Mediterranean Sea this morning."
    1   2   4   5

The focus of this sentence is squarely where you <u>don't</u> want it now—on your company—and you can't leave anything out. But you can do this:

"Oil was spilled in the Mediterranean Sea this morning by Multimajor. . . ."

And now, since no rule requires you to fill the slot where "by Multimajor" occurs, you <u>can</u> leave it out. "Oil was spilled in the Mediterranean Sea this morning" is fine, just like that. (This isn't possible in all languages; Arabic, for example, doesn't permit it.) What you did was this:

1. You promoted one nominal—the oil—into the subject position, which can't be left empty.

2. You demoted another nominal—Multimajor—all the way to the end of the sentence, into a slot that <u>can</u> be left empty.

3. And then you got rid of the demoted nominal altogether by simply deleting it.

I want to make one thing clear: I'm not suggesting that you actually go through all of these steps in your head before you use such a sentence, or that you would ordinarily be consciously aware of putting one nominal in one place, moving another one, taking one out, etc. However, this way of describing what happens is the simplest way I know to make the <u>strategy</u> clear, so that you can use it deliberately when it suits your needs.

When you're talking about yourself and your own actions, rather than about your company, this particular pattern is often not suitable or useful. Politicians do try it, in desperation, but in daily life you'll rarely be able to get away with it. Suppose that in your letter about the heirloom dish you'd tried this sentence:

". . . A mutual friend called me this morning to tell me that the little dish that was mistaken for an ashtray at your home last night belonged to your great-grandmother, and that it may have been permanently stained. . . ."

That sounds absurd. It sounds as if you were pretending not to <u>know</u> that you did the mistaking and the staining. In a case like this, you will want to use one of the other English patterns for bumping nominals up and down the focus ladder. Let's look at the most common ones, using the sentence about the oil spill.

Basic Sentence:

1. Multimajor spilled oil in the Mediterranean Sea this morning.

Focus-shifted Sentences:

1á. Oil was spilled in the Mediterranean Sea this morning.

1b. What was spilled in the Mediterranean Sea this morning was oil.

1c. It was oil that was spilled in the Mediterranean Sea this morning.

1d. The oil that was spilled in the Mediterranean Sea this morning . . .

The strategy used in the sentence in Paragraph Two is the pattern shown in the partial sentence #1d. You can't get yourself <u>out</u> of the sentence this time without looking as if you're a liar, but you have demoted yourself into a decent obscurity. "The little dish I mistook for an ashtray at your home last night belonged to your great-grandmother . . ." is not about you or about what you did; its focus is that elaborately described dish. Now look at this sequence.

Basic Sentence:

2. I may have permanently stained the dish with my cigarettes.

Focus-shifted Sentences:

2a. The dish may have been permanently stained by me, with my cigarettes.

2b. The dish may have been permanently stained by my cigarettes.

When you use this strategy in your second paragraph you provide needed balance after your strong personal focus in the first one. You don't want to lay blame on yourself so thickly that you start sounding sarcastic (Outraged Lamb), or as if you were groveling

(Worthless Worm). In addition, this shift in emphasis helps provide a transition to your final paragraph, in which you plan to point out to Mrs. Kensington that she isn't totally blameless herself.

You close the paragraph with "I am so very sorry." Just like that, without elaboration or excuses, and without one unnecessary word.

Third Paragraph

> In future I will pay more attention to what I am doing, and I will be more careful. I hope that you, in future, will not hesitate to tell me at once if I'm about to make a mistake of this kind again. I will be grateful if you will allow me to have the dish sent to someone who is an expert in repairing the sort of damage I did, at my expense. Perhaps we can remove the <u>evidence</u> of my carelessness; I know there's no way I can remove the memory. I should have realized that someone with your good taste would not furnish her home with anything that is ordinary.

Now, having made it very clear that you know you behaved badly and that you accept the responsibility, you bring your hostess into the context of guilt by suggesting that she change her behavior and warn her guests of potential pitfalls. And you end with a mild compliment that presupposes Mrs. Kensington's good taste: your claim that anything found in her house, even a small inconspicuous dish, is unlikely to be ordinary.

Certainly this paragraph could be shorter. Suppose you feel that Mrs. Kensington was really out of line, just sitting there watching you ruin her heirloom without saying a word. Suppose you don't like her very much and you don't think she deserves this much attention. Suppose—although the intensity of the letter is tailored to your friend's reporting that this woman was "heartsick" about the damage, which is a strong word—you would feel phony going to such lengths. In that case, you drop all of the paragraph from "Perhaps we can remove . . ." to the end, leaving a dignified apology plus an offer to repair the damage if it can be done. You could also be less formal, if that's more to your taste. All you have to do is rewrite the paragraph using more contractions ("you're" for "you are," "I'm" for "I am," etc.), and changing the word "allow" to the less formal "let." Like this:

In future I'll pay more attention to what I'm doing, and I'll be more careful. I hope that you, in future, will not hesitate to tell me at once if I'm about to make a mistake of this kind again. I'll be grateful if you'll let me have the dish sent to someone who's an expert in repairing the sort of damage I did, at my expense. Perhaps we can remove the <u>evidence</u> of my carelessness; I know there's no way to remove the memory. I should have realized that someone with your good taste wouldn't furnish her home with anything that's ordinary.

The content of the message doesn't change, but the tone does, with the written tone having precisely the same effect that a change in tone of <u>voice</u> from lofty formality to friendliness would have. You may find this more appropriate for your personal circumstances.

"As You Know" Strategy

Once again you have refrained from writing things that would muddy the waters and cast doubts on your sincerity. The fact that there were no ashtrays probably means that Mrs. Kensington doesn't want people smoking in her home. If she had <u>said</u> so, and you had ignored her and smoked anyway, you'd have to bring up that issue. Since she didn't—and because the acceptability of smoking is a touchy matter at best, these days—you are very wise to simply leave it out.

When you bring up a controversial issue in conversation, the others present have an opportunity to state their feelings too, either supporting or arguing against your position. When you do the same thing in a letter, they don't have that opportunity, and they are likely to feel that you've invaded their privacy by setting down your personal opinions uninvited. The *Who Do You Think You ARE, Anyway?* reaction is dangerous; it's far better not to provoke it. If you find yourself in a situation where you <u>must</u> bring up something like this, I recommend starting with "As you know. . . ." As in "As you know, the claim that smoking is dangerous to people's health is silly nonsense based on incompetent research." This lets you sound as if you're under the impression that your reader feels the same way you do about the controversy, rather than as if you feel obligated to impose your opinions on others.

THE TRIPLE-F LETTER PATTERN

Now we've come to a point where some careful explanation is in order. I want to demonstrate to you that the model letters in this book are not based on "inspiration." Inspiration comes along now and again, but you can't count on it. You certainly can't count on it to light on your shoulder by lucky chance every time you flub, flounder, or suffer the effects of human frailties. There's a solid and coherent system behind these letters. A system that you can use to write any number of other letters as you need to write them, without any inspiration being required.

The basic pattern is shown in Figure X. It has six parts; three are optional.

FIGURE X—The Triple-F Letter Pattern

Dear . . . . .,

Paragraph One:

A.   Warning that something negative is coming. (OPTIONAL)
"I regret the need to write this letter."

B.   What prompted the letter—the actual facts of the Triple-F situation. (REQUIRED)
"Last night I put a dent in the fender of your car."

Paragraph Two:

A.   How you found out about it. (OPTIONAL)
"This morning your sister told me what I'd done."

B.   Apology. (REQUIRED)
"I'm sorry."

Paragraph Three:

A.   "In future" statement. What will be done to keep this from happening again; how things will be different. (Involve your reader here, if possible.) (REQUIRED)
"In future I'll be more careful—and you must tell me to drive my own car."

B. Compliment. (OPTIONAL)

"I'm glad you're not the kind of person who holds a grudge."

Sincerely,

We can simplify this even more by paring it down to its absolute bare-bones messages as in Figure X.

FIGURE X—The Bare-Bones Messages

1.	(Paragraph One A)	BRACE YOURSELF.	(Optional)
2.	(Paragraph One B)	SOMEBODY GOOFED.	(Required)
3.	(Paragraph Two A)	I FOUND OUT.	(Optional)
4.	(Paragraph Two B)	I'M SORRY.	(Required)
5.	(Paragraph Three A)	NEVER AGAIN.	(Required)
6.	(Paragraph Three B)	YOU'RE TERRIFIC.	(Optional)

Let's look at how Letters 1 and 4 fit the pattern. Here they are, in skeleton-sentence form.

Letter 1—Skeleton

1. (OPTIONAL—NOT USED)
2. "Last night I ran into Joe Trino and closed a deal."
3. "This morning I found out Trino had been <u>your</u> deal."
4. "I'm sorry."
5. "In future we'll spend more time together."
6. "Your preliminary work made it all possible."

Letter 4—Skeleton

1. "This letter—my best effort—should be better."
2. "I damaged your heirloom dish last night."
3. "A friend told me."
4. "I'm so sorry."
5. "In future I'll be more careful—and you must be more frank."
6. "I know you have good taste; I should have known the dish was special."

The difference between a list and a system is that the system can handle something <u>new</u>. To use the pattern, all you have to do is follow these four simple steps:

1. Identify—for your own personal Triple-F situation—the messages that would go into each of the six possible slots.

2. Decide whether you want to include any of the three optional messages.

3. Write down your letter in skeleton form, filling each slot with a brief summarizing sentence.

4. Expand the skeleton sentences as needed, to produce your final three-paragraph letter.

It's possible that you'll find yourself needing four paragraphs in a letter, or five, or even more. By all means go ahead and add them if they're needed. But unless you plan on only one sentence (maybe a despairing "Please forgive me!"?)it's best to have at least three paragraphs. And if three will do it, adding more is a mistake.

English speakers and readers love things in threes. We go for three wishes, Three Bears, Three Little Pigs, Three Billy Goats Gruff, third time's a charm, and lots more of the same. We like things to have three parts: a beginning, a middle, and an end. Even four-quarter football games come to us in a three-part package: two quarters, a half-time show, and two more quarters.

Furthermore, three paragraphs, even if each one is only a sentence or two, fit nicely on a single page. Remember, you don't have the advantages of body language going for you when you write letters. One of the resources you can substitute for them is a letter that <u>looks</u> good on the page . . . a letter that is an attractive language token in its own right and that would still be attractive even if the person looking at it couldn't read the language in which it's written. The graphic arrangement—three nicely spaced paragraphs bracketed by Salutation ("Dear X") and Complimentary Close ("Sincerely")—is a handsome one. It's the written-down equivalent of a pleasant voice and a nice smile and a good handshake.

CUSTOM-TAILORING YOUR LETTERS

You can adapt any sample letter in this book to many situations. You use its basic form as an example of the Triple-F Letter Pattern, but you plug in new chunks of language that are tailored to fit your personal needs, as shown below. The custom parts go into the slots between brackets—"[X]." The examples below will make this process clear.

Letter 4, Revised

Dear . . . . .,

This letter won't be the letter you deserve to receive; I'm not eloquent enough, or skilled enough, to write <u>that</u> letter. But it represents the best efforts of [a man who is filled with remorse because he has missed his favorite nephew's graduation from college.]

[This morning your mother told me that the whole family nearly missed the ceremonies because they kept waiting for me to arrive.] I am so very sorry.

In future, I'll be more careful. And I hope that in future you [and the rest of the family] will [simply <u>tell</u> me when something important is coming up that needs my attention, so that I won't make a mistake of this kind again.] I will be grateful if you'll [let me have your diploma handsomely matted and framed], at my expense. Perhaps I can [make some amends for my thoughtlessness]; I know there's no way to remove the memory. I should have realized that [in a close and loving family like ours, the celebration could only be complete if everyone was present.]

Sincerely,

Letter 4, Revised Again

Dear . . . . .,

This letter won't be the letter you deserve to receive; I'm not eloquent enough, or skilled enough, to write <u>that</u> letter. It represents the best efforts of [an old friend who is deeply ashamed of having damaged your car.]

[Yesterday your insurance agent called to tell me that the noise I heard as I pulled into your driveway—a noise

I inexcusably failed to investigate—was a tree limb scraping the top of the car.] I am so very sorry.

    In future, I will pay more attention to what I'm doing, and I'll be more careful. I hope that you, in future, will [tell me to drive my own car!] I will be grateful if you'll [let me have the car sent to a body shop for repairs], at my expense. Perhaps we can remove the <u>evidence</u> of my carelessness; I know there's no way to remove the memory. I should have realized that [a noise like that meant trouble, and checked it out—and I should most certainly have looked where I was going].

Sincerely,

    You might need to write a personal letter of this kind on behalf of your firm, your organization, or some other group. Your major change would then be a switch from "I" as writer to "we," and a less personal tone, as shown in the paragraph below.

Dear . . . . .,

    This letter will not be the letter you deserve to receive; no one here at Better Roads, Inc. is eloquent enough, or skilled enough, to write <u>that</u> letter. However, it represents the best efforts of a firm that is deeply sorry to have been forced to level your family's home to make way for our current highway project.

You see: The pattern is infinitely adaptable.

    The fact that you can do this so easily is one of the strongest proofs that you are an expert in the grammar of your language, no matter how you may have gotten along in "language arts" classrooms. You will never have any trouble knowing where the substitution slots are in a letter. Nor will you have any difficulty making the substitutions or tidying up the various snaps and zippers. You know all the rules involved in the process, as part of your internal grammar, and you can trust that grammar to guide you all the way from "Dear" to "Sincerely."

SUPPLEMENTARY LETTERS

LETTER 5
Flub: You've Exposed Someone's Flaming Past—
In Front of Her Inlaws

Dear Marilyn,

This letter won't be the letter you deserve. I don't have the faintest idea what that letter would say; I wish I did. However, this letter represents the best efforts of an embarrassed woman who accidentally betrayed your confidence—and who values our friendship too much to give it up without at least <u>trying</u> to set matters right.

I didn't need anyone to tell me that I'd put my foot in it after I told the story of the hour you spent trapped on the fraternity house fire escape while a dean searched the rooms. I could see by the look on your face that I had humiliated and hurt you. I <u>did</u> need someone to tell me that the couple on the couch who were my most fascinated audience were your husband's parents. I didn't know who they were, Marilyn; if I had known, I would <u>never</u> have told that story. That's not an excuse, and it's not much of an explanation, either. But it's important to me for you to know that I would never have done such a thing deliberately. I am so very sorry.

In future, I promise you that I won't tell others stories about the wonderful years you and I have shared without asking you for permission, no matter where we are and no matter who else is present. And in future I hope that I can count on you to speak up and stop me if I am about to embarrass you, instead of sitting there in horror and letting me do it without so much as opening your mouth! I can't undo the damage I have done. It's too late to take back my words, and anything I might say to your inlaws would only make matters worse. (It's not as though I could tell them I'd made the whole thing up.) It is my good fortune—probably undeserved—that you're not the sort of person who would refuse to forgive a friend who truly did not intend to do harm and is heartily sorry for her thoughtless behavior.

                                   Miserably,

LETTER 6
Flub: You've Damaged Someone's Prized Possession

Dear Fred,

This letter will fall far short of what it would say if I were skilled enough and eloquent enough to get it right. I know that; nevertheless I have to <u>try</u>. Because this letter comes from a man who has done something he is heartily ashamed of and would like to make amends for—a man who listened to your warnings with only half an ear and then proceeded to ignore them, with significant negative consequences.

I do remember, Fred, that you were reluctant to lend me your boat, and that you warned me it wasn't easy to handle. I even remember the specific instructions you gave me about water in the engine. But it wasn't until this morning, when my son told me the boat wouldn't start, that I really heard what you were saying—and then of course it was too late. I've damaged the engine (and a few other things) in exactly the ways you were afraid I would. I am more sorry than I can say.

In future I promise to <u>listen</u> when you're talking to me, and to be more careful; I hope that you, in future, will stick to your guns and refuse to let me borrow your property. In the meantime, I've taken your boat to the best repair place in this part of the state and I've told them to do whatever has to be done and send the bill to me. I know this doesn't make my carelessness any less inexcusable; perhaps, because you're not the sort of person who holds grudges, it will make it a little more forgivable.

                                   Your friend as always,

Chapter Four

"If I'd Only Known..."

Triple-F Scenario Three

Dear Madam:

I must confess that as I rode through the night to warn the people that the British were coming, I was not thinking about your tulips. Still, I deeply regret having trampled them into the ground as I did, and if you c̶a̶n̶ ̶f̶i̶n̶d̶ ̶i̶t̶ ̶i̶n̶ ̶y̶o̶u̶r̶ heart to forgive

Your o̶b̶e̶d̶i̶e̶n̶t̶

Paul R̶e̶v̶e̶r̶e̶

*L*ast Sunday night you had dinner with your family at your mother's house. It started as a friendly evening, with everyone relaxed and talking freely. But sometime during the meal you found yourself making an impassioned speech about the money the government is wasting on the unemployed in this country. You remember saying quite a few harsh things about "freeloaders" and "parasites"; you remember that the basic thesis of your argument was that anybody who doesn't have a job is just lazy. You remember that you didn't seem to be able to make the rest of the group understand how <u>important</u> it all was. And you remember how irritated you were because they kept trying to change the subject, when it should have been obvious to them that it really mattered to you and you really wanted to discuss it. You could tell that something was wrong, and before it was over you heartily wished you hadn't brought the subject up; but you couldn't seem to find a way to bring the episode to any kind of graceful close. Everything you tried only made the stress level worse.

It's all clear to you now, however—because you ran into a friend of your brother-in-law's and heard his tale of the hard times Frank is going through since he was laid off. Nobody had told you your sister's husband was out of work, undoubtedly because they know how busy you are and they didn't want to add to the things you have to worry about. If you'd known, you certainly would have kept your opinions to yourself as long as he and your sister were present.

You're very fond of your sister, although you rarely can find time to get together with her; for that matter, you're fond of her husband. The whole family's fond of Frank, and you can just imagine what they think of you and your big mouth. You still believe that most of the unemployed—but not Frank—are just too lazy to go out and get a job and pull themselves up by their bootstraps; you're not willing to back down from that position. Furthermore, it seems to you that someone ought to have warned you before the dinner, and that they should have let you in on information that was clearly known to everybody else in the family <u>except</u> you. Still, you'd like to be able to smooth things over, and you genuinely regret the pain you've inflicted. WHAT DO YOU SAY IN YOUR LETTER?

LETTER 7
Flub: You've Ranted about the Unemployed—in Front of Your Unemployed Brother-in-law

Dear Frank and Ellen,

There are people who always say the right thing; there are people you can always look forward to having around, because you can be sure it will be a pleasant experience. This letter doesn't come from one of those people. This letter comes from a man with a nasty case of foot-in-mouth disease, who has disgraced himself, embarrassed his family, and caused serious distress to two people he loves and admires.

Last night after a Little League game I ran into one of your friends at the Pizza Pit. He was kind enough to sit down and tell me how sorry he was about the trouble you've been having, and how he wished he had a job that he could offer to Frank. (He thought I already knew, of course.) I didn't tell him that what he was saying was a complete surprise to me, or that I'd already had an opportunity to demonstrate my ignorance of the facts. Frank . . . Ellen . . . I am so very sorry.

I can't promise you that I'll never sound like a conservative in public again; that would be a lie. But I can promise to pay more attention to the reactions of others when I start making speeches—so that if distress is one of their reactions I can stop talking before serious harm is done. And you two must promise me, please, that when you face problems in future you will help me out by taking me into your confidence as you would any other member of the family; I might then be able to do something useful on your behalf instead of causing you more grief. Unfortunately, I can't unsay the things I've said. But because you are the kind of caring and sensible people you are, I know I can count on you to forgive a clumsy man who doesn't always think before he speaks, but who truly would not have hurt you for anything in this world.

Affectionately,

Notice that although you express your regrets in this letter in the clearest and strongest terms, nowhere do you compromise your own principles or pretend to accept the opinions of others. You never say, falsely, "I didn't mean the things I said."

This is important. You're going to see your relatives again in future, and the subject of government spending is likely to keep coming up. You don't want to have to spend the rest of your family encounters pretending you hold opinions for which you actually feel only contempt. You also don't want to have to face an outraged family member saying, justifiably, "But in your <u>letter</u> you said you didn't <u>feel</u> that way about it!" The rule in situations like this is hard to apply, but easy to understand:

WHEN YOU DIDN'T MEAN TO CAUSE PAIN, BUT YOU DID MEAN WHAT YOU SAID, IT'S MUCH BETTER TO BE HONEST AND AGREE TO DISAGREE.

People who know you well are going to know when you're lying to them, and the falseness will contaminate the entire letter—they'll think that when you say you're sorry that's <u>also</u> false. (If in fact you <u>didn't</u> mean what you said, you should say so, certainly—but that's a different letter, and easier to write.)

Now let's move on to the analysis.

ANALYSIS OF LETTER 7

Paragraph One

There are people who always say the right thing; there are people you can always look forward to having around, because you can be sure it will be a pleasant experience. This letter doesn't come from one of those people. This letter comes from a man with a nasty case of foot-in-mouth disease, who has disgraced himself, embarrassed his family, and caused serious distress to two people he loves and admires.

This paragraph is written in the language behavior style called <u>Computer</u> Mode and is a sample of the application of another *Gentle Art* technique: the deliberate strategic use of the set of language patterns called <u>Satir Modes</u>. We'll begin with a quick introduction to the Satir Modes in speech, where they will be more familiar to you, and then extend that to written language.

USING THE SATIR MODES

Over the course of a lifetime of practice, therapist Virginia Satir noticed that when people are tense or under stress their language behavior tends to fall into one of five patterns: *Blaming, Placating, Distracting, Leveling,* and *Computing.* You may not be familiar with the underlined labels Satir chose for these language patterns, but you know them well; you will recognize them instantly when they are described to you and when you hear them used.

Blaming is openly hostile and confrontational, with obvious emphatic stresses on words and parts of words; its basic message is "I'm angry!" **Placating,** also with lots of obvious emphatic stresses, comes across as desperately apologetic; the basic message is "I'm sorry!" In both of these modes the language is intensely personal and filled with references to "I, me, you." People in Blamer Mode use sentences like these:

- "WHY can't you EVER do anything RIGHT?"
- "You NEVER think about what OTHER people might want to do!"
- "You could at LEAST get here on TIME!"

And people using Placater Mode say things like this:

- "Oh, YOU know ME! I don't care!"
- "Whatever YOU want is okay with ME!"
- "It's MY fault—I'm SORRY!"

Distracting cycles from one mode to another in hopeless panic, as in:

"Shoot, I don't care how long they make me WAIT! I didn't have anything to do at home ANYway! But I'm NOT GOING TO PUT UP with this kind of treatment! No rational person could be expected to do so."

That's two Placating sentences, a Blamer sentence, and a final sentence in Computer Mode. The basic message of the Distracter is "Help! I don't know what to say!" The only reason I can think of for ever writing in Distracter Mode is the one I've just relied on: in order to provide an example.

Extra emphasis on words and parts of words is a characteristic of Blaming, Placating, and Distracting. As a result, it's wise to keep your use of underlining (or italics) as an indication of focus in written language to a minimum. Look at this sentence:

"If you <u>really</u> had a <u>reason</u> to object to the clause, you should have <u>said</u> so at the <u>beginning</u>!"

A sentence like that sounds, in the reader's mental ear, like the speech of a whiny and overagitated child. It's annoying and it provokes only contempt. Avoid it at all costs.

Leveling is the expression of the simple truth, with none of the characteristics of Blaming, Placating or Distracting. Leveling can use the same words as any other Satir Mode, but the intonation—the tune the words are set to—is very different. When someone says "Whatever YOU want is okay with ME!" that's Placater Mode; Leveling would just be "Whatever you want is okay with me." And the Leveler, unlike the Placater, would <u>mean</u> it.

This leaves Computer Mode. Its most prominent identifying characteristic is its <u>neutrality</u>—a basic "I'm neutral on this" message—marked by the absence of emphatic stresses on words and parts of words. It's also marked by the near-absence of "I/you/me" language, and the substitution of references to hypothetical people and situations instead. Look again at the first sentence in Model Letter Three.

"There are people who always say the right thing; there are people you can always look forward to having around, because you can be sure it will be a pleasant experience. . . ."

The sentence refers to <u>hypothetical</u> people who say the right thing and are fun to have around. It doesn't mention "I" or "me." And the "you" that appears here is the hypothetical "you" that is the American equivalent of British "one." Few Americans would feel comfortable writing "There are people one can always look forward to having around, because one can be sure it will be a pleasant experience." The reader of the letter will be aware that this "you" is not a reference to him or to her.

The sentence that follows refers not to "my letter," but to "this letter." And the paragraph ends with a reference to "a man who" has done a particular list of things—still carefully avoiding all specifically personal language.

If you had written the paragraph in Leveler Mode you would have written sentences like these:

"I'm not one of those people. I'm a man with a nasty case of foot-in-mouth disease. I have disgraced myself, embarrassed my family, and caused serious distress to two people I love and admire."

Computer Mode conveys the same basic content, but it does it in a way that lets you avoid sounding like a person who's chosen the Worthless Worm strategy. It preserves your dignity. It gives you more room for "I/you" language later in the letter. And it keeps the regret you're expressing from seeming overdone and thus unbelievable. Whenever you want to defuse an emotional situation and cool things down, Computer Mode should be the first strategy you consider. Because taking the personal focus out of potential confrontations helps everyone involved to keep their emotions under control and maintain their perspective.[1]

Paragraph Two

Last night after a Little League game I ran into one of your friends at the Pizza Pit. He was kind enough to sit down and tell me how sorry he was about the trouble you've been having, and how he wished he had a job that he could offer to Frank. (He thought I already knew, of course.) I didn't tell him that what he was saying was a complete surprise to me, or that I'd already had an opportunity to demonstrate my ignorance of the facts. Frank . . . Ellen . . . I am so very sorry.

Paragraph One took care of the first two basic messages— BRACE YOURSELF, and SOMEBODY GOOFED. Paragraph Two covers I FOUND OUT and I'M SORRY. It switches out of Computer Mode and into Leveler Mode for a simple and truthful explanation of how you learned about your flub and how you feel about it having made it. It doesn't identify the man who spilled the beans to you, and it portrays him in a flattering light ("he was kind enough to . . .") in case Frank and Ellen recognize the source. It reinforces your claim that you misspoke out of ignorance rather than malice. And it doesn't beat around the bush in any way.

---

[1] For detailed discussion of the strategic use of the Satir Modes in speech, see any of the books or audio programs in the *Gentle Art of Verbal Self-Defense* series.

Paragraph Three

I can't promise you that I'll never sound like a conservative in public again; that would be a lie. But I <u>can</u> promise to pay more attention to the reactions of others when I start making speeches—so that if distress is one of their reactions I can stop talking before serious harm is done. And you two must promise me, please, that when you face problems in future you will help me out by taking me into your confidence as you would any other member of the family; I might then be able to do something useful on your behalf instead of causing you more grief. Unfortunately, I can't unsay the things I've said. But because you are the kind of caring and sensible people you are, I know I can count on you to forgive a clumsy man who doesn't always think before he speaks, but who truly would not have hurt you for anything in this world.

Your first sentence in this paragraph lets you take the moral high ground. It says, without being confrontational, that you won't lie and pretend to take back what you said. The second sentence states what you are willing to do in future to avoid making similar flubs—this is your NEVER AGAIN message. The third sentence brings in Frank and Ellen (and, indirectly, your entire family) and points out that they have to take some portion of the blame. But it doesn't say "It's your fault for not telling me" (Leveling) or "It's <u>your</u> fault for not <u>telling</u> me!" (Blaming). It asks Frank and Ellen to help you be a more effective member of this family—and it makes it hard for them to respond to you angrily. Like the compliment in the paragraph's final sentence, it puts them in a position where being gracious and courteous back at you will seem like the obvious response.

People with their backs to the wall, people whose perception is that they are being challenged and insulted, feel obligated to defend themselves by fighting back. People trying to cope with a Worthless Worm, watching the Worm grovel and writhe, feel obligated to get themselves out of the embarrassing contact as quickly and completely as possible. But people who have just been told NEVER AGAIN and YOU'RE TERRIFIC have no reason to feel either of these obligations. You've made it easy for them to be the nice people they would like to be, with no loss of face on either side.

MAKING EXCEPTIONS

One more item we need to take up here: Do you want to add
to the letter a sentence saying that, although you meant what you
said about freeloaders and parasites, you don't think those terms
apply to your brother-in-law? Think it over carefully. Can you explain
why Frank is an exception? "Because he's my brother-in-law" won't
do it. "My family right or wrong" won't do it. Unless you can make
that explanation, and do it sincerely and without hesitation, don't
make the change. If you can explain comfortably, Paragraph Three
is the right place to do it. Like this:

> "Unfortunately, I can't unsay the things I said. What I
> can do is assure you that they don't apply in any way to
> either one of you. Because [INSERT YOUR EXPLANA-
> TION HERE.] And because you are the kind of caring
> and sensible people you are, I know I can count on you,
> etc."

When you make an exception of this kind in speech, it may
be accepted because your body language and the situation make it
so clear that you're desperately sorry and trying to make amends.
The words go by quickly, and they're not available for leisurely
examination. When you write something you don't believe or can't
support, you lose both of those advantages. Don't do it unless you're
absolutely sincere and certain of your facts.

This was a bad episode. No one likes to hurt a family member,
spoil a family occasion, and look like an arrogant and unfeeling boor
to others. But at least it was family! Suppose it had been a business
dinner where you ranted about the waste in a new government bill
for retarded adults—and then you learned that one of your company's
guests had a fourteen-year-old retarded daughter? That would have
been far worse. Here's Letter 8, for that terrible situation.

LETTER 8
Flub: You've Griped About the Disabled—In Front
of a Client With a Disabled Child

Dear Mr. Edwards:

There are people who always say the right thing; there
are people you can always look forward to having around,
because you can be sure it will be a pleasant experience.

This letter doesn't come from one of those people. This letter comes from a man with a nasty case of foot-in-mouth disease, who has disgraced himself, embarrassed his firm, and caused serious distress by the careless and uninformed public statement of his opinions.

Jerry called me into his office this morning to tell me of your personal tragedy—and of my inexcusable behavior in the context of that tragedy. It is important to me for you to be aware that I was totally ignorant of the information Jerry shared with me; if I had known, I would never have made those callous remarks. That is no excuse, I know; it is intended as an explanation. Mr. Edwards, I am deeply sorry.

I can't promise that I'll never sound like a conservative in public again, or that I will never say things I will later regret. Like any human being, I make mistakes, and I am sure to make many more in future. I <u>can</u> promise to pay more attention to the reactions of others around me when I start making speeches—so that if distress is one of the reactions, I can stop talking before serious harm is done. And I can tell you frankly that I have learned from this experience that it would be better for me to <u>refrain</u> from making speeches when I have not been invited to do so. Unfortunately, I can't unsay the things I've said; I wish I could. I only hope you can find compassion enough in your heart to forgive a clumsy man who doesn't always think before he speaks, but who truly would not have added to your burdens for anything in this world.

Sincerely,

Getting to Computer Mode: Three Resources

Getting to Blamer, Placater, or the (very unlikely) Distracter Mode in written language is difficult. Telling those Modes from Leveler Mode in written language is equally difficult. The differences are obvious in spoken language, where you can hear the melody that goes with the words, but English punctuation doesn't transmit that melody clearly. Fortunately, we don't have to concern ourselves about this. Because there are no good reasons—none—for learning to write in Blamer, Placater, or Distracter Mode. Computer Mode, however, as shown in the analysis of Letter 3, can be extremely useful in your letters. It's therefore worthwhile to discuss the linguistic strategies available for using it. The basic principle of Computer Mode is this:

DEMOTE THE PERSONAL; PROMOTE THE HYPOTHETICAL.

That is: Use every resource English offers for changing the focus of a potential confrontation so that the people involved will be able to maintain some emotional distance. Here are three of the most effective of those resources.

Resource #1—Use the "Third Person"

The words "I, me, we, us" are said to be "in the first person"; second person is signaled by "you." When your letter would ordinarily contain "I/me/you" language, substitute sentences that refer to you and to your reader in the <u>third</u> person, as if you were writing about someone else. Instead of sentences like "I am writing to you to tell you that [X]," use sentences like the ones below (and like similar examples in the model letters.)

- "This is a letter from a man who has made a serious error of judgment and regrets it deeply."

- "This letter comes from a woman who very much wants to make amends for having spoken thoughtlessly at last night's banquet."

- "This is a letter from a company that is fully aware of its responsibilities to the city of Toledo and is prepared to fulfill every single one of them."

- "This is a letter to a woman whose extraordinary patience is greatly appreciated and will be long remembered."

- "This letter is being written by an attorney who has only just learned that a major piece of evidence was omitted from yesterday's court presentation."

Resource #2—Use Focus Shift

Use the strategies for shifting focus discussed on pages 28–32 as a way of removing both writer and reader from the sequence of written language.

Don't use these Leveling sentences:

- "I discovered this morning that you have lost the Whipple file. It was a real shock to me."
- "My discovery this morning that you have lost the Whipple file was a real shock to me."
- "Your loss of the Whipple file, discovered by me this morning, was a real shock."

Instead, use these Computer Mode sentences to get both "I" and "you" out of the spotlight:

- "The loss of the Whipple file, discovered this morning, was a real shock."
- "This morning's discovery that the Whipple file had been lost was a real shock."

Don't write "I called your office yesterday afternoon when I learned that you had lost the Whipple file." That sentence focuses unequivocally on "I" and "you," and it leaves the reader no space at all. Instead, write:

"During a phone call yesterday it was learned that the Whipple file had been lost."

This still lets your reader know that the jig is up—that you know he or she has lost the file and that this is a serious matter requiring your attention. But the focus of the sentence is on the call and on the file, on the physical objects involved. This cools down the confrontation and lets you make a simple statement of facts instead of an <u>accusation</u>.

Some of these Computer sentences are more awkward than the basic "I/you" sentences they replace; I agree with you about that. And in situations where chances of an unpleasant confrontation are slim—when you write letters containing nothing but good news and positive information, for example—you should of course try to avoid awkward sentences. But when your choice is between a sentence that is likely to create a hostile or panicked reaction in your reader, and a sentence that might strike your reader as awkward, the less graceful sentence is always the better choice. To write awkwardly because you don't know any better and can't help it is a handicap; to write awkwardly for solid strategic reasons is a demonstration of skill. (For a more detailed discussion of what "awkward" actually means, see pages 125–126.)

Resource #3—Use Indefinites and Generics

Substitute indefinites ("someone, something, some [X]") and language generics ("people, everybody, lawyers, engineers") for language that is personal.

Instead of this Leveling sentence—

* "I know you're upset about our price changes."

—use one of these:

* "Price changes are often upsetting to customers."
* "People are often upset by price changes."
* "Customers often are upset by price changes."

Instead of—

* "I've been advised that you are angry about your long wait for spare parts."

—use one of these:

* "The problem of long waits for spare parts is one that distresses customers nationwide."
* "Customers object to long waits for spare parts."

Computer Mode is rarely the most <u>efficient</u> way to transmit information. That's why we just shout "Duck!" instead of yelling "Because people who remain standing are likely to be struck on the head, it would be advisable to duck!" We can be reasonably sure, however, that a message urgent enough to rule out Computer Mode is a message we wouldn't put in a letter anyway; we'd deliver that sort of information face to face or by telephone. When there's time enough for a letter, there's time enough for Computer Mode. And it is the most neutral, the most dignified, and the least dangerous way to deliver a message that might provoke a negative reaction. Letters written in Triple-F situations need those three qualities badly.

SUPPLEMENTARY LETTERS

LETTER 9
Flub: You've Cut Down the Wrong Three Acres of Trees.

Dear Mr. Cartwright:

There are companies that never make a business error; there are companies you can always look forward to doing business with, because any move made will be the <u>right</u> move. This letter doesn't come from one of those companies. This letter comes from a firm that is just getting started in its field, that has made a serious blunder due to inexperience, and that had the misfortune to make a mistake that cannot be corrected.

Yesterday afternoon Hightop Timber learned that one of its crews had cut down three acres of your standing pine trees by mistake. The instructions given to that crew, as well as the survey information, were in error. The crew should have been working on the north side of Braggart Mountain instead of the eastern slope where your property is located. Mr. Cartwright, we are deeply and sincerely sorry.

We cannot say that Hightop will never make a mistake again; we can't be sure of that. We <u>can</u> promise to double-check all our orders in future, so that if the information we have is incorrect we have a better chance of discovering that before serious harm is done. Unfortunately, the trees that were cut down can't be put back. The check that we are enclosing to pay for the timber can't change the fact that it's gone and that you didn't intend it for logging. But because you were once head of a new business yourself, and understand what that is like, we hope you can find it in your heart to forgive a firm that has caused you harm but was truly innocent of any <u>intention</u> to do so.

Sincerely,

LETTER 10
Flounder: You Said You'd Show Them 'Round Your Town—But You Didn't Mean It

Dear Mr. and Mrs. Jacobs:

There are people who always say the right thing; there are people you can always look forward to having around, because you can be sure it will be a pleasant experience.

This letter doesn't come from one of those people. This letter comes from a woman who has made a promise she cannot keep and who faces the unpleasant task of taking back that promise unfulfilled.

Last April when I had the pleasure of meeting you at the convention in Chicago, I told you that if you ever visited Boston I would be happy to show you around the city. Now my secretary tells me that you will be here in two weeks, and that you have called to say you are taking me up on my offer. And I have no choice but to tell you that I cannot possibly carry out that promise. My schedule is so tight that not one more thing can be fit into it, and I see no prospect of a change in the situation any time soon. I realize that the theater tickets I have enclosed as a token of my regret fall far short of what I promised. Mr. and Mrs. Jacobs . . . I am so sorry.

I can't tell you that I will never again make a promise I cannot keep; like any human being, I make mistakes. I can promise to think more carefully in the future before making careless offers, so that I will be less likely to do harm. Unfortunately, my error can't be repaired. But because you are kind and understanding people, I hope I can count on you to forgive an embarrassed woman whose only real intention was to be courteous and friendly.

Sincerely,

Chapter Five

"I'm Only Human..."

Triple-F Scenario Four

Dear Adam,
I never thought we would lose our beautiful home and garden, but the snake said, "If you'll just* ... just one little bit* ...
Your gonna love it!"

Sorrowfully,

Eve

You are the owner and manager of a pet store in an expensive urban district. Most of your customers are highly paid professionals or people from families that have been wealthy so long they take their money for granted. You provide personalized service, you sell only purebred animals and top quality merchandise, and you pride yourself on your image. Several weeks ago a woman new to your customer list arranged to buy your only purebred female German Shepherd puppy, just as soon as it was old enough to leave its mother. You agreed to notify her when it was time to come take the pup away. But—perhaps because, unlike most of your customers, she didn't stop in from time to time to check on the pup's progress—the agreement somehow slipped your mind completely, and yesterday you sold the pup to someone else.

Your memory didn't kick in until three o'clock this morning, when you came bolt upright out of a sound sleep, saying "Oh, <u>no</u>!" As early as you dared, you called the pup's new owner to find out if he would be willing to exchange the animal for another one of equal or even greater value, but he refused. And now you have no choice but to tell the customer what you've done.

This is <u>serious</u>. Not only because you've broken your agreement with this one customer and let her down badly, but because a business like yours survives on word of mouth. If she's angry enough to start spreading the story of your error, she can do you serious damage that won't be easily repaired; you've got to mend your fences with her somehow. WHAT DO YOU SAY IN YOUR LETTER?

I want to offer you a suggested letter here in two versions, each with its own analysis, to show you how you can add another *Gentle Art* technique to your letter-writing skills.

LETTER 11
Flub and Frailty: You Forgot—and Broke—Your Promise to a Valued Customer

VERSION 1: NEUTRAL MODE

Dear Dr. Ellison:

In the course of my fifteen years at McDole Pets, I have never written a letter that distressed me as much as writing this one does; I am frankly heartsick about this. Doctor Ellison, I have done the unforgivable—I have sold to someone else the puppy that you arranged to buy from me.

I have no excuse to offer you; I can only say that it was not done deliberately. I simply forgot our agreement, and had no safeguards in place to prevent the mistake. I woke up in a cold sweat at three o'clock this morning when I suddenly realized what I had done. I am so very sorry.

I will take steps immediately to be sure that nothing like this ever happens to a customer of mine again, I promise you. But that in no way solves the present problem! Let us suppose that, unforgivable behavior or not, you are willing to forgive me and let me make amends. If so, I am prepared to find a suitable replacement pup through my professional network as quickly as that can possibly be done, to have the dog brought here at my expense, and to provide her to you at 20 percent less than the price we originally agreed on. There's no need for you to write or call unless this arrangement does <u>not</u> meet with your approval. I've already set in motion the process of locating the replacement, and I will notify you when the dog arrives.

Sincerely,

ANALYSIS OF LETTER 11, VERSION 1

Paragraph One

In the course of my fifteen years at McDole Pets, I have never written a letter that distressed me as much as writing this one does; I am frankly heartsick about this. Doctor Ellison, I have done the unforgivable—I have sold to someone else the puppy that you arranged to buy from me.

This paragraph is written in strict Leveler Mode. In this situation, you really have no excuse. Your best bet is to throw yourself—in as dignified a manner as you can—on the mercy of the customer. Your first sentence warns Dr. Ellison that you're about to give her some bad news and tells her you're not happy about it. Your second sentence states baldly what you've done and admits that it's unforgivable. There are times when this is the best way to go, and the more quickly you do it the better. The only plea you've made here is your reference to "my fifteen years at McDole Pets," which lets you call the doctor's attention indirectly to the fact that you've been in business a long time. That wouldn't be the case if you made this sort of mistake often.

Alternatively, you could use the method and technique that was demonstrated in Letter 7, and write the paragraph in Computer Mode. Either strategy will serve. The Computing paragraph will be a slightly cooler and more formal sequence of language, like this:

> This letter is difficult and distressing to write, and it is written with the deepest and most sincere regret. This is a letter from a man who has done the unforgivable—who has sold to someone else the puppy that he had promised to save for you.

Notice that there's no way to avoid using "you" at the end of the paragraph. The rule in Computing is to avoid as much "I/you" language as possible, but there will be times, like this one, when the personal words have to be used.

Paragraph Two

> I have no excuse to offer you; I can only say that it was not done deliberately. I simply forgot our agreement, and had no safeguards in place to prevent the mistake. I woke up in a cold sweat at three o'clock this morning when I suddenly realized what I had done. I am so very sorry.

This paragraph continues in Leveler Mode. (Even if you had begun in Computer Mode, the switch to Leveling would be necessary at this point.) It was your conscience that finally made you aware of what you had done, and you're willing to report the event in dramatic language, stressing the fact that it was an accident and an oversight rather than a deliberate violation of the agreement. You want the customer to understand that although your business practices may be too casual, they are not dishonest or malicious. And then you apologize, as you rightly should.

Paragraph Three

> I will take steps immediately to be sure that nothing like this ever happens to a customer of mine again, I promise you. But that in no way solves the present problem! Let us suppose that, unforgivable behavior or not, you are willing

to forgive me and let me make amends. If so, I am prepared to find a suitable replacement pup through my professional network as quickly as that can possibly be done, to have the dog brought here at my expense, and to provide her to you at 20 percent less than the price we originally agreed on. There's no need for you to write or call unless this arrangement does not meet with your approval. I've already set in motion the process of locating the replacement, and I will notify you when the dog arrives.

Here you go on to explain what you plan to do in the future, but you don't try to involve your reader. Not this time. She is genuinely innocent of any responsibility for the mix-up. And then you insert one extra item into the pattern: You state what you are prepared to do to make up for your error. In order to make things as convenient for Dr. Ellison as possible, you specify that she doesn't have to do anything unless she disapproves.

If your business allows for this sort of thing, it's always a good move when you know the reader has just cause to be angry with you. It's a good move when a reputation for service is important to you. If you ask Dr. Ellison to call or write you and let you know what she wants done, that is one more inconvenience for her to be angry about and one more delay in the process of providing her dog. If, as is likely, she's willing to accept your offer, the wording you've used above lets her know that she doesn't have to take any action herself. Finally, offering the 20 percent discount acknowledges that you are at fault and owe her something for that fault, but it avoids the Worthless Worm Message that would be conveyed by a larger discount or an offer to let her have the dog for free. Remember: There was no malice in what you did, only sloppiness.

This is a letter you can be proud of. If Dr. Ellison isn't a vindictive and unreasonable woman—and if you follow through on your bargain this time—matters should go smoothly. We can go on now to look at another version of the letter.

VERSION 2: TOUCH MODE

Dear Doctor Ellison:

In the course of my fifteen years at McDole Pets, I have never tackled a task as rough as writing this letter; it hits me very hard. Doctor Ellison, I have done the unforgivable—I have sold to someone else the puppy that you arranged to buy from me.

I'd feel better if I had an excuse for this stumble, but I don't. I can only say that I didn't do it deliberately. Somehow, our agreement just slipped through the cracks in my memory, and I had no safeguards in place to prevent the mistake. I woke up in a cold sweat at three o'clock this morning when I suddenly realized what I had done. I feel terrible about it; I am deeply sorry.

You can be certain that I will take steps immediately to make sure no customer of mine ever runs into this problem again—you have my word on that. But that doesn't put an end to the present problem! Let us suppose that, unforgivable behavior or not, you are willing to forgive me and let me set things right. If so, I am prepared to find a suitable replacement pup through my professional network as quickly as that can possibly be done, to have the dog brought here at my expense, and to provide her to you at 20 percent less than the price we originally agreed on. There's no need for you to get in touch with me unless this arrangement does <u>not</u> meet with your approval. I've already set in motion the process of locating the replacement, and I will contact you when the dog arrives.

Sincerely,

ANALYSIS OF LETTER 11, VERSION 2

Traditionally, it would be said that Letter 11, Version 2 is "only Version 1 in a different <u>style</u>." Some people would prefer the first version, some would prefer the second, and the verdict would be that "there's no accounting for taste." That's a myth. There are <u>lots</u> of useful ways to account for taste. The style used in Version 2 has been chosen for good strategic reasons and is constructed systematically. Let's compare the first paragraphs of the two versions; the sections that differ are in italics to make comparison easier.

(V1)

In the course of my fifteen years at McDole Pets, I have never *written a letter that distressed me as much as writing this one does; I am frankly heartsick about this.* Dr. Ellison, I have done the unforgivable—I have sold to someone else the puppy that you arranged to buy from me."

(V2)

In the course of my fifteen years at McDole Pets, I have *never tackled a task as rough as writing this letter; it hits me very hard.* Dr. Ellison, I have done the unforgivable—I have sold to someone else the puppy that you arranged to buy from me.

Version 2 changes "written a letter that distressed me as much as writing this one does" to "tackled a task as rough as writing this letter." And it changes "I am frankly heartsick about this" to "it hits me very hard." In both cases the shared information is that knowing you must write the letter is very unpleasant for you. But the words are different; why? Please set aside the idea that it's just a random selection based on what "sounds good" or "looks okay" to the writer. There are solid reasons for the choices made, based upon one of the most useful techniques used in the *Gentle Art* system—the use of the language patterns called *sensory modes*.

USING THE SENSORY MODES

All human beings survive by processing information from their external and internal environments. They do this by using the sensory systems of sight, hearing, touch, smell, taste, and so on. Every human being discovers, usually no later than the age of five, that one of those sensory systems serves him or her better than the others for understanding, learning, and remembering. Some people process information more easily and effectively if they look at it; others do better with information that they hear; and still others need to get right in there and work with the information "hands on" to do their best. How strong the preference is varies from one individual to another. My husband, for example, has so strong a preference for sight that he can't listen to a cassette tape properly unless he has his glasses on! People reflect their sensory preference in the choices they make among the language behavior patterns called sensory modes. They will consistently choose a word or phrase from the vocabulary of their preferred sensory system, especially when they are tense or under stress. For example:

Sight Mode

- "I see what you mean by your latest proposal; it's perfectly clear, and it looks like exactly what we need."
- "From our company's point of view, your plan is definitely going to brighten the day."
- "Sorry—I can't see my way clear to adding that clause to the current contract."

Hearing Mode

- "It sounds like an excellent idea; let's do it."
- "That's music to our ears, my friend—it really rings a bell in this division!"
- "If I'm hearing you correctly, you're telling me that you're going to give us a lot of static."

Touch Mode

- "This feels like the perfect solution; how fast can you get it nailed down for us?"
- "I'm not sure you're in touch with the situation . . . you don't seem to be getting our message."
- "I'm afraid I've put my foot in it this time . . . I just don't have a firm grasp of the basic problems we're up against."

All of these example sentences are "correct," of course. You could use any one of them that fits your situation. However, when you know someone's preferred sensory mode, it gives you an advantage that should not be wasted. By using the language of that mode whenever possible, you can substantially increase your chances of getting through to that person.

Suppose that you, owner and manager of McDole Pets, know that the customer you've wronged is a surgeon, that she plays the piano rather well, and that although she has very little free time she belongs to a neighborhood group of amateur potters who share a small studio and a kiln. In that case you have excellent reasons to assume that she likes to do things with her hands and that her preferred sensory system is touch. This is information that you can put to good use. Here's the first paragraph of Version 2 again, with the words that are unambiguously touch mode language in italics.

In the course of my fifteen years at McDole Pets, I have never *tackled* a task as *rough* as writing this letter; it *hits* me very hard. Dr. Ellison, I have done the unforgivable—I have sold to someone else the puppy that you arranged to buy from me.

This conveys the same basic messages as Version 1, but it's worded to make it as convenient and painless as possible for Dr. Ellison to understand you. Psychologist George Miller once said something so important to communication that I have named it Miller's Law:

IN ORDER TO UNDERSTAND WHAT ANOTHER PERSON IS SAYING, YOU MUST ASSUME THAT IT IS TRUE AND TRY TO IMAGINE WHAT IT COULD BE TRUE OF.

There is an obvious corollary: "In order for other people to understand what you are saying, you must make it possible for them to apply Miller's Law to your language." The easier you make it for others to apply Miller's Law to your letters, the greater your chances are that what you're trying to tell them will be completely and correctly understood.

Suppose you knew that your customer spoke only French, and you were able to use French with ease. You would write to her in French, as a courtesy and to minimize the chances of misunderstanding. Writing to someone in his or her preferred sensory mode is exactly the same thing, though on a much smaller scale. It's courteous and considerate, and it says to the reader, "You and I speak and write the same language."

In addition, although everyone can use all the sensory modes at will, just as I'm doing here, people who are tense or angry or under stress tend to rely heavily on their preferred sensory mode. Since you know in advance that your announcement to Dr. Ellison about the sale of the promised puppy is going to upset her, using her preferred mode is a doubly wise move.

Finally, let's consider the worst case scenario. What if you're wrong, and Dr. Ellison doesn't prefer touch mode at all? What if she was forced to go into surgery by domineering parents? What if she only plays the piano and does pottery because she believes it will increase the strength of her fingers and wrists for surgery? It's unlikely, but it's certainly possible. In that situation, your strategic move to use touch language in your letter will be wasted effort. But no real harm has been done, because both versions of the letter are acceptable—it's not as if you had written a letter in French to someone who reads only Chinese. It was worth a try, and most of the time you would have been correct.

When you know people well, when you have an opportunity to hear the language choices they make and observe their behavior, you'll find that it's easy for you to determine which sensory mode they prefer. You'll automatically recognize the sensory mode of language you hear or read, because that's one of the ways your internal grammar cross-indexes your vocabulary; you just need to begin paying attention to it as information worth noting and remembering. You can then make good use of that knowledge in your language interactions.

The rules for using the sensory modes in spoken language are as follows (with sensory language in italics):

RULE ONE:
MATCH THE SENSORY MODE THE OTHER PERSON
IS USING IF YOU CAN.

Example:

Answer "How bad does it *look?*" with "I don't *see* it as a serious problem." This is SENSORY MODE MATCHING. "I don't *feel* that it's very serious" would be SENSORY MODE MISMATCH.

RULE TWO:
OTHERWISE, USE AS LITTLE OF THE SENSORY
VOCABULARY AS POSSIBLE.

Example:

Answer "How bad does it *look?*" with "I don't think it's a serious problem," to avoid sensory mode mismatch.

In writing a letter, where you often don't have an example of the other person's language available to respond to, you can't use these rules in the same way. But you can <u>adapt</u> them, like this:

RULE ONE:
IF YOU KNOW YOUR READER'S PREFERRED SENSORY MODE,
USE IT AS MUCH AS POSSIBLE.

RULE TWO:
OTHERWISE, USE AS LITTLE OF THE SENSORY
VOCABULARY AS POSSIBLE.

Version 1 of the model letter in this chapter was written without taking any thought for the choice of sensory modes. That is the most common situation, because few of us have learned anything about the sensory mode communication strategy in school or anywhere else. Version 2 was written with the specific intention of making maximum use of touch mode. Here are the other two paragraphs of the letter, with the touch language in italics for your reference.

> I'd *feel* better if I had an excuse for this *stumble,* but I don't. I can only say that I didn't do it deliberately. Somehow, our agreement just *slipped through the cracks* in my memory, and I had no safeguards in place to prevent the mistake. I woke up in a *cold* sweat at three o'clock this morning when I suddenly realized what I had done. I *feel* terrible about it; I am *deeply* sorry.
>
> You can be certain I will *take steps* immediately to make sure that no customer of mine ever *runs into* this problem again—you have my word on that. But that doesn't *put an end to* the present problem! Let us suppose that, unforgivable behavior or not, you are willing to forgive me and let me *set* things right. If so, I am prepared to find a suitable replacement pup through my professional network as quickly as that can possibly be done, to have the dog *brought* here at my expense, and to provide her to you at 20 percent less than the price we originally agreed on. There's no need for you to *get in touch with* me unless this arrangement does <u>not</u> *meet with* your approval. I've already *set in motion* the process of locating the replacement, and I will *contact* you when the dog arrives.

Our society has a very strong bias in favor of the sense of sight, followed by the sense of hearing. The touch vocabulary items, especially when used in quantity as in Version 2, are often judged less elegant, less intellectual, and less graceful. If you strongly prefer eye or ear language (as do most successful Americans who are not surgeons or sculptors), you may feel that the touch mode version of the letter is too "colloquial" for your taste. That won't make it any less the best version when your readers are those for whom touch language is the most accurate way to express their perceptions of the world. You might be wise to consider ignoring your biases in favor of their preferences.

To end this chapter, here are two more versions of Letter 11—one in sight mode and the other in hearing mode—with a few other wording variations provided for your reference.

LETTER 11, Version 3: Sight Mode 2

Dear Dr. Ellison:

In the course of my fifteen years at McDole Pets, no task has ever darkened my day as much as writing this letter has; it's like looking at a cliff face to be climbed in the dark. Dr. Ellison, I have done the unforgivable—I have sold to someone else the puppy that you arranged to buy from me.

If I could see any way to offer you an excuse for my mistake, this would be less painful. I can't. I can only say that it wasn't done deliberately. Somehow, I simply forgot about our agreement, and I had no safeguards in place to prevent the mistake. I could hardly look at myself in the mirror this morning after I realized what I had done. I am so very sorry.

I assure you, I will see to it that no customer of mine ever has this experience again. But that doesn't solve the present problem! Let us suppose that, whether my behavior is or is not unforgivable, you are willing to forgive me and to let me set things right. If so, I am prepared to find a suitable replacement pup through my professional network as quickly as that can possibly be done, to have the dog brought here at my expense, and to provide her to you at 20 percent less than the price we originally agreed on. I see no need for you to write or call unless this arrangement does <u>not</u> meet with your approval. I've already begun looking for the replacement, and I will let you know at once when the dog arrives.

Sincerely,

LETTER 11, Version Four: Hearing Mode

Dear Dr. Ellison:

In the course of my fifteen years at McDole Pets, no words have ever sounded as inadequate to me as those I'm using to write this letter; I wish I had a way to tell you properly how distressing this is. Dr. Ellison, I've done the unforgivable—I've sold someone else the puppy you arranged to buy from me.

I'd feel better if I had an excuse for my mistake, but I don't. I can only say that I didn't do it deliberately. Somehow, I forgot that you'd said you wanted the pup, and I had no safeguards in place to prevent the error. I woke up in a cold sweat at three o'clock this morning when I suddenly realized what I had done, as if I'd heard a thunderclap. I am so sorry.

You can be sure that I will take steps immediately to make certain that no customer of mine ever has to listen to this kind of sorry tale again—you have my word on that. But that's not a solution to the present problem! Let us suppose that, unforgivable behavior or not, you're willing to forgive me and to let me make amends. If so, I am prepared to find a suitable replacement pup through my professional network as quickly as that can be done, to have the dog brought here at my expense, and to provide her to you at 20 percent less than the price we had originally agreed upon. I won't expect to hear from you unless you are opposed to this arrangement. I've already set in motion the process of locating the replacement, and I will call you when the dog arrives.

Sincerely,

Sometimes English has a complete and perfect set of vocabulary items for the three sensory systems of sight, hearing, and touch. For example, when asked to offer your opinion of someone's idea, you can say "It looks right to me," "It sounds right to me," or "It feels right to me." Most of the time, however, the set is incomplete—as when the eye person can write "It's a sight for sore eyes" and the ear person can write "It's music to my ears" but there isn't any corresponding touch expression. (And you'll notice that I can call a person who prefers sight an eye person, and a person who prefers hearing an ear person, but there's no equivalent term in English for the person who prefers touch.) This means that there'll be times when you'll want to write a particular message in one of the sensory modes and there literally won't be any words for what you want to say. In such a situation, either use words from one of the other sensory modes or avoid sensory language entirely, according to your needs at the time. Don't struggle for perfection where perfection is impossible.

The letter in which you want to be most careful about matching sensory modes is the one for which your goal is to persuade your reader to do something, or to refrain from doing something. Sensory mode matching creates trust and good feeling, and it gives you just that little extra advantage that may accomplish your goal.

Finally, there are times when your letter will be addressed to a group rather than an individual, with a variety of sensory preferences to be considered as a result. That doesn't mean there's no way to use the sensory modes strategy. You have two choices. You can use examples of language from sight, hearing, and touch, all three modes, so that there'll be something in your letter for everybody. This is particularly useful for letters that have a teaching function— that contain instructions, for example, or substantial amounts of data to be understood and remembered. Or you can avoid sensory language completely, to make the letter sensory-neutral and equally acceptable to every one of your readers. This loses the advantage of being able to transmit the message "I perceive the world the way you perceive it; we speak the same language." But it avoids the message that you and your listeners are on completely different wave lengths, which is also a worthwhile strategy.

SUPPLEMENTARY LETTERS

LETTER 12
Flub and Frailty: You've Given Away the Job You Promised a Friend

Dear Joe:

I've been a manager here at Acmeco for more than fifteen years, and I've been through every conceivable kind of chaos and mess. But I have never had to deal with anything that was as hard for me to face as writing this letter is. There's no easy way to tell you what I've done. Remember the job I promised you? Joe, I gave that job to somebody else. Not because I didn't mean it when I said you could have it. Not because you aren't completely qualified to get it. But because, to my shame, I just plain forgot.

I don't know how this could have happened. I don't know how I could have forgotten, or why I didn't have sense enough to tell my secretary so that I didn't have to rely on my memory alone. I do know that I didn't do it deliberately and that if I could <u>undo</u> it I would. Joe, I am so very sorry about this.

I've set up some new files here to be sure that nothing like this ever happens again. For me, that's an improvement. But it's no help to <u>you</u>! Let's suppose that you're willing to accept my explanation and my sincere apology and let bygones be bygones. If so, I'm prepared to find a place for you somewhere else in the company, as quickly as that can be done. If that interests you, and you're still willing to work here, just give me a call and I'll start looking immediately; if you'd rather not, no need to call— I'll understand. I've already told the personnel people that if the man I hired doesn't work out, that job is yours.

Sincerely,

LETTER 13
Flub and Frailty: You've Spent the Money You Owe a Friend

Dear Charles,

You and I have known each other a long time, and we've been through a lot of unpleasant experiences together. We've always managed to keep our friendship intact. This time, it may not work. Charles, I've done something there's no possible excuse for: I've taken the money I was supposed to pay back to you Friday afternoon and bought a new CD player with it.

I don't have any excuse to give you. I don't even have an explanation. I can't get my money back, because I bought the unit at a clearance sale, no returns allowed. I can't even say I didn't do it on purpose. I <u>knew</u> I shouldn't buy it, no matter what a bargain it was and no matter how long I'd been wanting one. I just plain couldn't resist.

I wish I could promise you that I'd never buy anything I can't afford again; I can't. I know my weaknesses, and buying things on impulse is one of the worst of them. I <u>do</u> promise you that you'll have your money back in two weeks, with whatever interest you think is fair. And I promise you that I'll never again ask you for a loan. A lot of people would consider this incident the end of our friendship; I know you're not one of these people. And I know how lucky I am that that's true.

Sincerely,

Chapter Six

"It's Out of My Hands..."

Triple-F Scenario Five

Dear Madam:

I do indeed remember that when you invested in my expedition you were promised a supply of water from the fountain of youth. However, due to a succession of lengthy delays, mostly environmental in nature, we have been unable to procure

Respe

Ponce d

$\mathbf{Y}$ou are an executive vice president with a large staff, and you value your reputation as an executive who stays close to your people. Your relationship with the staff is critical to the smooth operation of your business, and that relationship depends heavily on <u>trust</u>. Ever since the movement for dress codes in the workplace began to spread around the country, you have been reassuring your staff: IT WILL NEVER HAPPEN HERE. But yesterday *your* boss called you in and informed you in no uncertain terms that: (1) a dress code is to be put in place immediately; (2) you are to write the memorandum to the staff announcing the rule; and (3) he is to get a draft copy of that memo for approval before you send it out. You fought him on it. You pointed out that it meant you had to break a promise—and he told you he was perfectly willing to take the heat. You suggested that in that case <u>he</u> should write the memo—and he told you that's why he has executive vice presidents, so he won't have to write memos. It is clear to you that the matter is not negotiable, and that you are going to have to be the messenger for this particular piece of bad news. WHAT DO YOU SAY IN YOUR MEMO?

LETTER 14
Frailty: There Will Be a Dress Code After All

MEMORANDUM

FROM: (Your name and title)   DATE:
TO: Staff names and titles, or just "All personnel"
SUBJECT: Change in company policy

This is a memorandum I never thought I'd have to write, and one I write with great reluctance. People, I promised you that a dress code would never appear in the procedures manual at Prittikin—I remember that very well. I promised you not just once, but <u>many</u> times.

I was wrong. I am advised by our president that starting Monday morning we <u>will</u> have a dress code, and that by Friday you will have a list of the specific details. I am truly sorry to be the messenger who brings you this bad news.

I wish I could tell you that I will never break a promise to you again; I can't. I wish I could tell you that I will always know enough about what's going to happen next to make it possible for me to make promises with complete confidence; I can't do that either. What I <u>can</u> do is give you my word that my future promises, like those of the past, will be based on my knowledge of the facts and my understanding of your best interests. You know you can count on me, although there are going to be times when I am overruled; I know I can count on you, though there are going to be times when you'd like me to do things differently. You have my deep appreciation, as always, and my regrets.

This memo follows the same pattern we've been using, but with a slightly different twist, like this:

1. BRACE YOURSELF.
2. SOMETHING HAPPENED.
3. I FOUND OUT.
4. I'M SORRY.
5. NEVER AGAIN, IF I CAN HELP IT.
6. YOU'RE TERRIFIC.

The difference is that unlike letters about flubs and flounderings, a frailty letter usually reports something unpleasant that you are responsible for <u>only</u> because you're human. That is, you'd like to have been a person so skilled at persuasion that you won the argument with your boss, or a person so skilled at prediction that you would have seen this coming and been able to prepare the staff . . . you'd like to be a person who could turn back tornadoes and spin straw into gold, too. Because you are only human, things like this are going to happen, and that's the real world—that's frailty. You therefore substitute SOMETHING HAPPENED for SOMEBODY GOOFED; and you add IF I CAN HELP IT to NEVER AGAIN.

ANALYSIS OF LETTER 14

Paragraph One

This is a memorandum I never thought I'd have to write, and one I write with great reluctance. People, I promised you that a dress code would never appear in the procedures manual at Prittikin—I remember that very well. I promised you not just once, but <u>many</u> times.

Your warning message in the opening sentence is quite clear, and it immediately tells your readers that what you're about to announce came as a shock to you and upsets you a good deal. You've used the technique of focus-shifting here. You could have begun with "I never thought I'd have to write this memorandum, and I do it with great reluctance." That would have been a correct sentence and it would have expressed the facts accurately. But the shift in focus to "This is a memorandum I never thought I'd have to write," etc., lets you give yourself <u>explicit</u> distance from what has happened. It's a way of saying subtly, "Be angry with the message, not with the messenger."

Next, with "People," you speak to your readers directly, calling them by name, and you *Level*. You say what you know they are going to want to say: "But you told us over and over again that this was never going to happen! You <u>promised</u> us!" And although you do not say, yet, that a dress code will be put in place at your company, no one could possibly fail to get the message that something of that kind has come to pass. There could no other reason for what you've written.

You have not, fortunately, structured your message as a Hedge, as in this sentence:

"... I know I promised you—not once, but many times—that there would never be a dress code at Prittikin, but I was wrong. ..."

Hedges, remember, make people angry, and they should be rigorously avoided whenever that's possible. It's the linguistic foliage labeled "but" that provokes the anger; just clip it, as has been done here. And moving the "I was wrong" section into the next paragraph helps to keep your readers from hearing a Hedge in their mind's ears even though none is there.

Paragraph Two

I was wrong. I am advised by our president that starting Monday morning, we <u>will</u> have a dress code, and that by Friday you will have a list of the specific details. I am truly sorry to be the messenger who brings you this bad news.

In this paragraph you give them the bad news, and because you want to maintain the contract for mutual trust, you Level all the way through it. You begin with "I was wrong" and you end with "I'm sorry." Nothing ambiguous about that, and no weasel words. In between, however, you do some fancy focus-shifting. "I am advised by our president" says, equally clearly, "We're all in this together, being told what we have to do by somebody who outranks us." This is much better than writing, "The president tells me that starting Monday morning . . ." or "The president has decided that starting Monday morning. . . ." Your staff knows that you are the brass and they are the troops, sure. But it helps for them to know that at another level you *also* have to take orders. The fact that you acknowledge it openly, with "our president," tells them that you are aware of this, too.

The choice of the very formal "advised" and "further advised," is deliberate. It carries a metamessage for you. It says, "This is the message I am ordered, formally, to transmit. I'm transmitting it. But I don't have to like it! I don't have to make it *my* message." Bracketing all that formal reporting of language with the two personal messages is like setting the message off in a box with a label. This is a strategy you can use any time you are obligated to deliver a message that you don't approve of, unless your own typical written language is so formal that your reader would miss the metamessage.

Paragraph Three

I wish I could tell you that I will never break a promise to you again; I can't. I wish I could tell you that I will always know enough about what's going to happen next to make it possible for me to make promises with complete confidence; I can't do that either. What I can do is give you my word that my future promises, like those of the past, will be based on my best knowledge of the facts and my understanding of your best interests. You know you can count on me, although there are going to be times when I am overruled; I know I can count on you, though there are going to be times when you'd like me to do things differently. You have my deep appreciation, as always, and my regrets.

The construction of this paragraph (the NEVER AGAIN—IF I CAN HELP IT, and YOU'RE TERRIFIC paragraph) will repay your close and careful examination. It Levels with your staff; it tells it like it is. It says you're human and you can't always get everything exactly as you want it, but you do the best you can. It says you expect them to do the same for you. But it isn't done casually, off the top of your head. The tone of this paragraph includes a metamessage saying, "I don't take this lightly, and I don't consider it trivial; taking back a promise and putting new restrictions on your personal freedoms are grave matters to me." And that tone is created by heavy reliance on one of the most ancient of all language strategies: <u>parallelism</u>.

USING PARALLELISM

Suppose I'm making a speech, and you're listening. You hear me say "When winter comes, we will . . ." do something or other. That creates no particular expectations in your mind. However, you then hear me say "When spring arrives, we will . . ." do something or other, and the pattern-detector in your mind <u>notices</u>.

Once can't be a pattern, by definition. Twice probably is, especially when the two items are the first and second members of a larger set. Hearing or reading two similar chunks puts your pattern-detector on full alert. Three times can't be anything else <u>but</u> a pattern; that rule is part of your internal grammar. So that when you hear me say first "When winter comes, we will . . ." and then "When spring arrives, we will . . .," based on shared cultural knowledge, you automatically set up four files in your memory and label them "winter, spring, summer, autumn (or fall)." When I say, "On the first day of summer, we will . . . ," you'll already be waiting with the space in your memory assigned and labeled, and you'll be able to give your full attention to filing whatever information goes with summer in that space. The same thing will be true when I come to autumn in my talk; you'll be prepared, because the work of indexing for storage in memory has already been done.

The primary *purpose* of this kind of parallelism is not to be either formal or fancy. "I came; I saw; I won" is just as "parallel"—just as much a structural matching and balancing of linguistic items—as is "I came; I saw; I conquered." The point of such patterning is to structure your language in such a way that it will be easier for your readers or listeners to understand and remember what you're telling them.

Let's look at the paragraph again, in two versions: first, a version without deliberate parallelism, and then the version we've already seen. In the second version, the parallel sequences are in capital letters for clarity.

Without Deliberate Parallelism:

1. "I wish I could tell you that I will never break a promise to you again; I can't.

2. If I could say that I'll always know enough about what's going to happen next to make it possible for me to make promises with complete confidence, you know I would.

3. But I don't know any way to do that.

4. What I <u>can</u> do is give you my word that my future promises, like those of the past, will be based on my knowledge of the facts.

5. And they will be based on your best interests, as I understand them.

6. You know you can count on me, although there are going to be times when I am overruled.

7. And I know I don't have to worry about your loyalty, even when I'm not doing what you'd prefer that I do.

8. You have my deep appreciation, as always, and I regret that this step had to be taken."

WITH DELIBERATE PARALLELISM:

1. "I WISH I COULD TELL YOU THAT I WILL never break a promise to you again; I CAN'T.

2. I WISH I COULD TELL YOU THAT I WILL always know enough about what's going to happen next to make it possible for me to make promises with complete confidence; I CAN'T do that either.

3. What I <u>can</u> do is give you my word that my future promises, like those of the past, will be based on MY KNOWLEDGE OF THE FACTS and MY UNDERSTANDING OF YOUR BEST INTERESTS.

4. YOU KNOW YOU CAN COUNT ON ME, ALTHOUGH THERE ARE GOING TO BE TIMES WHEN I am overruled; I KNOW I CAN COUNT ON YOU, THOUGH THERE ARE

GOING TO BE TIMES WHEN YOU'd like me to do things differently.

5.   You have MY DEEP APPRECIATION, as always, and MY RE-GRETS."

It's important to understand that the difference between the version using parallelism and the version without it has a *scientific* basis, not just a stylistic one. One reason parallelism is so helpful in communication is that it tailors the language you're using to the capacity and operation of the human short-term memory (also called the "working" memory).

When people read, the words they see go first to the short-term memory for processing. There, decisions are made as to which parts of the language should be given attention, which can be ignored, which must be transferred to the long-term memory for indexing and storage, and so on. This is a lot of work, and it has to be done, for all practical purposes, simultaneously. But the short-term memory can only hold about <u>seven</u> chunks of information at a time, and it can only hold a chunk of information for about thirty seconds before losing it.[1] Anything you can do to make the short term memory's work easier is going to increase the chances that your message will be understood and remembered; that's why really good speeches contain so many examples of the strategy. (Look at the speeches of John F. Kennedy, Martin Luther King, and Winston Churchill, for excellent examples of parallelism skillfully used.)

It's not as critical to use parallelism in written language as in spoken language, because the reader who doesn't get what you're writing the first time can go back and look at your words again and review them for additional meaning. The problem is that you can't be sure that will happen. If the reader <u>thinks</u> he or she got your message, there will be no review; if the reader doesn't think the message is interesting or important, review is very unlikely. Using parallelism lets you nail things down more tightly and maximizes your chances for successful communication. When you can do it without sounding phony or melodramatic, it's an excellent strategy.

---

[1] So far as we know, "losing it" means that the information goes into the infinite storage space of the long-term memory, but without any index—which means there's no way to retrieve it later, and it might as well not be there for all the use it is to you. This is different from simple forgetting, where the memory can be "jogged."

WARNING: ALLOW FOR DOMINANCE DISPLAYS!

You'll remember from Scenario Five that your boss requested a draft of the memo for his approval before you sent it on to the staff. Any human being with the power to approve or disapprove someone else's written text is going to feel tempted (or obligated) to demonstrate that power by making some kind of change in the text. This is called a <u>dominance</u> <u>display</u>, and it is as predictable and inevitable as weather; your boss is unlikely to be an exception to the rule. If your letter is too perfect, and you leave the boss nowhere to make a dominance display, you'll be sorry. One of two unpleasant things will happen.

1. The boss will notice the perfection and refrain from making changes; but he will resent it, and resent the fact that he resents it. He will feel that he ought to be a superior person who has nothing but admiration for a subordinate's superb language skills, and he will dislike you for making it clear to him that he's not that sort of person after all.

2. The boss will notice only that he has a hard time deciding where to make changes, and he will be annoyed by <u>that</u>. His changes will spoil your letter, too.

It's always best to put in a few very obvious things that will draw the attention of the person who has the power to make changes—things that can be changed without doing any serious harm. Your letter has several such items. "With great reluctance" can be changed to "reluctantly." You underlined "many" in "<u>many</u> times"; the underlining can be deleted. The sequence "will not be allowed" can be fooled with to produce "will be forbidden." In the final paragraph, the boss can play with your punctuation—turning some of your semicolons into periods—if he wants to. If you are careful to salt your text with things like these, you increase your chances that the parts of the letter that really *matter* to you won't be tampered with.

When I had to write letters and memoranda that were subject to the approval or disapproval of university committees, I always deliberately salted my drafts with items from my native Ozark English. I could count on my university colleagues to spot those instantly and replace them with "Standard English" substitutes. This was usually enough to get the rest of my text past the red pencils. Other good candidates for dominance displays are deliberate minor errors in spelling, in dates and figures, and the like. The boss who has the opportunity to change your misspelled "portefolio" to "portfolio" and your mistaken "$370.45" to the accurate "$375.45" will often be satisfied with that and leave everything else alone. Just be sure you keep track of what you've done, so that an error that gets past the review won't go out uncorrected.

PROVIDING AN ILLUSION OF CHOICE

In Scenario Five, the most serious problem you faced in writing your letter was that you were being forced to take back a promise and violate an established trust. But there's another problem in this sort of correspondence, and it will be there whether you've made a previous commitment to your staffers or not: the problem of giving orders to adults about their personal behavior. People react to those orders with an automatic knee-jerk negative response that usually has very little to do with the <u>content</u>. The reaction is not to the specific command but to the <u>speech</u> act: to the fact that the message <u>is</u> a command. Women who have no interest in wearing slacks to work resent being told they're not allowed to; men who would rather wear ties at the office object to being told they're required to; smokers who actually welcome help in cutting down on their smoking nevertheless resent being ordered not to smoke on the job. Adults don't mind being told what to do when the message is directly related to their work; they understand that part of having a job is following orders. But they perceive policies on smoking, dress codes, and other personal matters very differently.

One way to lessen this negative reaction somewhat is to offer what therapist Gregory Bateson and his associates called "an illusion of choice." That is, although you can't offer your readers a choice about the order being given in your letter, you can offer them a choice about something <u>associated</u> with the order. Suppose your company has decided to bring in a series of consultants and presenters every month to do on-site training (obligatory rather than voluntary) in communication skills. Most of your employees are not in jobs that require them to interact with the public, and many of them will see no reason why improved communication skills should be part of their job description. This means that resistance to the obligatory training sessions is likely, along with bad feeling toward management and less than enthusiastic participation in the training sessions. In a case like this, especially if you had previously assured your people that training would be voluntary, offering an illusion of choice as shown in Letter 15 is a useful strategy.

LETTER 15
Frailty: The Training Sessions Won't Be Optional After All

MEMORANDUM

FROM: (Your name and title)   DATE:
TO: "All personnel"
SUBJECT: Change in company policy

It gives me great pleasure to send you this memorandum, and I'm confident that you will be as delighted with what I am about to announce as I am. People, I am advised that starting in August we will be having on-site communication skills training here at Prittikin for one full day each month.

I do remember having assured you in the past that participation in any such training sessions would be voluntary. That was an error on my part, and I am advised that every employee will be required to attend the sessions. I'm sorry to go back on a commitment I'd made to you; that's always difficult. But I am anything but sorry that these training sessions are going to be offered. They are a terrific opportunity, with major benefits down the road for every single one of us.

We wish we could set up the sessions so that each of you would have full control of the scheduling according to your own personal preferences. Since that's impossible, we need your input on the following question: When the training starts in August, do you want to schedule sessions for Fridays or for Tuesdays? Please write your preference at the bottom of this memo and drop it off at the personnel desk no later than tomorrow afternoon; we'll count the votes and let you know which day you've chosen. I know we can look forward to your wholehearted and enthusiastic participation, and we're grateful for your help with the scheduling problem.

ANALYSIS OF LETTER 15

Paragraph One

It gives me great pleasure to send you this memorandum, and I am confident that you will be as delighted with what I am about to announce as I am. People, I am advised that starting in August we will be having on-site communication skills training here at Prittikin for one full day each month.

This is a straightforward and uncomplicated paragraph, carrying the BRACE YOURSELF and SOMETHING HAPPENED messages for you. Starting with "It gives me great pleasure" and "I'm confident that you will be delighted" is different from previous Triple-F model letters. There will be times when you have to handle it this way, and adults in our society have a lot of experience with negative messages worded positively, going all the way back to "Guess what, honey? You get to go to the dentist this morning!" Your readers will understand that you have to appear to back the new training project enthusiastically, for the same reason that they have to attend the sessions. Whether you have reservations (and whether they do) is irrelevant for people who want to go on working at Prittikin, once the decision has been made by top management.

Paragraph Two

I do remember having assured you in the past that participation in any such training sessions would be voluntary. That was an error on my part, and I am advised that every employee will be required to attend the sessions. I'm sorry to go back on a commitment I made to you; that's always difficult. But I am anything but sorry that these training sessions are going to be offered. They are a terrific opportunity, with major benefits down the road for every single one of us.

In this paragraph you admit that you're breaking a promise, and you apologize. As in the first paragraph, you use "I am advised" to let your readers know that the decision was made for you, as it has been made for them, and that any objections you may have had were overruled.

Paragraph Three

We wish we could set up the sessions so that each of you would have full control of the scheduling according to your own personal preferences. Since that's impossible, we need your input on the following question: When the training starts in August, do you want to schedule sessions for Fridays or for Tuesdays? Please write your preference at the bottom of this memo and drop it off at the personnel desk no later than tomorrow afternoon; we'll count the votes and let you know which day you've chosen. I know we can look forward to your wholehearted and enthusiastic participation, and we're grateful for your help with the scheduling problem.

It's not lying to tell the personnel that you wish everybody could pick the training schedule they'd most like to have. That's like "We wish you could fly," an innocuous wish for an unattainable perfect world. The individualized schedule, like flying, is impossible, and you say so. But your mention of it lets you transmit a metamessage of respect and courtesy, saying: I KNOW YOU'RE ADULTS AND THAT YOU HAVE INDIVIDUAL NEEDS AND PREFERENCES THAT SHOULD BE CONSIDERED WHENEVER THAT'S POSSIBLE.

Certainly the choice you're offering between Fridays and Tuesdays doesn't change the fact that the employees have no choice about attendance at the training sessions. They're still being ordered to attend. But the Friday or Tuesday choice tones down the dictatorial nature of the memo a little, at no cost to those giving the orders. In the case of the dress-code notice in Letter 14, however, there was no option for an illusion of choice.[2]

This paragraph differs slightly from the Triple-F pattern; it doesn't say NEVER AGAIN (or NEVER AGAIN—IF I CAN HELP IT) anywhere. It's not possible to tell your readers that you're offering them something wonderful and at the same time to promise never to do anything like that again. If you want to add a NEVER AGAIN message, it would have to go into Paragraph Two, where you write that you know you're breaking a promise and you're sorry. You could add "I'll do my best not to let this happen again" at that point.

Finally, when you write that you "know" you can count on enthusiastic participation, you are using the factive "know" to presuppose that that is true. This is a compliment to your personnel and a clear statement of what is expected.

---

[2] The illusion of choice strategy is part of a *Gentle Art* metastrategy: to do everything possible to minimize loss of face for your reader or listener.

SUPPLEMENTARY LETTERS

LETTER 16
Frailty: The Health Insurance Deductible Will Go Up After All

MEMORANDUM

TO: (All personnel)   DATE:
FROM: (Your name)
SUBJECT: Change in company policy

This is a memorandum I never thought I'd have to write, and one I write with great reluctance. Ever since we began working together I have told you that the deductible for your health insurance would never be raised—and I meant that. It wasn't an empty promise.

Unfortunately, it's a promise I can no longer keep. Last Friday I met with our health insurance providers in an attempt to convince them to be reasonable. It was no use, and they were inflexible. The amount of money they're demanding for premiums is now so high that there's no way Prittikin can pay it. The choice we have is between no health insurance at all, and health insurance with a higher deductible. That's a rotten choice, but there it is. I'm sorrier than I can say.

I wish I could promise you I'll never go back on a commitment again; I can't. Things change too fast, and I'm not good enough at predicting the future. What I <u>can</u> do is give you my word that future promises will be like past promises: based on my knowledge of the facts and my understanding of your best interests. You can count on me to do my best for you, as always; I know I can count on <u>you</u> to understand that there will be times when my very best is not as good as I'd like it to be, and to understand that that's just part of being human.

LETTER 17
Frailty: You Have to Sell the Family Farm After All

Dear . . . . .,

This is a letter I never thought I'd have to write, and one I write with a heavy heart; it's going out to all the members of the family. There's no way to make it easier, so let me just say it and get it over with: People, I promised you I'd never sell the old farm, and now I have to take that promise back.

I've met with my accountant three times this month, trying to work out some way I could keep the farm under current tax law and still meet the rest of my financial obligations. We've explored every conceivable alternative, and it's no use—I just can't afford to keep the property any longer. I'm very sorry.

I can't promise you I'll never let any of you down again, but I think you can be sure that nothing like this will ever happen again. It's an unusual situation, and not likely to be repeated. In the meantime, if any or all of you would like to buy the property yourselves, or if you have some other idea that I may have overlooked, please give me a call immediately; you'll find me very willing to listen. Unless I hear from you before the 15th of July, I will have to proceed with the sale on my own; a copy of this letter is going to my attorney and to my accountant to let them know how matters stand. I know I can count on your good sense, your understanding, and your for-giveness.

Regretfully,

cc: _____, Attorney
cc: _____, CPA

Chapter Seven

"I Got Part of It Right..."

Triple-F Scenario Six

Dear Isabella and Ferdina[nd]
I did find a new w[orld]
not the one I was looki[ng for]
will never amount to much
but the climate is nice . . . . .

Sincerely

C. Columbus

Recently you gave a talk at a local Rotary meeting. Your city's Rotary is powerful and has a large membership. The meeting was well attended, and a reporter was there from your local newspaper. You thought you'd done well, your talk was well received by the audience, and you were proud of the story that appeared in the paper . . . until you read the terrific paragraph that was quoted word for word from your speech and realized that it wasn't your paragraph at all: it was Thoreau's!

You've been a Thoreau fan all your adult life, and you know his work so well that you honestly did not realize you were quoting. That doesn't help much. What you have to do now is confess your fault and apologize as quickly as possible. This is a classic "I wanted you to hear it from me first" situation; you need to get your correction on record before somebody else does it for you. You're going to need *two* letters: a letter to the editor of the newspaper, intended for publication, and a cover letter to the appropriate individuals at your company. WHAT DO YOU SAY IN YOUR LETTERS?

LETTER 18
You Need to Write a Cover Letter

Dear . . . . . ,

Attached is a letter that I've sent this morning to the editor of the *Independent*; I'm sure you will find it self-explanatory. I wanted you to hear it from me first.

With my sincere apologies,

LETTER 19
Flub: You've Been Quoted—But the Words Weren't Your Own

Dear Editor,

This letter should have been a pleasure to write. It should have been an enthusiastic letter of thanks for the feature story you ran on November 9th about my talk ("The New Ethics of Big Business") at this month's Rotary Club meeting. Unfortunately, it has to be a letter of confession and apology instead. I'm sure that by now many people have called or written to tell you that the paragraph you were kind enough to quote from my talk was written not by me but by Henry David Thoreau, and to ask you why you let me get away with it. That's what I would have done, in their place.

All my adult life I have been a passionate admirer of Thoreau's work. There's always one of his books on the table by my bed, and it's a rare day that ends without my reading at least a few paragraphs of his. As a result, I know his work well—<u>too</u> well! And that is why I failed to give him credit for the paragraph you quoted: I truly did not realize that those words were not my own when I said them. They were the words I wanted to say, and the words that best expressed my thoughts and feelings. Because Thoreau and I were, however briefly, on the same team, I completely forgot that <u>he</u> had brought the <u>ball</u>. This is not an excuse; it is, however, an accurate explanation. I regret the error, and I am greatly embarrassed by it.

I can't promise that I'll never make a mistake like this again. It is the nature of human beings to make mistakes. I <u>can</u> promise that speeches I write in future will be gone over with a fine-toothed comb in an effort to be absolutely certain that I haven't appropriated somebody else's words without giving proper credit for them. I am most grateful to your fine paper for giving me the opportunity to set the record straight and to offer my apologies to your readers.

Sincerely,

Now let's analyze these two letters to see what is accomplished and how it's done.

ANALYSIS OF LETTER 18

The cover letter doesn't follow the six-part pattern that is used for Triple-F letters. The function of a cover letter is to transmit just two metamessages. First: "HERE'S SOMETHING I WANT YOU TO READ." Second: "IT'S A(N)_____" You fill in the blank with an identification of what you're sending the reader: an apology, a contract, a manuscript for publication, a set of instructions, etc.

Cover letters should be as brief as possible, and they should not call attention to themselves. The only place where you have any wiggle room is in the close, where the model has "With my sincere apologies." If there's any question in your mind about whether a variation like that is appropriate, take no chances. Use the standard "Sincerely." When some kind of response from the reader is needed, add one of the following as a final sentence:

"I look forward to hearing from you."

"I look forward to hearing from you by [DEADLINE]."

"I look forward to hearing from you at your earliest convenience."

Above all, let whatever text you're sending *with* the cover letter speak for itself. It annoys readers when you appear to believe they can't be trusted to understand the item your cover letter refers to without your assistance.

ANALYSIS OF LETTER 19

Paragraph One

This letter should have been a pleasure to write. It should have been an enthusiastic letter of thanks for the feature story you ran on November 9th about my talk ("The New Ethics of Big Business") at this month's Rotary Club meeting. Unfortunately, it has to be a letter of confession and apology instead. I'm sure that by now many people have called or written to tell you that the paragraph you were kind enough to quote from my talk was written not by me but by Henry David Thoreau, and to ask you why you let me get away with it. That's what I would have done, in their place.

In this paragraph you will recognize the strategy of shifting focus from yourself to your letter. Each of your first three sentences is worded to put the attention squarely on the product instead of on the producer. You write "this letter" and "it should have been an enthusiastic letter" and "it has to be a letter of confession and apology." This is a reliable strategy, and it's one of the things you do to keep the more openly personal sections later in the letter from sounding like Worthless Worm Language. Notice also that the fourth sentence also shifts the focus away from you. That is, you could have done it this way:

> ". . . I'm sure that by now many people have called or written to tell you that I used a paragraph of Henry David Thoreau's without giving him credit for it, and wondering why you not only quoted it, but let me get away with it. That's what I would have done, in their place. . . ."

That would have been equally grammatical and informative, but it's a lot harder on you. The focus-shifted sentence suggests that people were calling and writing about the quoted paragraph, and moves you into a less conspicuous position.

That you were "sure that by now many people have called or written," etc., is of course not strictly true. Thoreau's writing is not on today's best-seller lists. The chances are good that most people in town are not Thoreau fans, and you certainly know that. To say you're sure that many people will have caught your error—using the factive word "sure," so that the embedded sentence is presupposed—is a courtesy, like asking "How are you?" when you haven't the slightest interest in knowing.

This sentence is a complicated one, and it has a number of other sentences embedded in it and presupposed. For clarity, let's list them.

- Embedded as [X] in "I'm sure that [X]":
  ". . . many people have called or written . . ." etc.

- Embedded as [X] and [Y] in "people have called or written to tell you that [X] and ask you why [Y] . . .", etc.

  [X]"the paragraph you were kind enough to quote . . ." etc.

  [Y]"you let me get away with it."

And though it's harder to spot because more things have been done to it, you have also embedded a sentence saying roughly "it was kind of you to quote the paragraph in question." Packing all these smaller statements and all this information into a single sentence is efficient, and effective. Unpacking it to argue with the presupposed items would be a lot of trouble for the reader.

Finally, by saying "That's what I would have done in their place," you're able to convey the message that you are as shocked by plagiarism (and by errors in newspaper stories that get past the copy editors and fact checkers!) as anyone else would be, without saying either of those things directly.

Paragraph Two

All my adult life I have been a passionate admirer of Thoreau's work. There's always one of his books on the table by my bed, and it's a rare day that ends without my reading at least a few paragraphs of his. As a result, I know his work well—<u>too</u> well! And that is why I failed to give him credit for the paragraph you quoted: I truly did not realize that those words were not my own when I said them. They were the words I wanted to say, and the words that best expressed my thoughts and feelings. Because Thoreau and I were, however briefly, on the same team, I completely forgot that <u>he</u> had brought the <u>ball</u>. This is not an excuse; it is, however, an accurate explanation. I regret the error, and I am greatly embarrassed by it.

You'll recognize this paragraph as straight Leveling. It states what happened, and why. It admits that your familiarity with Thoreau doesn't excuse your ripping him off. And it makes the crucial point: that the facts you are presenting are evidence that what you did was carelessness rather than plagiarism. You end the paragraph with a suitable statement of apology.

What is new in this paragraph appears in the sixth sentence, where you write that . . .

> "Because Thoreau and I were, however briefly, on the same team, I completely forgot that <u>he</u> had brought the <u>ball</u>."

This sentence yanks Henry David Thoreau without ceremony into the twentieth century and makes him just one of the guys. It dispels the image of you as a bookish person immersed in the intellectual ideas of long-dead philosophers and puts you right there in the locker room with everybody else. And it reminds your readers of a common context in their daily experience—team sports—where the team effort is what matters, and where strict honesty is not only not required but would get in the way of playing the game. It's <u>okay</u> in football or basketball to pretend you have the ball when you really don't. It's okay in baseball to pretend you're going to run for the plate when you're really going to stay on third base. Such tactics are not considered lies.

This is an example of the use of <u>metaphor</u> to accomplish three tasks:

1. To bring your readers into the letter as active participants.
2. To transmit a great deal of information in a very few words.
3. To persuade others to perceive a situation as <u>you</u> perceive it, by calling their attention to a shared experience and its links with this new experience that you've had all on your own.

Nothing has the potential to do you more good in a sequence of language than a well-chosen metaphor. Nothing has the potential to do you more <u>harm</u> than one that's badly chosen or unclear. When you can use metaphors skillfully in your correspondence you have at your disposal a tool that gives you major and substantial advantages over the average letter-writer. Metaphors are incredibly powerful. They presuppose entire <u>contexts</u>, and are worth discussing in detail.

METAPHORS AND HOW TO USE THEM

The basic pattern for a metaphor in its strongest form is simply "X is Y." For example:

"War is hell."
"Time is money."
"A city is a jungle."

The weaker form is almost the same: "X is like Y." As in poet Robert Burns's line, "My love is like a red, red rose."[1]

Metaphors will remind you of the equations used in math, and they share certain features with equations, but there's an important difference: Metaphors aren't always, or for that matter even usually, <u>reversible</u>. Suppose you have an equation, "X = Y." If one side of the equation is 2 plus 4 and the other side is 6, it makes no difference whether you say that 6 equals 2 plus 4, or that 2 plus 4 equals 6. However, to say "Hell is war" doesn't convey the same meaning as "War is hell," nor is "A jungle is a city" synonymous with "A city is a jungle." When a metaphor is fully reversible, it's a coincidence.

---

[1] This pattern is traditionally called a <u>simile</u>.

Metaphors in human societies are much like holograms; using only one small part is often enough to bring the entire metaphor into consciousness. You only have to use enough of a metaphor to let your reader recognize it, and the rest will be understood automatically.

When someone in our culture says or writes "Wagons—HO!" the entire unifying metaphor of The Old West (cowboys, covered wagons, brave sheriffs, dancehall girls with heart of gold, campfires and cows, Good Old Doc, and so on) is evoked. You don't have to write "This project we're now beginning is the trek westward across the prairies and the deserts to settle the frontier. Our CEO is the wagonmaster, our competitors are the resisting Indian tribes, we employees are the brave pioneers . . ." and so on. (You not only don't have to, you must be careful not to, because your reader would resent it.) Using a metaphor is a participatory strategy. If your readers share your culture, they will bring out all the missing pieces and put them where they belong, just on the basis of "Wagons—HO!" and in Letter 19 you don't have to write "My speech was like a ball game . . . etc." to get your point across. The team sport metaphors are so familiar in our culture, especially for adult males, that all you have to do is *refer* to them. You can rely on your readers to do the rest.

Using old familiar metaphors—The Old West, The Brave Ship Sailing, The Football Game, The Rose-Covered Cottage—lets you remind your reader of your shared heritage. It lets you tie unfamiliar information to what is already known, making it easier for the reader's short-term memory to process your words for understanding and remembering. And it is a way of making the reader feel solidarity with you, even when there is potential disagreement.

Using a fresh new metaphor lets you give your reader a fresh new way to perceive something. For example: I've always been annoyed when people I was visiting left their television set running all the time, even with nobody watching it. I couldn't understand it, it bothered me, and it made a bad impression that was likely to interfere with the interaction between me and my hosts. Then I read Camille Paglia's metaphor ("She Wants Her TV! He Wants His Book!" in *Harper's Magazine*, March 1991), where she says that the television set is the flickering-fire-on-the-hearth of the modern home. And suddenly I did understand. She is right; I am no longer annoyed by the phenomenon; and a potential source of misunderstanding has been removed forever from my life. I no longer perceive the omnipresent tv as a sign of carelessness or sloppiness or bad manners.

That attitude was my error of perception, and Paglia's metaphor has corrected it.

I know nothing else that has the power metaphors have to create changes in people's perceptions, often instantaneously and permanently. As is true for any sort of power, however, misuse or careless use carries serious risks. A few years ago I read an article in which a professor of obstetrics tried to help young doctors explain why their fees for delivering a baby were so high. He suggested that they compare those fees to fees for embalming dead bodies in their communities. No doubt he thought he had come up with a compelling comparison. Both procedures are important: one ushers human beings into this world and the other ushers them out. Both are assumed to require experts. Both cost money. But the metaphor was an <u>awful</u> blunder! When you say that X is Y, you mean that certain things about X match certain things about Y, and the person who reads your metaphor automatically begins making those connections, two by two. The professor's metaphor evokes, magically, all of the following unfortunate pairs—

- a newly born baby matches a newly dead adult—a corpse
- an obstetrician matches a mortician
- a delivery table matches a morgue table
- a cradle (or its hospital equivalent) matches a casket
- an ambulance or family car matches a hearse

—and so, grotesquely, on. That wasn't what the professor meant, but his intentions aren't relevant. THE ONLY PRACTICAL MEANING ANY SEQUENCE HAS IN THE REAL WORLD IS THE MEANING THE LISTENER OR READER UNDERSTANDS IT TO HAVE. People react to and act on their own understandings, not your intentions. When you choose a metaphor, take the time to make it explicit enough in your own mind so that you always review the list of its parts. Be sure that the context your metaphor creates in your reader's mind isn't grotesque or offensive or—unless it would be helpful to you—comic. Be sure your metaphor doesn't bring with it a lot of semantic freight you didn't intend to ship.

Now let's return to our analysis of Letter 19.

Paragraph Three

I can't promise that I'll never make a mistake like this again. It is the nature of human beings to make mistakes.

I <u>can</u> promise that speeches I write in the future will be gone over with a fine-toothed comb in an effort to be absolutely certain that I haven't appropriated somebody else's words without giving proper credit for them. I am most grateful to your fine paper for giving me the opportunity to set the record straight and to offer my apologies to your readers.

This paragraph, like the rest of the letter, fits the Triple-F pattern. NEVER AGAIN, it says, specifying what you will do in the future to make sure this is a unique event.

Notice that you <u>could</u> have involved the editors here. You could have said "And in future I hope that you will be more alert to possible errors of this kind in the stories your reporters turn in for printing." It is in fact true that the journalists and editors are supposed to be certain that what they report is accurate, that its sources are correctly identified, and the like. However, you would gain nothing at all by making this point. Everybody knows it already. You hinted at it when you suggested that readers would have spotted the error and contacted the paper about it; you hinted at it again when you said it was the nature of human beings to make mistakes. And you are equally responsible for making certain that the information you give to a paper is correct. People are far less likely to claim that what you did was deliberate if you refrain from claiming that what <u>they</u> did was incompetent.

You finish the letter with a compliment—"your fine paper"— using the possessive to presuppose its validity. In the same sentence, you state explicitly what it was that you intended the letter to accomplish. Unless your readers (and the members of your company you send the cover letter and copies to) are very unreasonable people, this letter will accomplish the stated goals.

USING QUOTATIONS SAFELY AND EFFECTIVELY

It's an excellent idea to use good quotations in speeches or letters. Not everyone is able to come up with a powerful sequence of language that sticks in the mind and makes a strong and effective impression, but everyone can notice such sequences in the writing of others and make good use of them. I recommend keeping a file of such sequences, adding each one as you come across it in your reading. The final page of *Forbes* Magazine is always a good source, and many collections of quotations are available in book form for your use. Just be sure you give credit where credit is due when you quote another person's words. It may seem like a great deal of trouble, but it will save you embarrassment and misunderstanding. The rules are simple:

1. In formal writing (or speaking), give a complete reference for the quotation: who first said or wrote the words, where they first appeared—in a book, a speech, an article—on what page, on what date, and so on. The only exception is with truly ancient sources (Aristotle, Moses, Confucius, Plato) or when the quotation and its source are so well-known that giving the reference would be "talking down" to your audience or reader.

2. In informal writing (or speaking), just <u>mention</u> the quotation's source. Like this: "As Thoreau said . . ." followed by the quotation itself.

SUPPLEMENTARY LETTERS

LETTER 20
Flub: You've Quoted Somebody—Incorrectly

Dear . . . . .,

It should have been a pleasure to write this letter; certainly it was a pleasure to see my article ("Communication Problems in Middle Management") in the most recent issue of our *Prittikin Newsletter*. Unfortunately, the pleasure has to be mixed with embarrassment. By now I suspect that someone in the company has called or written you to point out that when I quoted from Art Smith's fine paper I made several errors.

I've read Smith's paper so many times, and know it so well, that I thought I knew it by heart. I would have sworn I could also give every page its proper reference. I was wrong. The paper appeared in the June 1986—not 1985—issue of *Developments,* and the quotation should have read as follows:

> A well-chosen metaphor makes it possible to accomplish in a few seconds tasks that would otherwise take days or weeks to complete; there is no more efficient or more effective linguistic tool.

I should not have turned in my article to you without checking that reference, no matter how sure I was that I could trust my memory. Carelessness is the quickest and steepest road to error; I should have taken a different path. I'm embarrassed, and I do apologize.

I can't promise that I'll never make another foolish mistake; it's the nature of human beings to make mistakes. I <u>can</u> promise, however, that I will be scrupulously careful in future to check my facts before I send anything I've written off for publication. I have learned my lesson. I'd be grateful if you would find a place for this letter in an upcoming issue, so that I can set the record straight and let your readers know that I regret my error. Thank you for your courtesy.

Sincerely,

LETTER 21
Flub: You've Quoted Lincoln—But the Words Are Jefferson's

Dear . . . . .,

This letter should have been only an expression of my thanks for the opportunity to speak to your students last Thursday afternoon; that was the letter I had <u>intended</u> to write. I am sorry to have to admit that, although I still want to express my thanks, I must also express my dismay and offer my apologies. It pains me to admit it, but it's true: the quotation I used to open my talk was not from Abraham Lincoln, it was from Thomas Jefferson.

I have always been a dedicated admirer of Abraham Lincoln, and of his extraordinary speeches. As a result, I know his work well—but not as well as I thought! Certainly I don't know it well enough to be safe in assuming that I can instantly tell whether a quotation is or isn't Lincoln's. The words I used were words I knew Lincoln would have agreed with; they were words I could without hesitation imagine Lincoln saying or writing. Because Lincoln made so many touchdowns, I seem to have leaped to the conclusion that he was the only star on the team.

I know that's no excuse; please accept it as an explanation, along with my apologies for the error.

I won't promise never to make a mistake like this again, although I'll willingly promise to <u>try</u>. I do promise that next time I think I'm looking at the words of Lincoln I'll take time to make sure I'm right. I'd be very grateful if you would tell your students that the quotation came from Thomas Jefferson, and if you would explain to them that I truly had no intention to mislead.

Sincerely,

Chapter Eight

"It Just Slipped My Mind..."

Triple-F Scenario Seven

My dear nephew,

I do most assuredly agree that it was your kite, and that you are now permanently deprived of the pleasure of its use. I can plead only that in the heat of scientific passion, I simply forgot that the kite would be destroyed if the experiment were a success . . . . . .

Regre

Uncle Benj

Yesterday you and your boss went to a meeting with a client, and you made a very successful presentation for a major promotional campaign the client is planning. Not only was it the first time you'd taken the lead in a presentation for your firm, it was the first time you'd had to do one in front of your boss. You weren't absolutely certain about what strategies to use, so you did the best you could with the information you had available. When the client signed at the terms requested, you assumed you'd done well. You even assumed there'd be a few words of praise from the boss.

You were wrong. Much to your surprise, she's furious with you. Because, as she puts it, "You had the gall to take 100 percent of the credit for the project, and you did no more work on it than anybody else!" She said nothing about this in the meeting, and that strikes you as irresponsible. It seems to you that she could at least have thrown out a casual, "Tom and I both want to stress that this project was a team effort," or something of the kind, to give you a clue to her feelings. She claims that she would never have done that, because it might have embarrassed you at a time when it was critical for you to be relaxed and confident.

Now she insists that you write to the client, explaining the situation, with a copy to all the project members you failed to credit. You think that's a bad move. The point was to get the account, and you did that. You are sure you can count on the rest of your team to have sense enough to understand what happened and to agree with you. Furthermore, you feel that the letter will make Classco uneasy. You've offered to just pick up the phone and call them, but she says that won't do it. She's the boss, and she refuses to back down; you're stuck with it. How do you avoid losing face with the client? How do you keep from looking like a wimp? How do you avoid giving the impression that your company has internal problems? WHAT DO YOU SAY IN YOUR LETTER?

LETTER 22
Flub and Flounder: You Took All the Credit—For a Team Effort

Version 1: Informal

Dear . . . . .,

This is a letter I should not have had to write; I should have covered its content in yesterday's meeting. Fortunately, although I sometimes lose track of details in my enthusiasm for a project and my desire to get things moving, Charlotte is always here with a level head and a steady hand to see to it that those details are promptly taken care of.

Jim, what I did yesterday was fail to give you the names of all the people who were involved in putting our presentation together. When a football player makes a touchdown, everybody knows it would have been impossible without the efforts of the other members of the team; that goes without saying. I know my team, and I know their talents; that's my good fortune. I should have remembered, however, that you and your staff will also need that information as we go forward with the promotional campaign. You'll find a list of team members and a brief description of each one's primary responsibilities attached to this letter. If you have any questions, just contact me or anyone on the list, and we'll be happy to help.

In future I'll make sure my concentration on current matters doesn't distract me from my ongoing obligation to keep you fully informed. And you, in future, must call me on it if you feel that something may have been overlooked. I know I speak for every member of my team when I say that it's going to be a tremendous pleasure to work with you on this project.

Sincerely,

cc: [each of the persons on the list you attach]

This letter should satisfy your boss and square matters with your colleagues. With any luck at all, it will give the client the message your boss insisted on, <u>without</u> carrying any hazardous messages about conflict or carelessness at your end of the operation.

ANALYSIS OF LETTER 22, VERSION 1

Paragraph One

This is a letter I should not have had to write; I should have covered its content in yesterday's meeting. Fortunately, although I sometimes lose track of details in my enthusiasm for a project and my desire to get things moving, Charlotte is always here with a level head and a steady hand to see to it that those details are promptly taken care of.

WRITING IN CODE

It will be clear to you that much of this paragraph is in code. It begins with BRACE YOURSELF, addressed to the client. It goes on with a sentence that accomplishes three tasks:

1. It carries the SOMEBODY GOOFED message that's called for by the Triple-F Pattern. But it makes it clear, with the double reference to "details," that you consider the goof trivial.

2. It tells your reader that the goof was caused by something positive: your intense involvement in this project. And it uses possessive forms and nominalizations to presuppose your enthusiasm for the project and your desire not to let it be held back by "details," characteristics you can safely assume will be welcomed by Classco.

3. On the surface, it's simply a compliment to your boss. At the same time, it carries a more subtle message—it lets the client know that she, not you, is behind this letter. If the client agrees with her that it should have been written, you have just given her the credit due her for correcting your oversight; no problem. If the client, like you, feels that it's a letter about things nobody actually needed to discuss, that negative judgment won't be chalked up to you, and the client will realize that the sentence is really there for <u>Charlotte</u> to read. But there's nothing here your boss can object to, and nothing that could possibly be interpreted as critical of her or of her instructions. Again, no problem.

Notice also that you've used just a light touch of parallelism in the sentence, with "my enthusiasm for a project and my desire to get things moving" and with "a level head and steady hand." As always, this is a good move. However, this is a case in which it <u>is</u> done purely for stylistic reasons, to add to the gracefulness of the sentence and to impress the client with your skill in the use of language. Nothing here could possibly burden the reader's short-term memory.

People in business frequently find themselves needing to write letters that are not actually for the person they're addressed to. When (as in Letter 22) these letters are written only to satisfy the demands of someone higher in rank, or when they are written only to meet some abstract formal requirement, they are an unavoidable nuisance and otherwise unimportant. When, on the other hand, they are letters written not to give information to the addressee but to get it on record, they remain a nuisance but are very important indeed.

Suppose, for example, that the roles in Scenario Seven had been reversed. Suppose <u>you</u> were the one who wanted to be sure everyone who worked on the project got specific credit, and it was your boss who thought that was unnecessary. You could still have written almost exactly this same letter, but you would have refrained from making your boss responsible for it. The minor change shown below, in this one paragraph, is all that would be necessary.

> This is a letter I should not have had to write; I should have covered its content in yesterday's meeting. Fortunately, although I sometimes lose track of details in my enthusiasm for a project and my desire to get things moving, my staff can always be relied on to remind me of my oversight, so that those items are promptly taken care of.

The rest of the letter would have served your purposes without any need for further alterations.

Paragraph Two

> Jim, what I did yesterday was fail to give you the names of all the people who were involved in putting our presentation together. When a football player makes a touchdown, everybody knows it would have been impossible without the efforts of the other members of the team; that goes without saying. I know my team, and I know their talents; that's my good fortune. I should have remembered, however, that you and your staff will also need that information as we go forward with the promotional campaign. You'll find a list of team members and a brief description of each one's primary responsibilities attached to this letter. If you have any questions, just contact me or anyone on the list, and we'll be happy to help.

This is a "just the facts" paragraph. It tells the reader what you did. You've already let him know how your oversight was brought to your attention, in the sentence about Charlotte. In "I should have remembered" you are again writing for her eyes, but you have an additional purpose: to demonstrate to the client that there is no conflict in the ranks. That is, you're saying, "Charlotte told me I should have remembered to do this. As you can see by my inclusion of this message for her eyes, I am more than willing to defer to her judgment and accept the responsibility." This is intended to reassure your client and to demonstrate that you are not the sort of person who would allow a minor disagreement to interfere with reaching the goal.

You will have noticed one difference between this letter and the typical Triple-F letter: Up front, the I'M SORRY message is missing. You say "I failed to [X]," courteously accepting the fault, and you fill in the NEVER AGAIN message, but you don't apologize to your client. And that's exactly right. Because the disagreement in this case, as well as the communication breakdown, was not between you and the client. It was between you and your boss. The apology you could appropriately have made—"I'm sorry I didn't handle it the way you wanted it handled"—is not an apology to the client, but to your boss, and the letter itself, plus the act of writing it, constitute *that* message.

MORE ABOUT METAPHORS AND HOW TO USE THEM

When I discuss a letter of this kind with a client or in a seminar, one question always comes up: "Isn't there a danger that the boss will understand the code, too, and be even angrier with you?" The answer to that question is best understood in the context of the <u>metaphor</u> used in the paragraph. Look at the section in italics.

Jim, what I did yesterday was fail to give you the names of all the people who were involved in putting our presentation together. *When a football player makes a touchdown, everybody knows it would have been impossible without the efforts of the other members of the team; that goes without saying. I know my team, and I know their talents; that's my good fortune.* I should have remembered, however, that you and your staff will also need that information as we go forward with the promotional campaign. You'll find a list of *team members* and a brief description of each one's primary responsibilities attached to this letter. If you have any questions, just contact me or anyone on the list, and we'll be happy to help.

Business in the United States is saturated with the Football Game metaphor shown here. People use sports metaphors of all kinds, in both their personal and their business lives; but football language is the "Wagons—HO!" of American business communication.

First, because football allows for individual accomplishment, but it depends on the cooperation of a team that puts winning the game far ahead of glory for any one player. And second, because although football is unambiguously a game, with rules that apply only within the time and space boundaries <u>of</u> the game, it is at the same time serious business, as demonstrated by the salaries its players earn and the money people spend to watch it. In the context of business, only the two scenarios below are likely, and neither one is a threat to you.

1. Your boss shares the "business is football" metaphor, will certainly know what you are doing in your letter, and will respect you for the skill with which you do it.

2. Your boss does not share the metaphor, and will not perceive anything in your letter except the surface message it was supposed to contain.

You wrote a letter that transmits two metamessages at the same time, to two different targets. First, it says to the client: I AM IN CONTROL. Second, it says to your boss: I AM IN COMPLIANCE. In the context of the football metaphor and the football rules, this is not dishonest or contradictory or manipulative. Any more than it's dishonest in a football game to pretend you're going to throw the football when you're really going to run with it, or to tell your own team what you actually intend to do while giving the opposing team an entirely different message.

Your behavior in the presentation—when you behaved as though you had done all the work when really it had been a team effort—is consistent with the football metaphor. On the other hand, it's customary for the football star being interviewed by the media after the game to say "I couldn't have done it without the rest of the team!"; thus, writing the letter doesn't require you to abandon the metaphor or step outside its boundaries. And using the football metaphor makes it possible for you to comply with the wishes of your boss while at the same time achieving your own goals—avoiding both the "I am a wimp" message and the message that your company has internal conflicts.

Most of the time, people who seem unaware of the football metaphor in business, or who fumble in using it even if they are aware of it, are women. Men grow up playing football in our society; women don't. Many women spend a lot of time watching football or cheering it on, but that doesn't enable them to <u>internalize</u> the rules and strategy of the game—to learn them so well that they are essentially on automatic—as players do. As a result, many flubs and flounders result from attempts at communication between men who are operating from within the football metaphor and women (or men) who aren't. This is particularly troublesome when actions or words that are only part of the game are taken <u>personally</u>. As if you tackled someone in a football game, following the rules of the game, only to have them take it as a personal assault and sue you for it.

If you ever write a letter using a football metaphor and get back in response a chilly "This is not a game. This is <u>business!</u>", you'll know immediately that the writer is using some other metaphor. Bosses whose idea of a dominance display is to delete every example of the football metaphor are giving you clear signals that <u>they</u> are operating from inside some other metaphor. It would always be a good idea to find out what that metaphor is, if possible. It's dangerous to treat someone like a football coach unless you know that the person is both able and willing to fill the role.

The expression "it goes without saying" is never used to refer to anything that <u>does</u> go without saying, by the way. It always refers to something that must, for one reason or another, be said.

Finding good metaphors that fit your situation exactly and do the work you want done quickly and effectively isn't easy. Whenever you come across a good metaphor, even if you don't see a way to use it at that moment, make a note of it and file it somewhere accessible; you never know when you may need it badly and be grateful to have it ready to hand. Here are a few more examples from my own collection.

1. "It's time to stop driving this business and start <u>sailing</u> it!" That is: this business used to be a car, moving along routes already rigidly laid out, with very little freedom to maneuver. But things have changed. Now it's a sailing ship on the open sea. (And you can see how the variations on this would be

tailored to your own situation. "Our business was a wagon; now it's a car." "Our business was a plane; now it's a spaceship." And so on.)

2. "Everybody involved in this project is a pony-finder!" This one comes from one of Ronald Reagan's favorite anecdotes, in which a boy faced with the awful task of shoveling out a room full of horse manure says cheerfully, "I just know there's a pony in there somewhere!"

3. According to Robert Keidel, author of *Game Plans: Sports Strategies for Business,* most American businesses have as their dominating metaphor either football, basketball, or baseball. Looking at your own business, or a particular business situation, from within each of these possible metaphors, can be extremely useful.

Now we can return to the final paragraph of Letter 22 and finish the analysis.

Paragraph Three

In future I'll make sure my concentration on current matters doesn't distract me from my ongoing obligation to keep you fully informed. And you, in future, must call me on it if you feel that something may have been overlooked. I know I speak for every member of my team when I say that it's going to be a tremendous pleasure to work with you on this project.

Here you offer to make details more explicit in future—an offer directed once again more at your boss than at your client—and you let both boss and reader know that you'd appreciate it if they would let you know which details are important to them. You then end the letter with a compliment in which you speak not as star of the team but as spokesperson for all the players.

THE FORMALITY CONTINUUM

The tone of this letter was rather informal. Formality isn't an all-or-nothing matter. It's a continuum, ranging from the completely casual memo of the "Hey, you forgot to send me this week's sales figures!" variety to the completely formal letters used when discussing the terms of complicated contracts or in anticipation of possible lawsuits. On a scale from one (least formal) to ten (most formal), Model Letter 9, Version 1 falls somewhere between three and four. Let's assume that your business is one in which more formality is required, and rewrite the letter to fall closer to the other end of the scale.

VERSION 2: Formal

Dear . . . . .,

I regret the need to write this letter, inasmuch as its content was properly part of the agenda for yesterday's meeting. Fortunately, although my enthusiasm for a project and my desire to minimize delay occasionally cause me to overlook details, Charlotte Pritchard is always here with a level head and a steady hand to ensure that my oversights are promptly rectified.

What I did yesterday, Mr. Ardmore, was fail to provide you with the names of all our personnel who were involved in putting our presentation together. When a football player makes a touchdown, everyone is aware that it could not have been accomplished without the efforts of the other members of the team; that goes without saying. I have the good fortune to know my team and to know their talents. However, I should have remembered that you and your staff will also need that information as we go forward with the promotional campaign. Attached to this letter, therefore, is a list of the individuals I neglected to mention, together with a brief description of each one's primary responsibilities. Should any questions remain, please feel free to contact me or anyone on that list; we will be delighted to assist you.

In future, I will not allow my concentration on current matters to distract me from my ongoing obligation to keep your firm fully informed. I will be grateful if Classco, in its turn, will inform me of any perception that something may have been overlooked. On behalf of everyone involved in this project, let me say that we look forward with great pleasure to our association with you.

Sincerely,

The additional formality of this version is due for the most part to <u>word choices</u>. Often the words you use in a letter are available in several flavors, corresponding to various points on the formality continuum. For example:

LEAST FORMAL	MORE FORMAL	MOST FORMAL
let	allow	permit
try	attempt	endeavor
because	. . . . .	inasmuch as
help	aid	assist
fix	repair	rectify
leave out	. . . . .	omit
give	supply	provide
everybody	. . . . .	everyone
happy	pleased	delighted

You can find more formal (or less formal) alternatives for words in your letters, like the sets shown above, in any good thesaurus or large dictionary.

SUPPLEMENTARY LETTERS

LETTER 23
Flub and Flounder: You Failed to Give Credit Where Credit Was Due

Dear . . . . .,

This is a letter I should not have had to write. I should have cleared up all possible misunderstandings during yesterday's meeting at your office. However, because we were working against time and a number of your people has planes to catch, I decided to let things go at the time and clarify them by letter. Fortunately, although I did create a certain amount of confusion in my eagerness to get our project moving, no harm has been done and the matter is easily set right.

Marilyn, what I did yesterday was allow the impression to be created that I had come up with the new product name and slogan all by myself. That's not accurate, and I should have been much more specific on the spot. I want you to know that both Charles Klepper and Anita Phillips worked with me to develop those items and to prepare the presentation for the meeting. They are entitled to full credit, and I apologize for failing to say so.

In the future I'll make sure that my enthusiasm doesn't lead to this sort of carelessness. I know that you will understand how it happened <u>this</u> time, since you were there and under the same pressure to hurry things along as I was. Charles and Anita and I are all looking forward to working with you, and we are confident that the project will be a tremendous success.

Sincerely,

cc: Charles Klepper
Anita Phillips

LETTER 24
Flub and Frailty: You Failed to Acknowledge Help With Your Research

Dear . . . . .,

It's unfortunate that I must write this letter, and it's due entirely to my own carelessness. I should have noticed my error before my recent article in your journal went to press and corrected it in advance of publication.

Dick, what I did was neglect to say in the acknowledgments for my article that I had been greatly helped in my research by my two graduate students, Eleanor Jones and Clifford Wilks. It's a rare research project today that doesn't require that credit be shared among a number of individuals; my own project is no exception. I regret the error, and I apologize.

In future I'll try to be much more careful. And perhaps you, in future, might remind me of this incident and help me to carry out my good intentions; I'd appreciate that. I know I can count on you to find a small space somewhere in your upcoming issue to print a correction for me, so that Jones and Wilks are properly credited and your readers are not left with a false impression.

Sincerely,

cc: Eleanor Jones
Clifford Wilks
Glenn Mallard, Chairman, Department of Ethnology

Chapter Nine

"I Can't Imagine How This Happened!"

Triple-F Scenario Eight

My dearest sister,

We were three days at sea before I discovered, to my horror, that I had accidentally packed your best blue silk gown among my things. I am absolutely devastated by my carelessness, and I hope that you can find it in your heart to forgive. . . . .

With

Ad

*R*ecently you published a scholarly article in your academic field, and you're happy about that. It was well received, and it was a publication you badly needed for promotion and tenure. However, you have a problem. When you wrote your bibliography you left out an article on a related subject, written by an older woman who is a full professor in your department. It was a genuine oversight; you simply forgot.

But you know she'll find that hard to believe. You're careful always to treat her courteously, but she can't possibly be unaware that you consider her work outdated. She's sure to think you left her article out deliberately. You have to see her every week at faculty meetings, you have to serve on committees with her, and there are many ways she can interfere with your future career. And even if none of that were true, you're ashamed to have done something so careless and so hurtful. You know quite well that it would be better to talk to her about this in person, but you just plain can't face her! A letter will have to serve, at least for starters. If it's cowardly, so be it, you're a coward. Everybody does something cowardly once in a while; it's your turn. WHAT DO YOU SAY IN YOUR LETTER?

LETTER 25
Flub and Frailty: You've Left a Colleague's Work Out of Your Bibliography

Version 1: Informal

Dear . . . . .,

I don't know any way to tell you how much I regret that this letter has to be written, and that it has to be written to <u>you</u>, of all people. It's not the letter you ought to receive; I'm not eloquent enough, or skilled enough, to write that letter. But it represents the best efforts of a woman who is guilty not only of one of the worst errors a scholar can commit—the error of carelessness—but also of having insulted a colleague for whom she feels the highest respect and regard.

I didn't discover that I had omitted "The Peruvian Paradox: Four Essential Perspectives" from the bibliography for my recent article until I actually had the printed copies in my hand. It seems to me that the only way it

could possibly have happened is that I was so certain it
<u>was</u> there that I didn't even bother checking for it. This
is the only explanation that makes any sense at all to me;
it certainly isn't an excuse. I realize that for a junior colleague to fail to cite an article of yours is a minor matter
for you. For me, however, it is anything but minor. I am
so very sorry.

To say that I will be more careful in future is absurd.
I was <u>scrupulously</u> careful this time, and still I made this
dreadful mistake. This time I was fortunate—I insulted
a friend, whose understanding and good judgment I can
count on. Next time, it might be <u>much</u> worse! Elizabeth,
I am about to add imposition to injury; I am going to ask
for your help. Next time I prepare an article for publication, could I call on you to give it one extra reading for
me, to be sure that if I have made errors or omissions I
will have the opportunity to correct them? Your knowledge of the field, your wide experience, and your critical
skills would be invaluable to me, if you could find the
time to share them with a colleague who clearly has need
of them. (If it would be a burden, you must of course say
no at once; I will understand.) In the meantime, I am
grateful to you for accepting my apology.

Sincerely,

This letter may not do it; it depends. If she is wise, she will
accept it graciously and tell you not to worry about it any more. If
she is wise, she will also tell you that she's sorry to have to turn
down your request for help, but she just can't manage to add that
to her already heavy workload. She may or may not be that wise.
The letter offers her all the appropriate messages and opportunities.

ANALYSIS OF LETTER 25, VERSION 1

Paragraph One

I don't know any way to tell you how much I regret that
this letter has to be written, and that it has to be written
to <u>you</u>, of all people. It's not the letter you ought to receive;
I'm not eloquent enough, or skilled enough, to write that
letter. But it represents the best efforts of a woman who

is guilty not only of one of the worst errors a scholar can commit—the error of carelessness—but also of having insulted a colleague for whom she feels the highest respect and regard.

You will recognize many of the strategies in this paragraph. Let's list the major ones here, for a quick review.

1. You have used the factive word "regret" to presuppose the truth of two statements:
   - This letter has to be written
   - This letter has to be written to you (of all people).

2. You have used focus-shifting several times. Instead of "I have to write this letter" you have used "This letter has to be written," from the very beginning, and you continue to refer to "it"—the letter—in every sentence of the paragraph. And in the final sentence you use the strategy of referring to yourself as if you were someone else, with "It represents the best efforts of a woman who. . . ."

3. You have followed the Triple-F Letter Pattern, transmitting the two basic messages: BRACE YOURSELF; SOMEBODY GOOFED.

4. Because you are unquestionably in the wrong here, you have used Leveler Mode to say for your colleague all the harsh things she might otherwise have felt obligated to say herself. This has the additional advantage of letting you set the tone and choose the wording, emphasizing the fact that the omission was neither deliberate nor malicious, just careless. But you haven't spared yourself, and you haven't tried to diminish your responsibility with Hedges. You didn't write "I know I was careless, but it was because" you'd just gotten over the flu or you had two new courses to teach this semester or anything of that kind. You haven't weakened or canceled your frank statement of the facts.

Well done! And a great deal accomplished in a single brief paragraph.

Paragraph Two

I didn't discover that I had omitted "The Peruvian Paradox: Four Essential Perspectives" from the bibliography for my recent article until I actually had the printed copies in my hand. It seems to me that the only way it could possibly have happened is that I was so certain it <u>was</u> there that I didn't even bother checking for it. This is the only explanation that makes any sense at all to me; it certainly isn't an excuse. I realize that for a junior colleague to fail to cite an article of yours is a minor matter for you. For me, however, it is anything but minor. I am so very sorry.

Your colleague may very well not believe one word of this paragraph—that's okay. The point is that you have answered her predictable question ("How on earth did it <u>happen</u>?") in a way that is a compliment to her. You're telling her that the idea of an article on this subject that <u>didn't</u> cite "The Peruvian Paradox" as a reference seems so unacceptable to you that you just took it for granted that the reference was there. You've admitted that that's no excuse, which is true; you should have checked. You've claimed that it's an acceptable explanation. Your reader can only disagree with that openly by accusing you of lying, which would be a drastic and alienating step on her part. And you have nailed your apology down tight by saying something you know you are expected to say: that someone like her—an established and respected scholar in her field—certainly could care less if someone like you—low woman on the same totem pole—failed to cite her work. Whether this is true or not is irrelevant. If such a trivial matter really <u>does</u> bother her, she'll be ashamed of that, and she certainly won't contradict you. You've used the factive "realize" to indicate that this is also something that can be taken for granted. If it's true that she's indifferent to your error, she will agree with you and all will be well. If it's false, she will still recognize your courtesy in paying the ritual compliment, and chances are good that all will still be well.

WRITING CAREFULLY CRAFTED TRUTHS

You don't greet another human being with, "Hello, you look awful. What an ugly shirt!" even if that happens to be what you're thinking. That's cruel and unnecessary, and it's evidence not of your honesty but of your lack of social skills. Similarly, you would not write to your colleague—even if it were the truth—anything like this: "I left your article out of my bibliography because it is so out of date and of so little importance that I don't want anybody to read it. And although I didn't leave it out on purpose, I'm sure that unconsciously I <u>forgot</u> on purpose." That sort of brutal honesty would be much worse than the offense that caused you to write the letter, and it would make no sense at all.

On the other hand, you did not say <u>anything</u> that could be called deliberate lying. You didn't write that "Peruvian Paradox" is a classic article and one of the major contributions to the field, for example. Suppose you <u>had</u> done that. Given the fact that Elizabeth knows you don't hold those opinions, she would quite rightly have suspected sarcasm, and that would have been a fatal flaw. Nor did you write that you told your secretary to add the reference to "Peruvian Paradox" and the secretary failed to do so, or any of the other half dozen "clerical error" excuses that might have tempted you. It's important to remember, when you are tempted to use what our culture calls "white lies," that lies in speech are one thing and lies in writing are quite another. The written lie is permanently available for later examination, and for having its validity checked by a reader determined to catch you in an untruth.

Except for what we could call Social Lies—letting little children believe there is a Santa Claus, asking "How are you?" when we don't care how people are, writing that no doubt many people in town noticed your faulty quotation of Thoreau, and so on—lying is ordinarily evidence of either laziness or incompetence. There is almost always something true that you can say or write instead of the lie; you just need to take time to figure out what it is. In this paragraph, you told the truth when you said you were so sure the reference to "Peruvian Paradox" was there that you didn't feel a need to check. It is in fact true that you thought it ought to be included, and that you didn't intend to leave it out, even if your reason was not respect for the article but your desire not to hurt Elizabeth's feelings. She is free to interpret your statement in any way she chooses, but it is a <u>true</u> statement. The same condition holds for your claim that this is not trivial for you; again, she can interpret your reasons for feeling that way as she likes. The claim is still true.

Whenever you find yourself faced with an unpleasant truth that does not <u>have</u> to be stated, stop and think. One alternative to that truth is an appropriate lie, and that's the easy solution. Instead of that, however, ask yourself: What could I say that would also be appropriate in this situation, and that would be <u>true</u>? You will find that there are always an abundance of possible true things to say once you've gotten into the habit of substituting them for the lie that comes so easily and seductively to mind. Instead of "I'm looking forward to seeing you on March 30th," when the truth is that you wish you never had to see this person again, write "Our next meeting is scheduled for March 30th," which is the truth. Instead of writing "Your editorial was well written," when the truth is that it was very badly written, fall back on the empty word "interesting," which can be interpreted in so many different ways.

Paragraph Three

To say that I will be more careful in future is absurd; I was scrupulously careful this time, and still I made this dreadful mistake. This time, I was fortunate—I insulted a friend, whose understanding and good judgment I know I can count on. Next time, it might be much worse! Elizabeth, I am about to add imposition to injury; I am going to ask for your help. Next time I prepare an article for publication, could I call on you to give it one extra reading for me, to be sure that if I have made errors or omissions I will have the opportunity to correct them? Your knowledge of the field, your wide experience, and your critical skills would be invaluable to me, if you could find the time to share them with a colleague who clearly has need of them. (If it would be a burden, you must of course say no at once; I will understand.) In the meantime, I am grateful to you for accepting my apology.

This paragraph transmits the basic messages NEVER AGAIN and YOU'RE TERRIFIC, and part of the compliment is the request for your reader's help. A request for help—framed as "You are wiser and more experienced and more skilled than I am; therefore I respectfully ask for your help"—is an ancient strategy that has survived the ages both because it is usually true and because it usually works. Since you and Elizabeth disagree on so many things, she probably knows you aren't really eager for her help; that's not the point. The point is that asking for it costs you nothing and is a compliment from you to her. You've done it very carefully, notice. You've specified that you will only ask at the last minute, when one final reading might catch something you missed. And you've given her an easy out with "If it would be a burden, you must of course say no at once; I will understand." (Suppose she takes you up on this offer. In the first place, she probably will find errors you've missed. In the second place, unless you are an extraordinarily prolific writer whose work is always accepted by the first journal you send it to, you're not likely to need to call on her more than once a year, at most.)

Finally, you've presupposed both that you can count on her to understand what has happened and to accept your apology. The factives "know" and "be grateful" take care of that.

This version of Letter 25 is not particularly formal. (If you're unfamiliar with the academic register, this may surprise you.[1] Version 2, below, is <u>very</u> formal. For it to be appropriate, two conditions would have to exist: (1) you work for a stuffy hyperconservative department, and (2) your slighted colleague is a distinguished senior scholar with very old-fashioned manners and habits.

LETTER 25, Version 2: Formal

Dear . . . . .,

It is difficult to express how much I regret that this letter must be written, and, in particular, how much I regret that it must be written to <u>you</u>. It is by no means the letter you deserve to receive; I am neither eloquent enough, nor skilled enough, to write that letter. It does, however, represent the best efforts of a woman who is guilty not only of one of the worst errors a scholar can commit—the error of carelessness—but also of having insulted a colleague for whom she feels the highest respect and regard.

I did not discover that I had omitted "The Peruvian Paradox: Four Essential Perspectives" from the bibliography for my recently published article until the printed copies were in my hand. In my opinion, there is only one way in which this could have happened: I was so confident that the reference was there that I felt no need to check for its presence. I am aware that this does not constitute

---

[1] The term "register" refers to a way of speaking or writing that is associated with a particular <u>role</u>. The child who says "Bye, Mom!" to his mother, "Goodbye, Mr. Martin!" to his teacher, and "Hey, man, gotta split!" to his friend demonstrates that he knows three registers: home, school, and peer group. The academic register used by college professors tends, even at its least formal, to be stuffy and encumbered with frills.

an excuse; however, I am convinced that it is the only explanation that has even minimal plausibility. I realize that for a scholar of your stature a junior colleague's failure to cite one of your publications is a minor matter. For me, however, it is anything but minor. I am deeply sorry.

To say that I will be more careful in future would be absurd. Were I asked whether I had been careful this time, I would insist that I was <u>scrupulously</u> careful. Nevertheless, the mistake occurred. It is my great good fortune that on this occasion I offended a colleague on whose understanding and good judgment I know I can rely. Next time it might be much worse. Dr. Paxton, I am about to add imposition to injury by requesting your assistance. When I once again have an article ready to go forward for publication, may I call upon you to read it through one last time, so that I may have the opportunity to correct any errors or omissions? Your knowledge of the field, your wide experience, and your critical skills would be invaluable to me, should you have the time and the inclination to share them with a colleague whose need for both is undoubtedly obvious to you. (If this task would prove burdensome for you, you must of course refuse; I will understand.) In the meantime, please allow me to express my appreciation and gratitude for your willingness to accept my apology.

Sincerely,

The differences that make this letter more formal are not exclusively differences in word choices; some of the changes are changes in grammatical structure. Let's go through this version again and discuss them briefly. You'll notice that the sequences that make up the actual apologies required almost nothing in the way of "formalizing." This is because apologies in writing are usually done very formally, even in a letter that is otherwise informal in tone.

ANALYSIS OF LETTER 25, VERSION 2

Paragraph One

It is difficult to express how much I regret that this letter must be written, and, in particular, how much I regret that it must be written to <u>you</u>. It is by no means the letter you deserve to receive; I am neither eloquent enough, nor skilled enough, to write that letter. It does, however, represent the best efforts of a woman who is guilty not only of one of the worst errors a scholar can commit—the error of carelessness—but also of having insulted a colleague for whom she feels the highest respect and regard.

The changes in word choice will be obvious. "I don't know any way to tell you" becomes "It is difficult to express"; "has to be written" becomes "must be written"; "but" becomes "however"; and so on. Two small chunks of academic jargon—"in particular" and "by no means" are added. This changes the tone and formality of the written language, just as a difference in tone of <u>voice</u> can place spoken language at any desired point on the formality continuum.

The structural change is "I am neither eloquent enough nor skilled enough" for "I'm not eloquent enough or skilled enough." This is an easy change—just substitute "neither" for "not" and "nor" for "or," straight across the board—and one that adds instant formality. The only way you can go wrong with "neither/nor" is by adding it to a sentence that is otherwise extremely casual, which creates the same effect as wearing sneakers with your best suit.

Paragraph Two

I did not discover that I had omitted "The Peruvian Paradox: Four Essential Perspectives" from the bibliography for my recently published article until the printed copies were in my hand. In my opinion, there is only one way in which this could have happened: I was so confident that the reference was there that I felt no need to check for its presence. I am aware that this does not constitute an excuse; however, I am convinced that it is the only explanation that has even minimal plausibility. I realize that for a scholar of your stature a junior colleague's failure to cite one of your publications is a minor matter. For me, however, it is anything but minor. I am deeply sorry.

The major structural change here is the revision of the second sentence to include "in which." You've changed "the only way it could possibly have happened" to "there's only one way in which this could have happened." That little two-word sequence, "in which," is so well established as a marker of formality that young students in "English comp" classes frequently throw it into sentences where it not only doesn't belong but makes no sense. (For example, I have often seen student sentences like "This is the notebook in which I keep my class notes in.") To write "This is the room where we'll meet" or "This is the room we'll meet in" is informal; the formal version is "This is the room in which we'll meet."

The other pattern that should be mentioned is again a standard marker of formality: a sentence that begins with an embedded statement and a semicolon (;), followed by "however," and a contrasting statement. Here are a few examples of this formalizing strategy, with appropriate word changes.

1. "It's going to be hard to meet this deadline, but we'll find a way to do it."

1a. "It will be difficult to meet this deadline; however, we will find a way to do it."

2. "You told us you would deliver five tons of material, but you only shipped four."

2a. "You advised us that you would deliver five tons of material; however, your shipment contained only four."

3. "We told you we would hire you if we had a job for you. Unfortunately, nothing suitable is open right now."

3a. "We advised you that you would be hired if we had a position for you; however, we have no suitable openings at this time."

Paragraph Three

To say that I will be more careful in future would be absurd. Were I asked whether I had been careful this time, I would insist that I was <u>scrupulously</u> careful. Nevertheless, the mistake occurred. It is my great good fortune that on this occasion I offended a colleague on whose understanding and good judgment I know I can rely. Next time it might be much worse. Dr. Paxton, I am about to add imposition to injury by requesting your assistance. When I once again have an article ready to go forward for publication, may I call upon you to read it through one last time, so that I may have the opportunity to correct any errors or omissions? Your knowledge of the field, your wide experience, and your critical skills would be

invaluable to me, should you have the time and the inclination to share them with a colleague whose need for
both is undoubtedly obvious to you. (If this task would
prove burdensome for you, you must of course refuse; I
will understand.) In the meantime, please allow me to
express my appreciation and gratitude for your willingness to accept my apology.

This paragraph, in addition to the many shifts to hyperformal
vocabulary, contains two items that mark it unambiguously as
hifalutin language.

First: It moves a preposition (on) into a sentence from its much
more natural position at the end, changing "whose understanding
and good judgment I know I can rely on" to "on whose understanding
and good judgment I know I can rely." This is like "in which," and
every English reader recognizes it as formal language. Grammar
books and grammar teachers are forever presenting an alleged rule
that goes: "Never end a sentence with a preposition." This doesn't
keep people from doing so in ordinary speech. Because their internal
grammars tell them that the rule is phony, and that saying "To
whom did you wish to speak?" instead of "Who did you want to
talk to?" only makes you sound ridiculous. In written language,
however, the "in whiches" and "to whoms" take the place of body
language messages indicating that the speaker considers formal language necessary.

Second: it uses the English <u>subjunctive</u>. This construction is so
rare in American English that it is confined almost entirely to frozen
expressions like "If I were the President," "had I known then what
I know now," "were I a Democrat," and "Long live mutual funds!"
It is certainly too rare to be worth a lengthy explanation here; I've
used it only for demonstration purposes. If you ever have a genuine
need for it in anything except the "if I were" slot, you'll find it
discussed in detail in grammar textbooks. The obvious subjunctive
sequences in the model letter are "were I asked" and "should you
have the time and the inclination."

It's good to have one model letter of this kind around, just in
case you need it someday. Most of the time, however, a letter like
Letter 25, Version 2 will be unsuitable for business correspondence,
and even <u>more</u> unsuitable for personal letters. The most important
thing to remember about your choices with regard to formality is
this: BE CONSISTENT. A letter that has a hyperformal first paragraph
and a hypercasual second paragraph is the equivalent of a tuxedo

jacket with blue jeans; avoid it. Sometimes the use of one or two very informal items in an otherwise formal sequence—or vice versa—can be extremely effective. However, unless you're absolutely sure you know what you're doing, it's better not to mix formality levels in that way. The only exception is when a letter contains something that is a formal speech <u>act</u>: an apology, a serious warning, a promise with legal force, or something of that kind. Such sequences should be written in formal language, even in an otherwise informal letter.

What "Awkward" Really Means

This is a good place to settle the question of what it means to say that a written sentence is "awkward." People tend to assume that it just means that the sentence is too long. That's sometimes true—but it's based on a misconception about <u>what</u> is too long. Look at the pair of examples below, please.

1. That you were unwilling to accept my apology for having neglected to include you in the bibliography surprised me.

2. It surprised me that you were unwilling to accept my apology for having neglected to include you in the bibliography.

Sentence #1 is nineteen words long. Sentence #2 is one word longer. But the nineteen-word sentence is very awkward indeed, while the twenty-word sentence is fine. The number of words, by itself, isn't what matters. What matters is *the number of chunks the reader's short-term memory has to keep track of in processing the sentence.*

Awkwardness has little to do with style; it's a psycholinguistic problem. Reading an English sentence, roughly speaking, requires the following steps:

STEP ONE: Find the verb.[2]
STEP TWO: Assign each of the nominals a role with
                    regard to the verb.

This isn't as technical as it sounds. Assume the sentence you're reading is "George Washington chopped down the cherry tree with a hatchet." You find the verb, "chopped down." Then you sort the nominals, assigning "George Washington" the role of Chopper, "the

---

[2] To avoid tormenting you with a grammar lecture, I've described this process as if all predicates were verbs. For English that's often not true. You'll find the other possibilities discussed in the glossary at the end of this book, under "Predicate."

cherry tree" the role of What's Chopped, and "a hatchet" the role of Instrument For Chopping. That's easily done. In example sentence #1 above, however, the verb "surprised" doesn't come along until almost the end of the sentence. The reader has to hold a seventeen-word subject in short-term memory until "surprised" is found. That's hard to do, and it's awkward, in the scientific sense of the term. In example sentence #2, on the other hand, "surprised" is the second word in the sentence, and the short-term memory has no such burden interfering with its task.

You will remember that the short-term memory can only handle approximately seven chunks at a time. When you write a sentence like #1, it overburdens your reader's short-term memory and makes understanding and remembering difficult. You would be wise to avoid that when you can, despite the fact that written language is available to the reader for re-reading.

SUPPLEMENTARY LETTERS

LETTER 26
Flub and Frailty: You've Left a Committee Member Out of Your Press Release

Dear . . . . .,

I don't know any way to tell you how much I regret the need to write this letter. It's not the letter you ought to receive, because letter-writing isn't one of my strong suits. It does, however, represent the best efforts of a man who is heartily ashamed of his carelessness.

I didn't find out that I'd left your name out of my news release on the Airport Relocation Committee until I actually saw the article printed in the Globe. I know only one way that could have happened: Because the committee's work couldn't possibly have been done without you, I just took it for granted that your name was there. (That's no excuse, of course.) I know that for someone as active in civic affairs as you are this is a trivial matter, but it's not trivial to me. I am genuinely sorry about it, and I have sent the newspaper a letter setting the record straight.

I could say I'll be more careful in future, but I was careful <u>this</u> time, and the mistake got past me anyway. I'm just lucky that the person I insulted is someone whose good sense and understanding I can count on. Maybe the next time I try my hand at anything for publication I ought to run it by you and let your more experienced eye find my errors. (If I thought you had time for that kind of thing, I'd be tempted to ask you to do it!) In any case, I'm grateful to you for accepting my apology.

Sincerely,

LETTER 27
Flub and Frailty: You've Left the Local Expert Off Your Panel

Dear . . . . .,

It embarrasses me greatly to find myself obliged to write this letter, especially since it has to be written to <u>you</u>. I only wish I were eloquent enough, and skilled enough, to make it the letter you deserve to receive; I'm not. All I can offer you is the best efforts of a careless woman who has managed to insult someone for whom she has only respect and high regard.

I didn't realize until I saw the printed program for the upcoming San Diego conference that I had made a serious mistake. Bob, I was in charge of putting together the panel on home equity loans. I carried out the task assigned to me, but I goofed—I didn't invite you to serve on that panel. I know it won't matter a great deal to someone with your reputation in the field, but that's not the point. It matters to <u>me</u>, because like me you are a resident of Willow Green. And it will matter to the audience at the conference, which would have benefited from hearing your expert communication on the topic. I am so very sorry, and I have no excuse to offer. I just plain forgot.

I will be more careful in the future, certainly. I've learned the necessity for carefulness, and I won't forget it. But that doesn't help much, since the panel is filled and I can't withdraw the invitations I've already sent.

I'm in so deep already that I'm going to add imposition to injury and ask you for your help. As you know, people often agree to serve on panels and then drop out down the road. If that happens, could I call on you to fill the vacancy? (If you'd rather not do that, you must say so at once; I'll understand.) In the meantime, I'm grateful to you for accepting my apology.

Sincerely,

Chapter Ten

"I Could Cut My Tongue Out"

Triple-F Scenario Nine

Dear Louis,

When I said, "Let them eat cake," I had no idea I would start a revolution. Nobody ever paid any attention to what I said before! Bu̲ _____ sensible and keep our head ____ sure we can work so ____

Your loving,

Marie

*L*ast Friday night you attended your company's major "office party" of the year, with personnel there from divisions scattered all over the country. You remember having a wonderful time. However, you are not ordinarily much of a drinker, and the fruit punch that was served was apparently far more powerful than you suspected from its taste . . . much of the evening is a blur in your memory.

You arrived at your office Monday morning to find your boss waiting for you in a very surly mood. According to him, during that blur you made a sexist and abusive remark to a visiting vice president. He is even able to quote your exact words. He reports that you said to her: "If YOU were a REAL woman, you'd be home taking care of your KIDS instead of playing OFFice!" Your protestations—that you are not and never have been a sexist man, that if you said anything of the kind it must have been a joke, and that you're sure it has to have been clear to the executive that it was a joke—make no impression on your boss at all. He makes it very clear: Your remark didn't sound like a joke to anybody who heard it, and a lot of people did. Furthermore, if it *was* a joke, it wasn't one the company would tolerate. You will, he says grimly, write a suitable letter of apology immediately, and you will FAX it before noon today, with a hard copy in the mail and a dozen roses.[1] WHAT DO YOU SAY IN YOUR LETTER?

LETTER 28
Flub and Frailty: You've Made a Sexist Remark to a Visiting V.I.P.

Dear . . . . .,

This is a letter that I never expected to find myself writing; it isn't going to be easy. It isn't going to be the letter you deserve to receive, because I don't know *how* to write that letter. I wish I did. I wish I were eloquent enough, and skilled enough. Inadequate as the letter is, I want you to know that it represents the best efforts of a man who doesn't like himself this morning and doesn't expect other people to like him much either. This letter, Ms. Cartwright, comes to you from a man who is quite frankly sick at heart.

---

[1] The roses may seem to perpetuate sexist stereotypes; however, I'm certain this is what the boss described above would say.

Donald Torina called me into his office the minute I got to work this morning and told me what I said to you last Friday night. It was hard for me to believe. It would be easy to say that it was the killer punch talking, but it wouldn't be true. It was *me* talking; me and my big mouth. I am sorry, and I am ashamed, and I would give anything to unsay those ugly words I said to you.

I can't promise I'll never say anything like that again. The simple truth is that I am an old-fashioned man who treasures women and who believes that a mother's place is in the home. I know I'm wrong; I know that most mothers today, whatever their personal preferences may be, have to work to provide their children with the necessities of life. I know they don't have the good fortune my mother had; she was <u>always</u> there when my brother and I came home from school, and always our safe haven. I keep trying to go back to the world as it was then, and that's not possible. I <u>can</u> promise that I will be a great deal more careful in the future about what I drink, because it is also the simple truth that if I hadn't had so much of that punch I would have kept my opinions to myself (or, if it was appropriate to express them, I would have expressed them very differently). If you can find it in your heart to forgive the clumsy man who insulted and hurt you, you will have demonstrated to him once again a principle he already holds to fiercely: That it is <u>women</u> who keep this old world from falling completely apart.

Sincerely,

This letter is longer than the other model letters presented up to this point. You could, if you like, set it up as four paragraphs, with the final paragraph starting at "I <u>can</u> promise that I will be a great deal more careful in the future . . ." Either way is acceptable.

ANALYSIS OF LETTER 28

Paragraph One

This is a letter that I never expected to find myself writing; it isn't going to be easy. It isn't going to be the letter you deserve to receive, because I don't know <u>how</u> to write that letter. I wish I did. I wish I were eloquent enough, and skilled enough. Inadequate as the letter is, I want you to know that it represents the best efforts of a man who doesn't like himself this morning and doesn't expect other people to like him much either. This letter, Ms. Cartwright, comes to you from a man who is quite frankly sick at heart.

Before you decide that this paragraph is overdone, stop, please, and do a small experiment. Look at the sentence below, the sentence that caused all this uproar. Read it aloud, giving strong emphasis to each of the words or parts of words in capital letters, and listen to it carefully, remembering that this was said to a woman in public, loudly and belligerently, in front of a crowd of her colleagues and their guests.

"If YOU were a REAL woman, you'd be home taking care of your KIDS instead of playing OFFice!"

Well? Is the paragraph overdone? I don't think so. The sentence is a vicious and inexcusably brutal example of an English Verbal Attack Pattern (VAP, for short), packing two cruel presupposed insults. It would be <u>hard</u> for the person who said it to be overly apologetic for this one! And keep in mind the fact that in much of the balance of the letter you not only express your opinions but you defend them. You aren't going to spend three whole paragraphs groveling. Just as a basis for comparison, look at the following example, which would be typical Worthless Worm language in this situation.

This is a letter that I never expected to find myself writing; it isn't going to be easy. It isn't going to be the letter you deserve to receive, because I'm too *stupid* to write that letter. This is a letter from a man so despicable, so completely worthless, so unfit to associate with decent people, so loathsome and ignorant and . . . .

All right? You're not doing that. You're just saying that you are shocked at your own behavior and sick at heart about it. This isn't Worthless Worming. It's Leveling when you know you've done something genuinely awful, and it's not overdone.

ENGLISH VERBAL ATTACK PATTERNS (VAPs)

The English VAPs are learned along with the patterns for questions and commands and every other sort of utterance. Children not yet old enough for Head Start get a head start on participation in our violent society when they learn to say things like "If YOU were a REAL daddy, YOU'D let me watch TELevision!" Many children grow up in homes where the VAPs make up almost the entire linguistic inventory in family disagreements, and they carry that pattern on into their own adult lives, business as well as personal. The VAPs are language toxins whose only purpose is to demonstrate power and cause pain; you don't want them in your letters, or in your life. Here are the insults tucked into the presuppositions in the offending sentence, their meanings clear to any native speaker of English:

"If YOU were a REAL woman, you'd be home taking care of your KIDS instead of playing OFFice!"

1. You're not a real woman; real women stay home and take care of their kids.

2. You're not a real business executive, either—you're just playing office, like a child.

It's not the words in VAPs, unpleasant as they frequently are, that identify them as VAPs. It's the <u>tune</u>, the melody that the words are set to, called <u>intonation</u>. A great deal of the time, the very same words set to a different tune would not be verbal attacks. They might be clumsy, or rude, or a lot of other negative things, but they would not be VAPs. For example, compare "Why did you leave early?" with "WHY did you leave EARly?" "Why did you leave early?" is just a request for information, from somebody who wants to know. The same words, pronounced with heavy emphasis on "WHY" and "EARly," are an attack, from somebody who may have no interest at all in knowing the answer to the question, but is <u>very</u> interested in starting a fight and causing trouble. When people say "It wasn't what they said, it was the way they said it!" this is what they're talking about.[2]

---

[2] For a detailed discussion of how to recognize and respond to the English VAPs in speech, see any of the books or audio programs in the *Gentle Art of Verbal Self-Defense* series.

It's important to remember this when you read letters and memos and reports written by other people. Because without the information provided by the intonation, you cannot know whether the words are <u>intended</u> to be attacks. English punctuation does a rotten job of conveying intonation for written language, and you should always give the writer the benefit of the doubt. There's often a way to get the information you need, however; just follow these steps:

1. Spill coffee on the letter, over the sequence you find suspicious.

2. Call the writer on the phone and say you've spilled coffee on the letter—which is the truth.

3. Ask the writer to say the words aloud, because now it's hard for you to read them—also the truth.

4. Listen carefully.

Now let's go back to the analysis of the model letter.

Paragraph Two

Donald Torina called me into his office the minute I got to work this morning and told me what I said to you last Friday night. It was hard for me to believe. It would be easy to say that it was the killer punch talking, but it wouldn't be true. It was <u>me</u> talking; me and my big mouth. I am sorry, and I am ashamed, and I would give anything to unsay those ugly words I said to you.

In this paragraph (which is entirely in Leveler Mode) you give your boss full credit for calling your behavior to your attention, without saying that he has ordered you to write the letter. This is good strategy. Your reader is an experienced executive; she will know exactly what Torina said after he called you in. But you don't want to emphasize the fact that the letter is written under orders by setting that information down in black and white. And when you write that it was hard for you to believe you said the offending sentence, you're explaining why the order was necessary. If you feel this is too subtle, you could add a more explicit statement of the facts, like this:

Donald Torina called me into his office the minute I got to work this morning, told me what I said to you last

Friday night, and ordered me to send an immediate apology. And I am very glad he did, because I could hardly believe what he was telling me. I truly have no memory at all of saying those words, and I wouldn't have known that an apology was needed if it hadn't been for his timely intervention.

The problem with this version is that it also places unwanted emphasis on one of the facts, and it happens to be a most unsavory one: that because of your overindulgence at the party you can't even remember what you may have said or done. In my opinion, the original version is safer.

Now, suppose that the next thing in the paragraph was this old saw: "It wasn't me talking, it was the punch." Your reader's immediate response to that would be something like "Hah! That's easy to say!" You would like very much to blame the incident on the punch—not on your overindulgence, but on the punch itself, which was too strong and so disguised by the fruit juice that people couldn't tell how much they were drinking. But you want to avoid the cliche. You do that by saying what you did, and then admitting without reservation that the fault lies with "you and your big mouth," another cliche. Avoiding the first trite sequence gives you enough slack to make it possible to use the second one.

You end the paragraph with an apology that has just enough parallelism to make it memorable, and that tells the truth. Whether you are sorry and ashamed and wishing you could unsay your words because you hurt this woman, or only because you've gotten yourself into an undignified mess, the words of the sentence are true.

Paragraph Three

I can't promise I'll never say anything like that again, because the simple truth is that I am an old-fashioned man who treasures women and who believes that a mother's place is in the home. I know I'm wrong; I know that most mothers today, whatever their personal preferences may be, have to work to provide their children with the necessities of life. I know they don't have the good fortune my mother had; she was always there when my brother and I came home from school, and always our safe haven. I keep trying to go back to the world as it was then, and that's not possible. I can promise that I will be a great deal more careful in future about what I drink, because it is also the simple truth that if I hadn't had so much of that punch I would have kept my opinions to myself (or, if it was appropriate to express them, I would have expressed them very differently). If you can find it in your heart to forgive the clumsy man who insulted and hurt you, you will have demonstrated to him once again a principle he already holds to fiercely: That it is <u>women</u> who keep this old world from falling completely apart.

USING THE PERSONAL ANECDOTE

This long paragraph has three parts: an introduction; a brief essay on motherhood, with your own mother as a specific example; and a conclusion. If we take out the essay we get this:

> I can't promise I'll never say anything like that again, because the simple truth is that I am an old-fashioned man who treasures women and who believes that a mother's place is in the home. I <u>can</u> promise that I will be a great deal more careful in future about what I drink, because it is also the simple truth that if I hadn't had so much of that punch I would have kept my opinions to myself (or, if it was appropriate to express them, I would have expressed them very differently). If you can find it in your heart. . . .

And so on, to the end.

You may prefer this. It may be that you're uncomfortable with anything remotely like a narrative approach. You may feel that a personal item, almost an anecdote, has no place in a letter of this kind. You may have an image—as a tight-lipped strong silent type—that you value and want to preserve. In that case, take out the sequence about your own childhood. But think it over carefully. Because many people will forgive you for wanting all women to be like your own mother; they will find that touching, even charming. They are not as likely to forgive you for wanting all women to meet your set of personal abstract standards about what women should be and do.

This is the paragraph where you defend yourself, without in any way diminishing your apology. You want the vice president to know you're aware that the problem wasn't only what you said, it was especially the <u>way</u> you said it. You want her to know that, but for the overly powerful punch, you would have said something like what you're <u>writing</u>, instead of verbally abusing her, and although she might have disagreed with you, she wouldn't have been insulted. You want her to know that your opinions come not from your conviction that women are inferior beings incapable of understanding business, but from your conviction that mothers in the home are indispensable to the successful rearing of children. The two positions are very different, and it's important for you to make it clear which one is yours. You want this executive, the next time she encounters you, to say, "Oh, yes! You're the man who thinks women can't bring up their children unless they're at home all the time!", not "Oh, yes! You're the sexist pig who thinks women are so stupid they ought to stay home!" Your paragraph makes this clear. And considering the amount of information you had to convey, it does it very economically.

USING THE "GROUP" COMPLIMENT

In the final sentence, you compliment not just the woman your letter is addressed to but <u>all</u> women; it's unlikely that your reader will take exception to the sentiment you've expressed here. This sentence is an example of a variation that is useful in many situations. Here's the basic pattern of the compliment to a class rather than to an individual, with examples.

> "If you can find it in your heart to forgive [X], you will have demonstrated to him/her once again a principle he/she already holds to fiercely: That . . . .
>
>> it is <u>judges</u> who make it possible for our system of law enforcement to survive in the present epidemic of legislative meddling."
>>
>> it is <u>men</u> who suffer the gravest consequences from the communication barriers between the sexes."
>>
>> it is the <u>senior</u> executive who is able to look at problems and see them in their entirety instead of as a collection of largely unrelated symptoms."

And so on, tailored to your situation. This handy pattern lets you compliment your reader, compliment the entire population your reader represents, and, at the same time, state one of your own opinions or philosophical positions.

A WARNING ABOUT VAPs IN WRITTEN LANGUAGE

People know the verbal attack patterns the way they know the rest of their grammar—as internalized information that never has to be rehearsed and is never forgotten. For that reason, even though the words themselves don't make a sequence of language a VAP, you would be wise to avoid writing a sentence that could be interpreted as one. (You can't count on other people to know about the coffee-spilling technique!) Look at the pair of sentences below, for example. Read them both aloud, giving extra emphasis to words and parts of words that are all in capital letters.

"If you really want to close the Armstrong deal, you'll learn that list of sales figures by heart before the meeting."

"If you REALLY want to close the Armstrong deal, you'll LEARN that list of sales figures by HEART before the MEETing!"

Hear the difference? The second sentence, with "really" heavily stressed, presupposes (a) that you *don't* want to close the Armstrong deal and (b) that you can't be counted on to know the sales figures well enough at the meeting to close it. The first example sentence doesn't do that. It may be a nosy sentence that intrudes on your own ideas of how to close the deal and meddles in your business in a way you don't appreciate—but it doesn't carry the verbal abuse that the second sentence does. The problem is that in written language people can't tell which of these sentences they're reading. Even if some of the words in capital letters are underlined by the writer—the usual way to indicate emphasis—there's no sure way to tell whether the writer is just being forceful or is being abusive. The only "correct" punctuation option, in either case, is underlining.

Since that is true, you can't count on someone who reads a sentence of yours that <u>looks</u> like a VAP not to assume that it would sound like one if you were saying it, and take offense. Try, therefore, to scrupulously avoid sentences patterned like any of the common English VAPs. They're all potentially boobytrapped, and they are likely to get you into situations where you can only ask in bewildered outrage: "What on earth did I <u>say</u>?" Examples of the most common structures that might be mistaken for VAPs are shown in Figure 1 (see pages 140–141), with explanatory notes where needed. No attempt has been made in the examples to indicate intonation. In Figure 2, the same sentences are shown (for clarification, especially for non-native speakers of English) with the abusive melody made explicit by capital letters and punctuation.

Look over any letter you write, to be sure it doesn't include sentences like those shown in Figure 1. If you find one, rewrite it so that it will convey the message you want to transmit, but cannot be mistaken for one of the VAPs. For example: Rewrite "You could at least notify the clerical staff" as "One step that might be helpful would be to notify the clerical staff."

WRITING RESPONSES TO VERBAL ATTACKS

Suppose that you are absolutely certain that the language in a memo or letter sent to you was intended to be abusive and insulting. Suppose, for example, that it contained language conveying a message like one of those listed below.

1. "WHY can't you EVER get anything done on TIME?"
2. "WHAT'S THE MATTER with you lately, ANYway?"
3. "WHEN are you going to DO something about JOE?"
4. "What MAKES you so obnoxious and uncooperative?"
5. "DON'T you have ANY consideration at ALL for other PEOPLE?"

There's only one way, in my opinion, to respond to language like that in the examples. Here it is.

LETTER 29: Let's Talk This Over

Dear . . . . .,

I'm sure you are unaware of the abusive nature of the language in your recent letter.

Let's get together and talk this over.

Sincerely,

SUPPLEMENTARY LETTERS

LETTER 30
Flub: You've Called Your Doctor a Quack—in Front of the Staff

Dear Dr. . . . . .,

This is a letter I never expected to find myself writing, and it's not going to be easy. I wish I were skilled enough

FIGURE 1

1. "If you really wanted to get ahead in this business, you'd learn Japanese."

2. "If you really cared about the company, you wouldn't want to move the headquarters offshore."

3. "A person who really understood the economy wouldn't be worried about the budget deficit."

   (This one is just a Computer Mode variation on "If you really understood the economy, you wouldn't be worried about the budget deficit.")

4. "Even someone your age can operate this equipment with ease."

5. "Everyone understands why you are unable to complete the project before the deadline."

6. "Some managers would be furious if their direct reports came in late to every staff meeting."

7. "Why do you always insist on having this procedure carried out the way they do it at the home office?"

   (The potential problem here comes from the <u>combination</u> of "why" plus "always" or "never." With "why" only, this question isn't likely to be interpreted as a verbal attack.)

8. "You could at least notify the clerical staff."

9. "You're not the only person in the firm who has trouble with the new computers."

10. "Even if your sales figures do drop below an acceptable level, you can count on our support."

FIGURE 2

---

1. "If you REALLY wanted to get ahead in this business, YOU'D learn JapaNESE."

2. "If you REALLY cared about the company, YOU wouldn't WANT to move the headquarters offshore."

3. "A person who REALLY understood the economy wouldn't BE worried about the budget deficit."

4. "EVEN someone YOUR age can operate this equipment with ease."

    "EVEN someone YOUR age can operate THIS equipment with ease."

5. "EVERYONE underSTANDS why you are unable to complete the project before the DEADline."

6. "SOME managers would be FURIOUS if their direct reports came in late to every STAFF meeting!"

7. "WHY do you ALways insist on having this procedure carried out the way they do it at the HOME OFfice?"

8. "You could at LEAST notify the CLERical staff."

9. "YOU'RE not the ONly person in the firm who has trouble with the new comPUTers."

10. "EVen if your sales figures do drop below an acceptable level, YOU can count on OUR support."

    NOTE: Other intonations are possible—for example, you often hear "If you really CARED . . ." instead of "If you REALLY cared . . ." The examples above are the most typical ones.

---

to do it the way it ought to be done; I'm not. Nevertheless, I want you to know that this letter represents the best efforts of a man who doesn't admire himself very much this morning. I want you to know that I am disgusted with myself.

When I was in your office last Thursday afternoon, I lost my temper and made a scene in front of you and your staff; as I recall, I called you an unprincipled quack. It would be easy to blame that on how worried I was about my heart and about the tests you'd ordered, but I'm not going to do that. Let's just blame it on my bad temper and be done with it. I'm sorry, and I'd give a great deal to unsay all the ugly words I said.

I can't promise I'll never do it again; I can only promise that I'll try in future to think before I speak and keep a sense of proportion. If you are willing to forgive my outburst and go on with the doctor/patient relationship we have had up to now, you will have demonstrated to me once again something that I have always considered to be true: That it is <u>doctors</u> who see human beings at their worst, and must deal with them at their worst. I'll call your office next week to find out if I can make another appointment to see you.

Sincerely,

LETTER 31 (TO A MOTHER-IN-LAW)
Flub: You've Said Terrible Things About Her—and She Knows

Dear . . . . .,

This is a letter I never thought I'd have to write; it isn't going to be easy. It isn't going to be the letter you deserve, because I'm just not eloquent enough or skilled enough to write that letter. I want you to know, however, that inadequate as it is, it represents the best efforts of a man who doesn't like himself very much this morning and has no reason to expect *you* to like him, either. This letter, Helen, comes from a man who is quite frankly sick at heart.

Carolyn just called me to tell me that she'd told you the things I said to her about you yesterday over lunch. That was hard for me to believe. Not only because I couldn't believe I'd been fool enough to say them, but because I couldn't believe she could be that cruel. I shouldn't have said what I did; I had no right to do so. But for her to *tell* you only made a rotten situation worse. I want you to know that I am sorry, and that I apologize, and I want you to know that I apologize both for my own behavior and for Carolyn's.

I can't promise I'll never say anything I shouldn't say again. It's the nature of human beings to make mistakes, and I'm sure I'll make many more before I die. I <u>can</u> promise that I will do my best to think before I speak, and to make both my thoughts and my words more charitable. I don't know whether you can find it in your heart to forgive me; I hope so. I know that you are a person of extraordinary character and graciousness, and it may be that you will be willing to believe me when I tell you that those were the hasty words of a man who deeply regrets having said them and wishes he had kept his mouth firmly shut.

I'll call you next week for your decision; in the meantime I want you to know that I feel nothing but affection and respect for you, as always.

Sincerely,

Chapter Eleven

"But I Never Dreamed You Were Serious"

Triple-F Scenario Ten

Dear Madam:

When I said, "I shall return," I didn't mean tomorrow. At the moment I am having a property dispute with some very disagreeable people. As soon as I have settled this problem I . . . . indeed return . . . .

Faithfully Yours,

D. MacArthur

*S*everal months ago at a cocktail party, you found yourself in a conversation with an official from a local charity organization called JOINHANDS. His description of its activities was amazingly interesting. You became so enthusiastic about what you were hearing that he asked you to serve on a learning disability resource committee being set up by the group. You were taken aback by the request, and you said so, but he was very persuasive and insistent. There seemed to be no way you could gracefully say no, and you didn't know what to do. In the end, you reluctantly agreed, not knowing what else you could do to bring the conversation to a close. You hoped it was only party chatter and that you'd never hear from him again. As the weeks went by, you became certain that that was the case. You were wrong. Your secretary has just brought you a letter from JOINHANDS enclosing an announcement of the first scheduled meeting of the task force, with your name listed as one of the members.

This is bad. You not only don't have time to be part of a complex project like this, you wouldn't want to do it if you <u>did</u> have time. You have no interest in investigating local resources for dealing with learning disabilities. You'd be nothing but a liability to the group. However, the members and supporters of JOINHANDS include many influential local people. Some of them are already your clients. All of them are in a position to hurt your business by negative word of mouth if they choose to do so. This isn't one of those situations where you can just have your administrative assistant call and withdraw your name, with pro forma apologies. You have to get out of your commitment, but you have to do it in a way that doesn't alienate the group and anger its members. WHAT DO YOU SAY IN YOUR LETTER?

LETTER 32
Flub and Frailty: You've Got to Cancel—Much Too Late

Dear . . . . .,

You cannot imagine how much I don't want to write this letter, or how tempted I am just to ask my assistant to give you a call. But that won't do, and I have gathered my courage to do this myself. Forrest, this letter comes to you from a man who has to tell you that he won't be serving on your committee after all, and that you should be <u>grateful</u> that he won't.

Until my secretary handed me your letter announcing the meeting scheduled for February 9th, with my name on the list of members, I had taken it for granted that you were no more serious when you asked me to serve than I was when I said I'd do it. After all, the very last thing you need is a man who has three different urgent tasks already competing for every ten-minute slot in his day. Forrest, I'd be no use at all to your committee. I'm doing JOINHANDS a favor by withdrawing. (If I'd realized that you were serious, I would have done so much sooner!) I know the check I'm enclosing to support JOINHANDS doesn't make things right. I can only say that I am genuinely sorry for the misunderstanding, and for the inconvenience to your group.

I promise that when you ask me to do something in future I will demand to know if you <u>really</u> mean it, so that I don't say yes when I should be saying no. And in future I hope I can count on you to give me a call the following day and confirm that we both meant whatever it was we said. We're both very busy people with a thousand things on our minds, easily distracted, with no time to waste. Neither one of us should rely on an informal agreement made in the middle of a social event, perhaps only in an effort not to spoil the occasion with serious discussion and an argument. I have learned from this; I regret that I had to learn at your expense.It's my good fortune that I can be absolutely certain that JOINHANDS, under your able direction, will manage just fine without me. It is <u>your</u> good fortune that the task force won't be burdened by a member whose already impossibly full schedule would make his contribution inadequate at best.

Sincerely,

ANALYSIS OF LETTER 32

Paragraph One

You cannot imagine how much I don't want to write this letter, or how tempted I am just to ask my assistant to give you a call. But that won't do, and I have gathered

my courage to do this myself. Forrest, this letter comes
to you from a man who has to tell you that he won't be
serving on your committee after all, and that you should
be <u>grateful</u> that he won't.

This is a Leveling paragraph, very informal in its tone, getting
right down to the necessary business. It admits your frailty, and
your acknowledged reluctance to transmit this negative message
yourself is consistent with the explanation you are about to give
your reader. You are someone who hates to rain on other people's
parades, it says; you are someone who makes an effort, in spite of
your many heavy burdens, to be agreeable. You are also someone
who, when something negative <u>must</u> be said, doesn't do any tapdanc-
ing around the points to be made.

Paragraph Two

Until my secretary handed me your letter announcing
the meeting scheduled for February 9th, with my name
on the list of members, I had taken it for granted that
you were no more serious when you asked me to serve
than I was when I said I'd do it. After all, the very last
thing you need is a man who has three different urgent
tasks already competing for every ten-minute slot in his
day. Forrest, I'd be no use at all to your committee. I'm
doing JOINHANDS a favor by withdrawing. (If I had
realized you were serious, I would have done so far
sooner!) I know that the check I'm enclosing to support
JOINHANDS doesn't make things right. I can only say
that I am genuinely sorry for the misunderstanding, and
for the inconvenience to your group.

This paragraph goes right on Leveling, pulling no punches.
And it continues to make the case that although you're not doing
what he wants you to do, or what you said you would do, he should
be grateful for that. This is an aggressive way to handle the situation,
but it's a strategy that can be useful when your only excuse is that
you're human.

The paragraph makes your apology, at some length. It also
begins making your <u>case</u>—that he is also to blame for the mess—
indirectly. That case has three interacting points:

1. Forrest should have known you were a poor choice for his task force; he knows how busy you are.

2. You should have been safe assuming that an able man like Forrest, knowing you were a poor choice, was asking you to serve only to pass the time and be friendly.

3. Forrest should have known that an able man like you, knowing you could count on him, was agreeing to serve only to match friendly gesture with friendly gesture.

Paragraph Three

I promise that when you ask me to do something in future I will demand to know if you <u>really</u> mean it, so that I don't say yes when I should be saying no. And in future I hope I can count on you to give me a call the following day and confirm that we both meant whatever it was we said. We're both very busy people with a thousand things on our minds, easily distracted, with no time to waste. Neither one of us should rely on an informal agreement made in the middle of a social event, perhaps only in an effort not to spoil the occasion with serious discussion and an argument. I have learned from this; I regret that I had to learn at your expense. It's my good fortune that I can be absolutely certain that JOINHANDS, under your able direction, will manage just fine without me. It is <u>your</u> good fortune that the task force won't be burdened by a member whose already impossibly full schedule would make his contribution inadequate at best.

You will recognize the slight shift in tone in this paragraph, toward a greater degree of formality. There's a metamessage here: UP TO NOW, I'VE BEEN CASUAL; NOW I'M GOING TO GET SERIOUS. You accomplish the tone shift by switching to slightly more formal word choices and by using a judicious amount of parallelism.

The opening sentence is an example of another use of the power of presuppositions: presupposing with <u>time</u> words.

PRESUPPOSITIONS AND TIME WORDS

When English speakers talk or write about something that hasn't happened yet, or that is entirely hypothetical, they often use what is called an "if/then" construction. (The "then" often doesn't appear in ordinary sentences, but is understood to be there all the same.) They do it without realizing that the if/then pattern brings with it a presupposition that can be a barrier to accomplishing their goals. For example:

"If you buy our products, you will find that they are the best available in today's market."

"If you go to St. Louis, be sure you see the Arch."

The problem is that in English, "If [X]" presupposes "not [X]." "If you buy our products" presupposes that you won't buy them. "If you go to St. Louis" presupposes that you won't go there. How strong the negative presupposition will be for any particular sentence depends on the situation, the other words used, and the like. But it's almost always possible to avoid "if/then" altogether and bring in a *positive* presupposition instead. Since that's true, it seems foolish to risk even a hint of negativeness unless some legal technicality makes it obligatory to use "if/then."

To presuppose that something will happen, will be done, etc., use time words and phrases that carry that presupposition instead of using "if." Like this:

"When you buy our products, you will find that they are the best available in today's market."

"While you are in St. Louis, be sure you see the Arch."

These two sentences presuppose that the reader <u>will</u> buy the products and <u>will</u> see the Arch. Similarly, instead of "If you pass the state exams, you will qualify for a promotion," write "After you pass the state exams, you will qualify for a promotion."

You can also presuppose that something will happen by starting a sentence with the word "suppose." Don't write "If you decide to hire our firm, your sales figures will show a substantial improvement in the first ninety days of the contract." Instead, write "When you decide to hire our firm . . ." or do it this way:

"Suppose you decide to hire our firm. Your sales figures will show a substantial improvement in the first ninety days of the contract."

The first sentence in paragraph three of the model letter uses this strategy. It doesn't say "I promise you that if you ask me to do something in future. . . ." Instead, with "I promise you that when you ask me to do something in future . . ." it presupposes that that will happen. As if—despite the writer's having let the reader down badly this time—it could be taken for granted that there'll be another chance.

This is such an easy strategy to use, and has so much to recommend it, that it should be added to your letter-writing grammar immediately. Always give any sentence starting with "if" a careful second look and ask yourself if it could be rewritten to guarantee a positive presupposition.

LAYING PAPER TRAILS

Two problems are reflected in Letter 32. The first—the difficulty the writer has saying a firm and final no—is not an appropriate topic for this book. The second problem, however—how to take back a yes that you regret—is directly and immediately relevant to a book of letters. You should do it by writing a letter very different from the one we just analyzed, which had to be written because the situation was so badly handled. You protect yourself against this kind of social and business catastrophe by laying a swift paper trail.

Suppose you've found yourself unable to say no to this high-powered charity official, for any of a number of reasons. What you do, *as soon as you're at your office again,* is send a followup letter like this one.

LETTER 33
Flub: You've Got to Cancel—Immediately!

Dear Forrest,

Last night at the cocktail party you were kind enough to invite me to serve as a member of the learning disability resource committee you're now setting up for JOINHANDS. I want you to know that I appreciate the invitation, and that I would have felt very awkward refusing.

However, you and I both know that the last thing you need on your committee is a man who has three urgent tasks competing for every ten-minute slot in his schedule. I'm reasonably sure that at this very moment you're sitting at your desk wondering how on earth you can take back the invitation.

Let me set your mind, and mine, at rest. Forrest, I can't serve on your committee, and I have better sense than to try. My contribution would be inadequate at best. What I <u>can</u> do is send you a donation for JOINHANDS; you'll find my check enclosed with this letter.

Cordially,

A letter like this will acknowledge what happened, make it unambiguously clear what your motivation was at the time and what your intentions are now, and take you gracefully off the hook. Certainly you could just pick up the phone and call, but that's not nearly as good a strategy as sending this letter. Remember: You got into the quandary in the first place because you couldn't say no when you were talking to this man. If you talk to him again, either in person or on the phone, you're giving him yet another opportunity to try to persuade you to do what he wants. There's no reason to think you'll find it any easier to resist his skillful armtwisting than you did the first time. And if you say yes <u>twice</u>, it's going to be a great deal harder to get out of your foolish commitment. Send the letter. Send it <u>fast</u>. You never want to make it possible for the reader to come back at you with a justified claim that even if you didn't mean it when you said yes, you've waited so long to say so that it's now too late for you to change your mind.

You would be very wise, after <u>every</u> interaction in which negotiations take place and decisions are made, to send a quick letter or memo that sets out exactly what happened, as you perceive it. A more formal example, easily adapted to almost any business situation, is Letter 34, below.

LETTER 34
You've Got to Lay a Paper Trail: Letter

Dear . . . . .,

It was a pleasure to see you again at yesterday's meeting. I think we made real progress and I look forward to working closely with you over the next six months to complete this project.

It's my understanding that we've all agreed on the following four items:

1. Your company will gather the background data and supply it to us no later than the middle of March.

2. You will immediately begin searching for a temporary replacement for the engineer on your staff who has a maternity leave coming up shortly, so our joint project will continue to be fully staffed.

3. We will arrange to have the modified software programs in your hands by the 15th of this month.

4. We are postponing the discussion of a potential additional funding source until a later meeting, to allow everyone time to consider all the ramifications.

If you disagree with anything here, or if you feel that I've left something off the list, please give me a call as soon as possible and we'll straighten it out. If I don't hear from you by Friday, I'll know that the list reflects your perceptions of the meeting as well as mine.

Sincerely,

(Notice that the "if/then" sentences in this letter trigger negative presuppositions that you do want. "If you disagree" presupposes that the reader won't disagree; "if you feel that I've left something off the list" presupposes that the list will be perceived as complete. And "if I don't hear from you by Friday" presupposes that you won't have any reason to make contact, which is the desired outcome.)

Again, you could do this by telephone. But each verbal interaction not backed up by something in writing only increases the number of potential misunderstandings. You're inviting a conversation like this one . . .

YOU: "I just wanted to call and very quickly run through the list of items we agreed on yesterday, to be sure everything is clear."

HIM: "Sure! Good idea. What's first?"

YOU: "According to my notes, your company is going to get all the background data together and supply it to us no later than the 15th of March."

HIM: "Oh? Are you sure? As I recall, we talked about the data but nobody said anything about a deadline."

YOU: "I'm sure somebody from your outfit said the 15th of March."

HIM: "I don't remember that. Do you know who it was?"

And so on, through each item on your list. Part of this is the other person's need to make a dominance display. Part of it is natural human cussedness. Part of it may be that you in fact <u>did</u> misunderstand what went on at the meeting. But when you send a letter, nobody has to go through this hostility-breeding process. With a letter, your reader can look over everything you said, take all steps necessary to find out what the decisions actually were—checking notes and minutes, and talking to others who were present if necessary—without feeling defensive or flustered because you're putting him or her on the spot. It doesn't take very long to write a letter like Letter 34, and it will pay you back many times over in confrontations and complications avoided.

Many people don't bother to do this. They think they'll remember what was said, how they felt about it at the time, what others' reactions were, and so on. They're wrong. And when the time comes to implement the decisions that were made, they don't have any documentation to prop up their memories with. Few things waste more time and more resources than a followup session where neither side has a clear understanding of the previous session's results and neither one can provide documentation. This is as true of the results of a quick phone call as it is of a three-hour meeting, though you may want to handle the phone call with a quick memo, like this:

LETTER 35
You've Got to Lay a Paper Trail: Memo

MEMORANDUM

TO: (Name)   DATE:

FROM: (Your name)

Ellen, this is just a quick followup to our phone conversation earlier this morning. If I understand you correctly, we're agreed that the deadline should be moved back to April 4th and that the index will be prepared by Breckenridge. If I've got this wrong, let me know. If I don't hear from you in the next week or ten days I'll assume everything's okay as stated. Thanks again.

LETTER 36
Flub and Frailty: You Can't Make That Speech After All

Dear Mr. Metcalf:

I can't begin to make clear to you how much I would rather not write this letter, or how tempted I am just to have my secretary give you a call. But that won't do; this is something I have to have courage enough to do myself. Mr. Metcalf, this letter comes to you from a woman who has to tell you that she will not be giving the keynote address at your upcoming conference after all, and that you should be grateful to her for that decision.

Until I opened your letter with the draft conference program inside and saw my name listed as keynote speaker, I had taken it for granted that you were only making casual conversation when you asked me to speak. After all, what you need for your conference is someone with the time and the energy to prepare a compelling speech, something that will set the tone for the entire conference and fire up everyone present. Mr. Metcalf, I don't have that kind of time and energy and I am not that kind of public speaker. I wish I were, naturally. And I wish I'd made this clear to you when you asked me. I know the list of suggested speakers I'm enclosing with this letter doesn't take care of the inconvenience I've caused you. I can only say that I am genuinely sorry.

I promise you that when you ask me to do something in future I will take you seriously, and respond more carefully. We're both busy people, and neither of us needs this sort of mixup to make our lives even more complicated. It's my good fortune that I can be sure the conference, under your able direction, will be a total success without me. And it's <u>your</u> good fortune that I'm not so foolish as to agree to do something I truly cannot do.

Sincerely,

NOTE: With only very minor changes, this letter could be used to withdraw a promise to write a paper or other item for publication, rather than a promise to speak.

LETTER 37
Flub: You Shouldn't Have Volunteered Your Spouse

Dear . . . . .,

You can't imagine how much I hate writing this letter or how tempted I am to have somebody else do it for me. I know that won't do, and I'm doing it myself—but I hate it. This is a letter from a man who has to tell you that he's really put his foot in it this time, and that his wife will _not_ serve on your Beautification Task Force.

The note from you thanking Doris and welcoming her to the task force arrived at our house in the morning mail. I want you to know: I really did think she'd like to do that, and I really did intend to tell her I'd volunteered her for it. I was wrong on both counts. She doesn't have time, and she's not happy that I forgot to tell her what I'd done. She is correct in telling me that my behavior is inexcusable. I'm sorry, and I'm ashamed.

Let's just suppose that sometime in the future you ask me if I can suggest someone for one of your volunteer roles, and you again hear me say, "I'm sure my wife would be delighted to do that!" Will you do me a favor? Will you remind me that I am making a terrible mistake, and instruct me (in the sternest voice you can muster) to either volunteer my _self_ or shut up? I'd be grateful. In the meantime, I'm enclosing a small check to help out the beautification group and to repay you in some measure for the inconvenience I've caused. I know you'll manage in spite of my bungling, and I'm grateful for that.

Sincerely,

Chapter Twelve

"*It's Not My Fault!*"

Triple-F Scenario Eleven

Dear Sir:

You can be sure that if my husband Daniel had known the bear belonged to your traveling show he would certainly not have killed it. The bear however, was not wearing anything to indicate that it was something more than just another wild bea...

Sincerely,

Mrs. D. Bo...

You are an executive in a large publishing firm. On the basis of interest expressed very strongly (and, in your opinion, very indiscreetly) by another executive, a small press has not only prepared a lengthy proposal for a series of children's books but has actually lined up an author and an illustrator and signed contracts with both individuals. Now your firm has decided not to go ahead with the series, and this will cause financial hardship and embarrassment for the small press. No written agreement was made, and in that sense there is no legal problem. On the other hand, everyone knows the small press was responding to your junior colleague's expressed desire for haste. In ethical terms, your firm has clearly wronged the smaller company.

Your colleague agrees with you that Bonafide Press has a right to feel betrayed. He even claims to be sorry for what he's done. But he flatly refuses to apologize either by phone or by letter; he intends to behave as if the whole thing never happened. Worse yet, he complains loudly and at length that he is the victim in this mess. According to him, Bonafide kept pressuring him; Bonafide took his remarks out of context; Bonafide wouldn't take no for an answer; he was only trying to be polite and Bonafide took advantage of his good nature . . . and so, lamely, on. You know from long past experience that he won't back down from this Outraged Lamb position. You believe that an apology is required as a matter of common decency. Furthermore, you don't want Bonafide Press going around saying (truthfully) that your firm not only backed out of an agreement but didn't have even the minimal courtesy to apologize.

You know that you should have seen this coming and stopped it before it got out of hand. You've worked with your indiscreet associate for years; you know how he operates. You should have checked with Bonafide to find out what was going on. There has to be an apology, and making it by telephone would put you in the awkward position of listening to negative comments about your colleague that you personally think are right on target. It has to be a letter, and it's obvious that there won't be one unless you write it. WHAT DO YOU SAY IN YOUR LETTER?

LETTER 38
Flub and Frailty: You've Got to Correct a Colleague's Foolish Mistake

Dear Mark:

I very much regret the need to write this letter, and every member of our firm shares my regret. Any publisher feels dismay when a project that seemed to have great promise, as did your new children's book series, must be abandoned; this firm is no exception to that rule.

I learned this morning that a final negative decision had been made, and that you had been notified. Mark, on behalf of the firm as well as personally, I am sorry.

We look forward to seeing proposals from you in the future as we have in the past. It's always a pleasure to work with a publisher of the quality and taste that is consistently shown by Bonafide Press.

Sincerely,

ANALYSIS OF LETTER 38

Paragraph One

I very much regret the need to write this letter, and every member of our firm shares my regret. Any publisher feels dismay when a project that seemed to have great promise, as did your new children's book series, must be abandoned; this firm is no exception to that rule.

You'll notice that you didn't mention your colleague (we'll call him Harry Smith) openly in this brief paragraph. But you've brought him in, willing or not, by writing that "every member of our firm" shares in the feeling of regret about what's happened. Then you have deftly shifted focus to the "any publisher" platitude, written for the most part in Computer Mode. And you have added support to your legal position by your reference to the canceled project as one that only "seemed" to have great promise. The choice of this word "seem" is important, because it is one of the set of words and phrases I call "Trojan Horses."

USING, AND AVOIDING, TROJAN HORSES

The "Trojan Horse" metaphor comes from the ancient tale of the wooden horse built by the Greeks, which was pleasing to the eye but was actually concealing armed soldiers ready to attack. A Trojan Horse word or phrase is like that—it looks entirely harmless and innocuous, even pleasant, but it contains dangerous presuppositions. In many contexts the word "seem" presupposes "but it didn't" or "but it wasn't." When you say that the proposed children's book series from Bonafide Press "seemed" to have great promise, the implications are: (a) that no one was <u>certain</u> that it had promise, and (b) that it turned out <u>not</u> to have promise, confirming the initial uncertainty. "Seem" is especially deceptive, because its dangers depend on its combination with other words. "You seem to be tired" is usually a harmless utterance, and the multitude of such utterances lulls us into letting "seem" pass without examination. But think of "you seem to be qualified," or "you seem to be innocent," or "you seem to have fulfilled the terms of the contract." None of those is harmless, and we often demonstrate our understanding of that fact by responding with "Whaddaya mean, *seem?*"

Another Trojan Horse is the word "manage," which presupposes that whatever was done was only done with great difficulty and effort. Suppose you write, "We are delighted that you managed to pass your board exams." The presupposition is that the reader passed, but had a very hard time doing so; it's not a compliment. "Humor" and "indulge" are Trojan Horse verbs; to say "It was our pleasure to humor/indulge you on this point" presupposes, "Your behavior with regard to this point was so childish that we gave in to you as we would have given in to a child."

The point is not that you shouldn't use Trojan Horses. As was shown in Letter 38, they can be very useful. The point is that you should always be aware that you are using one and aware of the message it carries, and that you should always be sending that message <u>deliberately</u> rather than by accident. Trying to convince someone after the fact by saying "But that wasn't what I <u>meant!</u>" is usually a useless effort.

Paragraph Two

I learned this morning that a final negative decision had been made, and that you had been notified. Mark, on behalf of the firm as well as personally, I am sorry.

Here, by saying that a "final" negative decision has been made, you continue to bolster your legal position. The implication is that any earlier decision was known to be only preliminary, and your use of the factive word "learn" lets you presuppose that this is true. Apologizing "on behalf of the firm" lets you spread the blame around, which is always useful, and it lets you drag Harry in again and put an apology in his mouth as well.

Paragraph Three

We look forward to seeing proposals from you in the future as we have in the past. It's always a pleasure to work with a publisher of the quality and taste that is consistently shown by Bonafide Press.

In this paragraph you let your reader know that so far as you are concerned the relationship between your two firms is unchanged. "We look forward to seeing proposals" is like "when we see your proposals in the future"; you have not said "if." And you end the letter with a vague compliment of the "This book has nice wide margins" or "This applicant has neat handwriting and unusual ideas" variety.

The letter is very brief, and that's appropriate for two good reasons. First: you're writing a letter that properly should have come from someone else. You can't know all of the intimate details of the interactions between Harry and Bonafide, and the less said under such circumstances of limited information the less likely you are to make an error that could be used against your firm. Second: although your legal department feels that Bonafide has no case against you, anyone can launch a nuisance lawsuit. It is an unfortunate fact about our lawsuit-prone society that when even the slightest possibility of legal action exists, the best move is to write or say only what *must* be said and to say it as briefly as possible.

With any luck, Bonafide Press will read your letter, realize that nothing can be done, and let the matter drop. With a bit more luck they will take you up on your offer to look at other book proposals and give you an opportunity to make amends with better treatment the next time. But you can't always be lucky. Suppose that in this case things don't go as you had hoped. Suppose the scenario continues and you get a nasty letter back from Bonafide. . . .

TRIPLE-F SCENARIO, CONTINUED

Here's the letter that appears on your desk the following week, sent by registered mail.

Dear Ms. Hefflane:

We got your letter this morning, and we are not impressed. You know, as we know, that Harry Smith gave us his firm commitment to the LEISURE POND series. It was on the basis of that commitment that we proceeded with the project. He insisted that speed was imperative, and we did everything in our power to accommodate him, including a substantial investment of both time and money.

Let's not pretend that a verbal contract is not a binding contract, Ms. Hefflane. We know better, and so do you. It is not true that the decision reported to us was the final one. The final decision had already been made, in our favor, and it was conveyed to us by Harry Smith.

We look forward to working with you on this project.

Very truly yours,

ANALYSIS, CONTINUED

Does this unpleasant development mean that you did the wrong thing in writing the letter? Maybe. Maybe the letter was more flounder than frailty; maybe you were wrong in thinking that it was the correct move. Certainly Harry is going to think so, and you can be sure he will have a lot to say about how you should have listened to him and let well enough alone. On the other hand, if you <u>hadn't</u> written, it's quite possible that the next piece of paper coming at you from Bonafide Press would have been a letter from its attorneys announcing an intention to sue. You can't know with any degree of certainty. In my opinion, the carefully written letter of apology was exactly right. But what do you do now?

The first thing you do, of course, is try to find out exactly what happened. The abstract facts are these:

1. Bonafide Press is correct in saying that a verbal contract is as binding as a written one.

2. Every standard book contract specifies that money will be paid on receipt of an "acceptable" manuscript, providing an easy out eventually, and Bonafide certainly knows that.

3. Despite #2, if Bonafide were to go ahead and sue your firm it would be unpleasant and inconvenient and expensive.

The facts that are in question here are the concrete ones. The details. You need to know what, <u>exactly</u>, Harry said or wrote to Bonafide Press that made them feel they had been given a binding contract. In a perfect world, Harry would have laid a careful paper trail, so that every discussion he had with Bonafide was followed up by a memo from Harry outlining the points of agreement and including a careful <u>disclaimer</u>.

WRITING DISCLAIMERS

You know those letters you get from sweepstakes companies? First they say you've won, then they tell you what you've won, then they say you are guaranteed to have won. And then they add the disclaimer, telling you that all that holds "if your number is the winning number" or "if your entry is one of the first fifty we receive" or whatever. You know that Harry kept giving Bonafide strong expressions of encouragement. Ideally, he also saw to it that his communications included disclaimer statements like those shown in italics in the examples below.

"I continue to feel that the prospects for this book series are bright, and *I sincerely hope that we will be able to reach an agreement on the project.*"

"*Although you never know what's going to happen until a formal contract has been negotiated,* things look very good to me."

"I'd like to urge you to get started on the series, so that *if we do decide to offer you a contract* there will be a minimum of delay."

"The $40,000 advance is no problem for us, provided you are able to meet the March 1st deadline. *With any luck at all, we will be able to give you a final decision one way or the other in the next week or two.*"

"The LEISURE POND proposal just looks terrific to me, and *I have to admit that I'm going to be very disappointed if we can't arrive at a mutually acceptable agreement to publish.*"

In a perfect world, Harry will have documentation like those examples. But we know Harry. Harry is the man who got your firm into this mess in the first place. Harry is the man who adopted the Outraged Lamb position and refused to do anything to try to clean the mess up. If, as is likely, Harry has nothing but his memories of conversations with Bonafide, it's his word against theirs. And they may have detailed notes of <u>their</u> perceptions of those conversations.

At this point, it's often best to turn the whole matter over to your legal department. Let's assume, however, that things aren't quite that bad. Let's assume that the business relationship your firm has with Bonafide Press is one that matters to you, and that you'd much rather not bring attorneys into it if that can possibly be avoided. You'd like to come to some kind of friendly resolution by your own efforts. In this case, you would write another letter, running it by your attorney for a quick review before you mailed it. Letter 39 offers one of the best ways to do that.

LETTER 39
Answering the Furious Response to Letter 38

Dear Mark:

Your response to my letter of [date] arrived this morning. Frankly, I was surprised by its tone. I am certain that it was written in haste, and that it does not represent the actual feelings of anyone at Bonafide. I am equally certain that it was not your intention to accuse me of having lied to you.

Prior to your letter, no one here was aware that you felt you had been offered a verbal contract. If we'd known that, we would have contacted you to discuss the matter and to try to resolve it in some mutually agreeable fashion. We regret the confusion.

I'm sure you know that our standard series contract is for the first book in the series, with subsequent volumes contingent on our judgment that we find the manuscript we receive for the first one acceptable. Given the strong negative feelings about the LEISURE POND series here, you would probably hesitate to risk going forward with Book One on that basis. However, you are of course free to take that risk if you wish. We look forward to hearing from you at your earliest convenience.

Sincerely,

All right? Let's analyze this letter to see what it does—and perhaps more importantly, what it doesn't—do.

ANALYSIS OF LETTER 39

Paragraph One

Your response to my letter of [date] arrived this morning. Frankly, I was surprised by its tone. I am certain that it was written in haste, and that it does not represent the actual feelings of anyone at Bonafide. I am equally certain that it was not your intention to accuse me of having lied to you.

This paragraph's force is dependent on its many presuppositions. You use the factive "be certain" repeatedly, to presuppose that Bonafide wrote you in a moment of haste, that what was said bears no resemblance to real convictions, and that when they called you a liar it was a sort of accident of passion, much too trivial for you to pay any attention to. Nothing in this paragraph is confrontational; you are in fact flatly refusing to participate in a confrontation, if that is what Bonafide had planned. It would be confrontational for you to write a paragraph like this:

> I am outraged by your letter, and doubly outraged by your absurd accusations. I am not a liar; I did not lie. This firm has always been, and continues to be, scrupulously honest in its dealings. I deeply resent the fact that you took it upon yourself. . . ."

And so on. Wisely, you didn't write any of that.

Whenever you find yourself writing a letter that has an angry or hostile or simply emotional tone, no matter how deeply you feel that it says what you want to say, follow this rule: PUT THE LETTER AWAY FOR AT LEAST TWENTY-FOUR HOURS AND THEN READ IT AGAIN BEFORE YOU SEND IT. This is true without exception, and it is doubly true when you are writing for possible publication. It's a rare month when I don't see at least one "letter to the editor" in a professional journal that clearly would have been drastically changed if its writer had observed a twenty-four hour cooling-off period. The tone of the paragraph in the model letter—cool, calm, and tactful—is the proper one for any potentially confrontational situation.

Paragraph Two

Prior to your letter, no one here was aware that you felt you had been offered a verbal contract. If we'd known

that, we would have contacted you to discuss the matter
and to try to resolve it in some mutually agreeable fashion.
We regret the confusion.

Notice: this paragraph doesn't argue about whether Harry offered a verbal contract to Bonafide or not. Since there's no proof
either way, it would be foolish to argue about it. However, you've
chosen your words carefully. You've claimed that no one realized
Bonafide felt it had been offered a contract, and you've used the
factive "be aware" to presuppose "You felt you had been offered a
verbal contract." (This is the same strategy you followed when you
wrote that the book series had "seemed" to show promise.) You
admit nothing and you deny nothing, but you don't argue. And
you say, politely, that this "feeling" of theirs is evidence of confusion
on both sides, not ill will, and that you regret that confusion. It is
also important to note that nothing you write in this paragraph is
untrue.

Paragraph Three

I'm sure you know that our standard series contract is
for the first book in the series, with subsequent volumes
contingent on our judgment that we find the manuscript
we receive for the first one acceptable. Given the strong
negative feelings about the LEISURE POND series here,
you would probably hesitate to risk going forward with
Book One on that basis. However, you are of course free
to take that risk if you wish. We look forward to hearing
from you at your earliest convenience.

This paragraph is written entirely in code. Here's what it really
says:

If you want to take the position that we offered you a
verbal contract, fine. We won't argue, and you therefore
won't be able to take us to court. And after you go to all
the trouble and expense of finishing the first book, we'll
tell you that we don't find it acceptable, and you'll have
done it for nothing. And you still won't be able to take
us to court.

You could of course just write that paragraph, Leveling all the
way. But there are two important reasons why you shouldn't do
that.

First, this would be an excellent way to get your firm sued by Bonafide. Any moderately skilled lawyer would be able to point out a variety of unethical and illegal tactics in this paragraph. Especially the part that says in effect, "No matter what you send in, we're going to say that it's not acceptable." When you ran this paragraph by your <u>own</u> lawyer, you would be told to modify the third sentence as follows:

> "And after you go to all the trouble and expense of finishing the first book, *unless the manuscript is very different indeed from our present expectations for it,* we'll tell you that we don't find it acceptable, and you'll have done it for nothing."

Second, and independent of the legal hazards, the Leveling paragraph would guarantee a major loss of face for Bonafide. Suppose this were a physical, rather than a verbal, confrontation. Someone who is much stronger than an opponent can get all kinds of warped satisfaction from holding the weaker person helpless in an undignified position, demonstrating power and shaming the loser. That's winning, no question about it, <u>in the short term</u>. In the long term, however, it's a foolish and damaging move. The loser will never forgive the winner for doing it, the loser will become a permanent enemy, and the victory will inevitably backfire over the course of time. People who have been shamed have very long memories. The paragraph in the model letter, which transmits the necessary messages but leaves Bonafide its dignity, is the better way to go.

You will have noticed that Letter 39 doesn't follow the pattern used for all the other model letters. It's different because it is a response to someone else's letter, and its content is in part determined by that other letter.

SUPPLEMENTARY LETTERS

LETTER 40
Flub and Frailty: You've Got to Overrule a Colleague's Offer to a Customer

Dear . . . . .,

I very much regret that this letter has to be written, and I know I speak for every member of the firm when

I say that. No company is comfortable when a misunderstanding arises and causes a good customer to suffer inconvenience. This is especially true in a situation like this one, where every aspect of the current project seemed to be going so well.

I learned yesterday afternoon that you had been given incorrect information about the discount available on the bulk orders for the EC-1783's. I also learned that when our parts division manager called to correct the error he found you more than a little distressed by the situation. I want you to know that everyone here at Acmecorp is genuinely sorry.

A company with your long years of business experience is well aware that no human being can guarantee a universe free of errors; mistakes happen in spite of our best efforts. When we process your orders in future, however, you can rely on us to do everything possible to make sure that nothing like this happens again. You are one of our most valuable customers, and we look forward to working with you in the future as we have in the past.

Sincerely,

LETTER 41
Flub and Frailty: You've Got to Take Back a Job Offer

Dear . . . . .,

I write this letter with a genuine feeling of regret, and that sentiment is shared by every member of our firm. When someone suffers a serious disappointment because of a misunderstanding, that's not trivial, and no one here takes it lightly.

I learned this morning that the position in our home office which you had discussed with Charles Gordesky is not going to be available in the near future, and that you had been notified. Ms. Norton, on behalf of the firm as well as personally, I want to offer you our sincere apology.

We have put your resume and your letter of application in our files, so that if an appropriate position should become open here at Acmecorp we would able to let you know immediately. However, we realize that with your excellent qualifications you will have no difficulty finding employment in this area; our loss will no doubt be some other company's gain. We wish you the very best of luck.

Sincerely,

Chapter Thirteen

"Somebody Was Supposed to Tell You..."

Triple-F Scenario Twelve

Dear Mr. Lincoln:

It is with deep regret that we write to inform you that the three cents you walked so many miles to return to us yesterday is not our money. It would seem that our bookkeeper fou— and has just brou— If you would like— claim your money, it—

Sincer—

T. Phinias

*E*very year, at a New Year's Eve banquet, your company gives several awards to managers and executives. The most coveted is the Golden Hawk Award, which goes to the employee considered in every way the most valuable to the firm during the preceding year (based on sales totals, innovativeness, leadership, community service, and so on).

You know that manager Claire Ward—your firm's only woman executive—expects to get the Golden Hawk this year. She has plenty of reasons to think it will be hers, not the least of which is the fact that the vice presidents she reports to have repeatedly failed to say no when she's asked them about it. She was one of the people considered for it, and she came very <u>close</u> to winning. Her own staff takes it for granted that she'll win and is planning a private Golden Hawk celebration after the banquet, in her honor.

The problem is she <u>isn't</u> getting the award. And everyone who knows that has been putting off telling her, with a variety of excuses, like not wanting to spoil her Christmas. Now the banquet is only five days away, and you feel that she *must* be told, to avoid the horrible alternative: that her first clue to having lost would be at the banquet, when she hears the winner's name read. You feel that it's important for her to get the news in private, so that if she loses her composure there'll be nobody she has to feel embarrassed with afterward. If she were a man, you'd just <u>tell</u> her; on the other hand, if she were a man the confusion would never have been allowed to go on for so long. The same problems of male/female communication that kept everyone from being frank in the first place face you now, and you don't feel comfortable with the idea of telling her in person and having to deal with her reaction, especially since you would have to defend (or at least explain) not only your own behavior, but that of everyone else involved.

This incident is made especially difficult by the climate of tension in American business today between men and women. A few years ago it might not have seemed like such a big deal. Right now, with all the commotion over sexual harassment and sexual discrimination and the "glass ceiling" that is alleged to hold career women back, it looks like a major difficulty. Nobody is sure how Claire Ward will react; nobody wants to take the chance of finding out. Your colleagues have all chickened out and left you to take care of the problem. WHAT DO YOU SAY IN YOUR LETTER?

LETTER 42
Frailty: She Won't Be Getting the Award After All—and You've Got to Tell Her

Version 1: Leveler Mode

Dear Claire,

I don't want to write this letter; I'd give a great deal to be able to hand the task over to somebody else. But it has landed in my lap, and I have to do it. Let me just get it over with, therefore, without any beating around the bush: Claire, you won't be winning the Golden Hawk Award this year.

I'm ashamed to have to tell you that the final decision was made more than a month ago. The fact that we haven't been able to bring ourselves to talk to you about it is a measure both of our clumsiness and of the high regard we have for you. Everyone has been putting this off, hoping that someone else would be the one to give you the bad news. We should have told you sooner, and we should have told you face to face. Needless to say, we're sorry.

We want you to know that this has taught us a valuable lesson, and that we will make absolutely certain nothing like it ever happens again; we only wish the lesson hadn't been at your expense. I know, however, that we can count on you not to let this incident spoil the banquet for you. I look forward to seeing you there as always, helping us celebrate the end of another successful year for the firm and another successful year for you.

Sincerely,

ANALYSIS OF LETTER 42, VERSION 1

Paragraph One

I don't want to write this letter. I'd give a great deal to be able to hand the job over to somebody else. But it has landed in my lap, and I have to do it. Let me just get it over with, therefore, without any more beating around the bush: Claire, you won't be winning the Golden Hawk Award this year.

This paragraph is straight Leveling, which is appropriate in this situation. Nothing could possibly be gained by stalling or being "subtle," not at this point. By the time Claire Ward has finished reading the first sentence, she'll know this is a letter telling her either that she's not getting the award or that she's being fired; this is the opening you'd use to announce a firing to an employee you were genuinely sorry to have to let go. There isn't some gentler way to do this, not without treating her like a child and as if she were a poor sport.

Paragraph Two

I'm ashamed to have to tell you that the final decision was made more than a month ago. The fact that we haven't been able to bring ourselves to talk to you about it is a measure both of our clumsiness and of the high regard we have for you. Everyone has been putting this off, hoping that someone else would be the one to give you the bad news. We should have told you sooner, and we should have told you face to face. Needless to say, we're sorry.

In this paragraph—which is still 90 percent Leveling—you use parallelism to give your words a dignified tone, to indicate that you take this matter seriously, and to signal that the letter is adult-to-adult. Because women can't take that for granted in business yet, it's important to make it absolutely <u>overt</u>. Notice that you didn't offer any phony pseudo-comfort, nothing along the lines of "Because you came so close to winning, we feel sure that you'll get the award next year." That would be more of the same waffling that was at the root of this misunderstanding, and it would be a very bad move to continue with it.

Your message here is that people let the confusion drag on too long not because they were malicious or careless, not because they were indifferent, but because they value Claire and care about her.

With "We should have told you sooner; we should have told you face to face" you make it clear that the apology isn't for giving the award to someone else—as if the standards for winning were different for a woman than for the male executives—but for your poor handling of the misunderstanding. The regret is for letting her think she was getting the Golden Hawk, even encouraging her to think so, and then lacking the courage to set her straight on the matter promptly.

And then there is the sentence just before the apology, the second half of which is false. You believe she should have been told sooner; that much is true. But when you write that she should have been told face to face, you're writing something you <u>don't</u> believe. It is a wise move, given that fact, to structure the sentence as a sort of abstract statement of what "people" ought to do in a similar situation, instead of beginning it with "We know" or "We realize"; it shades the falseness slightly. The truth is that the possibilities in a face-to-face announcement alarmed you.

She might have cried; and then she would have been ashamed of having done so, and embarrassed around whoever saw it happen. It's all right for powerful men, all the way up to the President, to get choked up and teary-eyed these days, but it's still held against a woman. In order <u>not</u> to cry, she might have insisted that she never expected to win and that anybody who thought she did was imagining things. Since everybody knows that that's not true, it would have been equally unsavory. She might have lost her temper and said harsh things about the executives who let her go on thinking she would win. The chances that she would have handled it magnificently, face to face, were too slim to risk. At which point the question arises: Is "you should have been told face to face" a <u>lie</u>?

I don't think so. I think it is a sentence in code, and I think it's justified. I think it transmits the following message: "Claire, we know that even if you would have dreaded being told face to face you'd feel obligated to ask <u>why</u> it wasn't done that way, and we believe it is courteous to relieve you of that obligation." It's unlikely that a woman who came so close to winning the Golden Hawk is incapable of understanding a little business letter code.

But suppose she does misunderstand . . . no harm will be done. Taken literally, the message is that you consider her the sort of superbly confident person who could have carried that face-to-face encounter off without a quiver, and with no loss of face for anyone involved. That is: The <u>worst</u>-case scenario is that she will mistake the sequence for a compliment instead of recognizing it as simple courtesy. Either way, the words are kind and they are appropriate; they are a way to maintain the confidence of another player on your team who's had a rough time.

Paragraph Three

We want you to know that this has taught us a valuable
lesson, and that we will make absolutely certain nothing
like it ever happens again; we only wish the lesson hadn't
been at your expense. I know, however, that we can count
on you not to let this incident spoil the banquet for you.
I look forward to seeing you there as always, helping us
celebrate the end of another successful year for the firm
and another successful year for you.

This paragraph (the NEVER AGAIN and YOU'RE TERRIFIC
paragraph) also contains statements that—because they are in code—
are false on the surface. Your perception and that of your executive
colleagues is that this disappointment is <u>certain</u> to spoil the banquet
for Ms. Ward. That perception was one of the primary reasons for
writing this letter. In addition, it's unlikely that after all this you
really are looking forward to seeing Ward at the banquet; that's also
false. The metamessage behind these two sequences could perhaps
be more easily summed up as NOW HEAR THIS. You want her to
be aware that failing to attend the banquet would be perceived as
a serious error on her part; you want her to know that she, like any
other member of the team, is expected to be on the field and ready
for uncomplaining team play. It would be cruel, and intolerably
rude, to say either of those things openly, like this:

We expect you to show up at the banquet as always, we
expect you to behave as if you were having a wonderful
time, no matter how you really feel; and if you don't do
both of those things, we promise you, you will regret it.

Claire Ward is a competent and capable woman—that's why
she was a finalist for the Hawk. She will understand why the two
sentences are there, and she will know what they mean.

I have no intention of making moral pronouncements about
this. That's not my role here. But let's suppose that you are someone
who strongly objects to the distance between this letter and the truth.
Let's suppose you'd like to do it differently. What are some possible
alternatives?

One possibility would be to *really* Level, saying something like
"Claire Evelyn, you're not going to get the Golden Hawk award
this year. If you'd had any sense at all, you wouldn't have let people

know you <u>thought</u> you were going to get it! You've made all of us uncomfortable and you've complicated our lives with your nonsense; the least you can do now is show up at the banquet and be a good sport about it." If that's your sort of thing, do not write a letter. Just stop by Ward's office, lean your head in the door, and <u>say</u> those words. That's no more confrontational than presenting them in writing, they won't be on the record, and the inevitable quarrel will be over faster. *Any* time you feel, for what you perceive as good reason, obligated to transmit a message that is unquestionably brutal and insulting, use spoken words rather than written ones. <u>Never</u> put anything like that in writing.

Another possibility, and more reasonable, would be to rewrite the letter in Computer Mode as shown below.

Version Two: Computer Mode

Dear Claire:

Anyone who must write a letter as difficult to write as this one wishes there were some way to avoid it, but nothing useful is accomplished by postponing what must be done. The message of this letter, therefore, with no beating around the bush, is: This year's Golden Hawk award will go to someone else.

The decision was made more than a month ago, and the members of the award committee have been aware for several weeks that it would be a surprise to many. The fact that there was no obvious way to convey the information, without at the same time causing distress to a woman greatly esteemed by everyone, has delayed this letter longer than can be justified. The delay is unfortunate and much regretted. A prompt face-to-face announcement would have been far better.

This unfortunate incident has taught a valuable lesson, making it unlikely that a similar problem will ever be allowed to occur in the future; that is the silver lining in this cloud. It is the company's good fortune to have on board a team member who can be counted on not to let this incident keep her from participating in the celebration of another successful year, both for the company and for herself.

Sincerely,

This letter is much less personal, much less intense, and much colder. It is <u>almost</u> free of false statements. "A prompt face-to-face announcement would have been far better" is always true when such an encounter can be gotten through without making matters worse. In the abstract (which is what Computer Mode provides) it is unquestionably better. You could achieve <u>perfect</u> honesty by leaving out the final sentence, of course. That would be essentially the same as answering your elderly mother's "How do I look?" with "Well, you're getting very wrinkled, and your waist is too thick, and the age spots on your hands are not attractive." Many things that are perfect in theory are undesirable in practice.

The question that has to be addressed here, no matter which version you prefer, is whether specific differences in the wording and structure of the letter were necessary due to the fact that it was (a) addressed to a woman and (b) written to a woman by a man. Suppose you'd had to write the same sort of thing to a man? Suppose the letter had been written from one woman to another woman? Would that have made a significant difference? For a coherent discussion of that question, we need a brief overview that will provide a context.

THE MAN/WOMAN COMMUNICATION PROBLEM—OVERVIEW

There was a time when it was taken for granted that women wrote a very different language from men and that men writing to women had to use a special form of language that catered to women's delicate sensibilities and weaker brains. These ideas were not only generally believed, they were openly stated in both speech and writing. In the United States, those days are long gone. But in some ways the ideas themselves have only gone underground. There is a much-repeated experiment in which two groups of people are asked to read the same written text and score it for logic, interest, coherence, persuasiveness, and so on. One group is told that the text was written by a man; the other group is told that the writer was a woman. Over and over again, the group that believes the text was written by a woman gives it lower scores than the group that believes it was written by a man. Since the words read are identical, this can only mean that the readers perceive women's language as inferior to men's simply because it <u>is</u> women's language.

Only a fanatic sexist today would propose that this perception is accurate, but that is not the point. FALSE PERCEPTIONS HAVE

REAL CONSEQUENCES. And both men and women have to deal with this one, just as surely as if it were true. They need to be aware that it exists, they need to watch for it in their language interactions, and they need to be sure it isn't reflected in their own language behavior.

Linguists and researchers in communications have spent a great deal of time and energy in the past few decades trying to find out whether American Mainstream English today actually is divided into two "genderlects," one used by males and another used by females. Most of this research has dealt with spoken language and nonverbal communication. If the subject interests you, you will find many books and articles available, often appearing on the best-seller lists.

Roughly speaking, scholars are lined up behind two basic theoretical positions. One is that the two genderlects exist; and that this drastic difference between male language and female language causes communication breakdowns in much the same way that language coming from two or more different <u>cultures</u> does. The other (which I support) is that there are no genderlects; that there is instead a kind of speech used by the dominant person in an interaction and a kind of speech used by the subordinate person; and that the subordinate patterns have come to be associated with women only because women so often <u>are</u> in the subordinate roles in our society.

This controversy is important for cross-gender spoken communication; no question about it. Fortunately, however, there is absolutely no evidence demonstrating that adult men and women use different varieties of <u>written</u> language. For business letters, what is important is that the letter be clear and courteous, that it be written as one adult to another adult, and that it contain the necessary information. This is true no matter what sexual gender the writers and readers are, and no other guidelines are needed. Writers of either gender who sit down to write a letter to a woman and find themselves thinking, "Now, this goes to a woman—I've got to be careful!" should realize that this is a distortion. The appropriate thought is: "This goes to another human being; I must be careful." The parts of male/female communication that most frequently turn up in sexual harassment complaints—obscene language, endearments like "honey" and "sweetie," open sexual overtures, and the like—aren't part of the vocabulary or grammar of business letters in any case, and should certainly not be a source of difficulty.

SUPPLEMENTARY LETTERS

LETTER 43
Frailty: He Won't Be Getting the Promotion After All—and You Have to Tell Him

Dear Bob,

Writing this letter is one of the worst tasks I've ever had to tackle; I won't deny wishing somebody else would do it for me. Since it's landed in my lap, however, I believe the best way to proceed is just to get it over with, without waltzing around it. Bob, I've been directed to tell you that we're bringing in someone from another division to fill the management slot in engineering that you had your eye on.

I'm embarrassed to have to admit that the final choice for the promotion was made almost a month ago. The fact that we haven't been able to bring ourselves to tell you is evidence both of our clumsiness and of the high regard we have for you. Nobody wanted to give you the bad news, everybody wanted to avoid causing you distress, and we kept putting off the inevitable. We've handled it badly, and we apologize—for failing to tell you sooner, and for writing a letter instead of telling you face to face.

Nothing like this is going to happen again at Brand & Brand, because we've learned our lesson; next time, we'll put all the information on the table as soon as it's available, as we should have done this time. We know we can count on you not to let this misunderstanding get in the way of your performance. We know we can count on you to continue giving us the same quality work you always have. And I assure you, we know how fortunate we are that that is true.

Sincerely,

LETTER 44
Frailty: She Won't Be Giving the Speech After All—and You Have to Tell Her[1]

Dear Dr. Forthright:

I am going to find it very difficult to write this letter; I tell you frankly that I wish someone else had been selected to write it. Since that didn't happen, and the task has been given to me, let me just get on with it. Dr. Forthright, I am extremely sorry to have to tell you that we will not be asking you to deliver the keynote address at this year's convention.

This decision was made some weeks ago, and should have been transmitted to you much sooner. Our reluctance to tell you was due only to our high regard for you; that makes it no less regrettable. Please accept our apologies.

I wish I could promise you that we'll never make a mistake of this kind again; human frailty being what it is, I suspect that would be foolhardy, and I won't do it. I _can_ promise you that we will take to heart the lesson we have learned from this experience, and we will make a real effort not to procrastinate in the future. It has been a pleasure and a privilege to have you as our speaker in the past, and we very much appreciate all your efforts on our behalf. We send you our thanks, and our very best wishes.

Sincerely,

---

[1] This letter is written to someone whose speeches for the writer's group were once satisfactory but are no longer appropriate. The reader should understand, from the fact that no reason is *given*, that the writer prefers not to transmit that information. If there had been a reason that would not have been hurtful—for example, if the convention this year were focused on a new topic that is outside this speaker's field of expertise—that reason would have been stated in the letter.

Chapter Fourteen

"I'd Give My Right Arm Not to Have to Tell You This...."

Triple-F Scenario Thirteen

Dear Mother
If I had known I was going to have to cross the Delaware River in a small open boat in the dark, I certainly would not have been carrying the gold watch~~ ~~ ~~ ~~ for Christmas. I cann~~ ~~ ~~ ~~ express my shame an~~ ~~

Your obe~~ ~~

George

You know how it is. People mean well; they have the best of intentions; but they nevertheless find reasons not to do things they can't face doing, and pretty soon a mess has been created. Your particular example of this kind of frailty goes like this:

You have a man in your company who has always been a tower of strength. Everybody respects and likes him, everybody relies on him; he's always been there for you and for anybody else who needs him. It's hard to imagine the company without him. But the passing years have not been kind to him. At first it was only little things. He forgot appointments; he agreed to things and then forgot to do them; he came into meetings prepared to negotiate on decisions that had been made in earlier meetings. Then, as time went on, his lapses became more serious. Now he argues fiercely over petty trifles, he gets his feelings hurt over even the most carefully chosen words, and it has begun to be hazardous to have him in meetings, because you can't rely on him not to embarrass everybody present. You are now right up against the hard, cold facts: Sad as it is, Jack isn't able to do his job. He can't cope any more. He's got to be told that he must retire, for the sake of the company as well as for his own sake.

You've handled this all wrong, and you know it. At the very beginning, when Jack's problems were minor, there were choices. You could have created a position for him where those problems wouldn't have mattered—kicked him upstairs, as the callous saying puts it. You could have tailored that position to last five years and then be phased out, giving Jack a natural retirement point to look forward to, and a dignified exit. It's too late for that now. Or you could have told him to retire <u>then</u>, and given him six months to wind things down. Either way, at that point you could have called him in and talked to him personally, and although he might have been hurt or angry he would have had no trouble holding up his end of the interaction.

You didn't do it that way. Nobody wanted to believe it had to be done. Everybody kept thinking it could be put off another week, another month, one more quarter. And now it's much worse than it would have been if the company hadn't procrastinated. A personal meeting now wouldn't be two strong competent adults discussing a problem; now one of those adults, like a child, is totally outranked. Because you and your colleagues were unable to bring yourselves to do this in a timely fashion—because of your human frailty—Jack would be humiliated now, not only by the message but by his own inability to handle the discussion. You already know what it would be like. You've tried asking him, casually, if he doesn't think he ought to consider retirement. Each time, he has reacted furiously, swearing that he'll leave only when he has to be carried out. For that reason, it's been decided that he should get a letter as a first step, and then—if <u>he</u> wants it—a personal meeting. WHAT DO YOU SAY IN YOUR LETTER?

LETTER 45
Frailty: You've Got to Tell a Respected Colleague that He Must Retire

Dear Jack,

Writing this letter breaks my heart. It breaks <u>all</u> our hearts. You've been the tower of strength for this company for more than thirty years; you've been the man who always knew exactly what to do and how to do it. You've been the man all of us wished we could be. Nobody ever thought the day would come when we'd have to tell you that—however much you're opposed to the idea—you <u>must</u> retire. We were wrong, Jack; that day is here.

It's our fault that it has to be done this way. We should have talked to you sooner; we should have <u>insisted,</u> sooner. We should have given you time to get used to the idea while there still <u>was</u> time. Jack, you meant too much to us; we just couldn't do it. If it had been somebody else, we would have counted on you to do it, and you would have. We put it off because of our respect for you, and we put it off too long. We are well aware that that's no excuse; we hope you will accept it as an accurate explanation. Jack ... we are all so very sorry.

We've learned a lesson from this, though. In future, I'm certain we'll be aware that postponing the bad news isn't doing anybody a favor. I promise you: It won't happen like this again. As always, it's you who has taught us where we are wrong and how we have to change; we only wish the lesson hadn't had to be at your expense. There's no way to express the respect each of us feels for you, or the gratitude; there are no words to make it clear to you how much you will be missed. If you'd like to set up a meeting to talk this over with me (or with someone else, if you prefer) just let us know. If you'd rather not, we'll understand that, and we'll let this letter take the place of what might be a difficult conversation. We know we can count on you to understand and to forgive our clumsiness; you always have. What we <u>don't</u> know is how we're going to get used to doing without you around here.

Sincerely,

ANALYSIS OF LETTER 45

Paragraph One

Writing this letter breaks my heart. It breaks <u>all</u> our hearts. You've been the tower of strength for this company for more than thirty years; you've been the man who always knew exactly what to do and how to do it. You've been the man all of us wished we could be. Nobody ever thought the day would come when we'd have to tell you that—however much you're opposed to the idea—you <u>must</u> retire. We were wrong, Jack; that day is here.

This is a straightforward Leveling paragraph, put together like a small essay. It has three parts, with the second part again divided into three parts, all tied together by an obvious use of parallelism. If we take this structure apart, it looks like this:

Part One—introductory statement

"Writing this letter breaks my heart. It breaks <u>all</u> our hearts."

Part Two—extended compliment

"You've been   the tower of strength . . . "

"You've been   the man who . . ."

"You've been   the man all of us wished we could be."

Part Three—closing statement

"Nobody ever thought the day would come . . . that day is here."

The opening and closing sentences of the paragraph carry the basic BRACE YOURSELF and SOMETHING HAPPENED messages, without much room for tinkering. In the center section, however, you could have used a variety of other traditional compliments. For example:

1. • You've been   the rock this company was built upon.
   • You've been   the man we knew we could turn to . . .
                    the man who was always ready and able
                    and willing to help . . . for more than thirty
                    years.
   • You've been   the man we all wished we could be.

2. • You've been   the quarterback on this team.
   • You've been   the man who always knew where the ball
                    was, and what the next play ought to be, for
                    more than thirty years.
   • You've been   the man we all wished we could be.

You don't want to overdo this sort of thing. You don't want to push it so far that it stops sounding like a compliment and begins to sound like sarcasm. But you'd be surprised how far carefully crafted sequences like these will go to make a painful message bearable, as long as the reader has reason to believe that they are true and are sincerely meant. Using this sort of parallelism and traditional three-part structure is sometimes called "old fashioned," but it helps when you have to write a letter that you know will hurt. It helps because the solemn and dignified tone you establish this way serves as evidence that the sequence was written with care and with conviction. It helps because the patterning makes the words memorable, and demonstrates to the reader that you don't consider the message an ordinary or trivial one. We've all been told that words are cheap, and that's often true; but words like these are valuable for their ability to soften an unavoidable hurt.

Paragraph Two

It's our fault that it has to be done this way. We should have talked to you sooner; we should have insisted, sooner. We should have given you time to get used to the idea while there still was time. Jack, you meant too much to us; we just couldn't do it. If it had been somebody else, we would have counted on you to do it, and you would have. We put it off because of our respect for you, and we put it off too long. We are well aware that that's no excuse; we hope you will accept it as an accurate explanation. Jack . . . we are all so very sorry.

Again, this paragraph uses parallelism to establish a solemn and dignified tone, as well as to make its message easier for the reader to understand and remember. Here are the clearly parallel items.

- we should have   talked to you sooner
- we should have   *insisted*, sooner.
- we should have   given you time . . .

- we put it off   because of our respect for you
- we put it off   too long

- we would have   counted on you to do it
- you would have   (done it)

- we   are well aware that that's no excuse
- we   hope that you will accept it

The sentence that says "If it had been somebody else, we would have counted on you to do it, and you would have" is one of the most important parts of this paragraph. It says, gently, that if Jack had been the one who saw another member of your team going downhill and needing to be retired he would not have hesitated to take care of the matter. That is a compliment to him, and a reminder of what his status has been until now. It gives him a little needed distance from the situation, and reminds him that *everyone* eventually reaches a point at which retirement is the proper decision—he is not alone. He will know that what you've said in this sentence is true, it will make it harder for him to argue about the decision, and it will to some extent reduce his feeling that he has to argue in order to save face.

Paragraph Three

We've learned a lesson from this, though. In future, I'm certain we'll be aware that postponing the bad news isn't doing anybody a favor. I promise you: It won't happen like this again. As always, it's you who has taught us where we are wrong and how we have to change; we only wish the lesson hadn't had to be at your expense. There's no way to express the respect each of us feels for you, or the gratitude; there are no words to make it clear to you how much you will be missed. If you'd like to set up a meeting to talk this over with me (or with someone else, if you prefer) just let us know. If you'd rather not, we'll understand that, and we'll let this letter take the place of what might be a difficult conversation. We know we can count on you to understand and to forgive our clumsiness; you always have. What we <u>don't</u> know is how we're going to get used to doing without you around here.

(If you feel that this paragraph looks too long on the page, you can break it into two shorter ones, starting the second at "If you'd like to set up a meeting . . . ." That's a natural break and would do the letter no harm.)

As in previous paragraphs, you use parallelism here to maintain the solemn tone of the letter. And you continue to point out to Jack how much he is valued—the sentence beginning with "As always" is a strong example of that message. It tells him that even in this sad situation, even in his manner of <u>leaving</u> the company, he has maintained his role as teacher and mentor and example for the rest of you.

USING PUNCTUATION TO ACHIEVE EFFECTS

Our English punctuation is basically an attempt to <u>write down</u> body language—to help readers supply all the nonverbal information that is otherwise missing from written language. We don't have the set of punctuation marks that would let us do that task adequately; it's probably impossible to construct such a set. But we tend not to do as much with the resources available as we could, because the way punctuation is usually taught gives us the false impression that the rules make no sense and were designed primarily as a mechanism for tormenting innocent students. Let's take a look at just one resource that is particularly relevant for our analysis of Letter 45.

Remember that you want above all to make it clear to your colleague that everyone takes this matter very seriously and that writing the letter is in itself a solemn action. If you were talking to Jack face to face, you'd do that with such things as the expression on your face and your tone of voice. In a letter, you don't have those resources available to you, and you have to fall back on punctuation to carry the message. Please look at the three examples below.

a. "I promise you it won't happen like this again."

b. "I promise you; it won't happen like this again."

c. "I promise you: It won't happen like this again."

In all three examples, you have a formal declaration that the sentence is a promise, and the <u>content</u> of the promise. Sentence (a) is the most casual and the most neutral of the three, and it contains the least information about body language. In Sentence (b), using the semicolon (;) tells the reader more about how the sentence would sound if it were said aloud, indicating that after "you" the pitch of the voice would drop slightly and there would be a brief pause. Sentence (c) does the same thing, but indicates that the emotional message carried by the body language is more intense. The drop in pitch would be a little greater and the pause would last a fraction longer. The extra information added by the colon(:) carries a metamessage roughly like this:

IF I WERE SAYING THIS SENTENCE YOU WOULD BE ABLE

TO TELL—FROM THE EXPRESSION ON MY FACE

AND THE TONE OF MY VOICE AND THE POSTURE

OF MY BODY—THAT I WAS TAKING THE SITUATION

VERY SERIOUSLY INDEED AND THAT I WANTED

TO GET THAT ACROSS TO YOU AS CLEARLY

AND AS THOROUGHLY AS POSSIBLE.

If you used a colon this way half a dozen times in a single letter, of course, or if you used it for trivial matters, it would lose all its force. It should be saved for those occasions when the information in the metamessage above would be part of what you wanted your reader to understand from your words. The situation in Letter 45 is exactly right.

There are other reasons for using (or not using) semicolons and colons. You'll find additional information about punctuation in Appendix B on pages 245–248.

You offer Jack the opportunity to request a face-to-face meeting to talk things over; he is entitled to that. At the same time, you offer him an easy way out of that meeting if (as you hope) he'd rather avoid it. You use the factive "know" to presuppose that he will understand and forgive; you use the possessive nominalization "our clumsiness" to presuppose the statement "We are clumsy." And you end the letter with a compliment that is an abrupt switch to a less formal, almost intimate tone.

The situation in Scenario Thirteen is a sad one, but it's one in which you really have no choice. You have to tell your senior colleague to retire, despite his opposition and his unhappiness with that decision. The problem is not his fault, and it's your fault only in the sense that you've made it worse by mishandling it. All of this is unambiguous, and the steps to be taken are obvious. Matters are equally clear when you have to write a letter offering someone a simple choice between making a requested change or being let go, as in Letter 46.

LETTER 46
Frailty: You've Got to Tell a Colleague to Shape Up—or Else

Dear Carolyn,

We regret the necessity to write this letter, and we wish that it could be avoided. We hope that you will look upon it as an attempt to offer you our help, and to make it possible for you to continue on the staff of Brand & Brand.

On two separate occasions we have met with you to explain that your habit of taking sums of money from petty cash for your personal use is not acceptable. We have informed you that any one of us might borrow from petty cash in an emergency, and no one would object. But your behavior—borrowing from petty cash for routine personal expenses—is different, and we have objected in the strongest terms. It is unfortunate that you have been unwilling to take those objections seriously.

The rest of the staff is unfairly inconvenienced when money is needed for legitimate purposes and none remains in petty cash because of your lack of consideration for others. In future, we will not just call you in for a discussion or a reprimand. With this letter, we are putting you on notice that any repetition of this behavior on your part will mean immediate dismissal. We are confident that you will respond to this notice by refraining from inappropriate use of petty cash, and we look forward to a more pleasant association with you from now on.

Sincerely,

This letter is unpleasant to write, of course, but it is again a response to a situation in which the alternatives are clear. Your firm has an employee whose behavior is unacceptable and who must choose between the behavior and the job; all you have to do is inform her that that is the choice. But what if it's not so simple? What if the relevant factors are differently mixed?

Suppose you face a situation in which, as in Scenario Thirteen, the employee is someone you value and would really hate to lose. And suppose that in contrast to Scenario Thirteen, where nothing can be done to correct matters, the employee's unacceptable behavior is something that he or she could control and should be able to change? Let's look at a scenario that illustrates this situation.

TRIPLE-F SCENARIO FOURTEEN

You have a staff member—we'll call him Joe—that you value highly. He's a top salesperson who consistently brings in sales figures significantly above the average for your sales staff. He's a "Type A" man . . . hard-working, hard-driving, competitive, determined to excel and to win. You'd hate to lose him. However, although Joe is Mr. Charm with clients and customers, he has a mean streak; toward those he outranks, he behaves like a petty bully. You need to make it clear to him that this behavior won't be tolerated, but you'd like at least a running chance at doing it without making him so angry that he quits. You don't trust yourself to do this face to face because you know he'll react with a defensive outburst that will infuriate you and is likely to lead to exactly the consequences you want to avoid. WHAT DO YOU SAY IN YOUR LETTER?

LETTER 47
Frailty: You've Got to Tell a Colleague to Shape Up—Please

Dear Joe,

I'm sorry this letter has to be written; I'd rather not write it. I'm sure you'd rather not read it. However, I need to ask you for your help and your cooperation, and this is the best and clearest way to do that.

Joe, you're under a lot of stress; you work hard. The sales figures you bring in reflect both of those things. At the same time, the load you carry has consequences that are less positive than your fine sales record. Specifically: when you yell at the secretaries, everyone here feels great distress, because the secretaries become very upset. This disturbs office workflow and decreases productivity all around.

I am confident that you can correct this problem. I'm confident that in the future you will find a better way to handle your interactions with the clerical staff. I know I can count on your good judgment and common sense, and I want to express my thanks—personally, and on behalf of everyone else at Brand & Brand—in advance.

Sincerely,

This letter follows the Triple-F pattern with only slight variations, and its strategies will be clear to you. It compliments Joe over and over again, so that he will not feel obligated to come charging into your office carrying on about his sales figures and how hard he works, and all the rest of that list. You've already said all that for him. You've <u>presupposed</u> that he will cooperate with you and make the requested change in his behavior. You haven't threatened him, you've made it clear that you value his presence in your firm, and you have carefully avoided <u>ordering</u> him to do anything. You have also put to good use another technique that is used in the *Gentle Art* system: the three-part message.

USING THREE-PART MESSAGES TO EXPRESS COMPLAINTS

No adult likes to listen to complaints; a negative reaction is almost inevitable. Complaints carry this metamessage: YOUR BEHAVIOR IS UNACCEPTABLE TO ME AND I AM ASKING YOU TO CHANGE IT, AND I HAVE THE RIGHT TO DO THAT. Much of the time people react not to the content of the complaint itself but to that metamessage; often the reaction is a kneejerk response that's way out of proportion. We all know this. But there are times when we *have* to transmit a complaint, as in Scenario Fourteen. In such cases, what we need is a way to minimize the automatic negative response so that the other person will understand the complaint and give it rational consideration.

An effective technique for doing that—the three-part message—was developed by Dr. Thomas Gordon, from an earlier technique called the "I-message." Gordon set up the following pattern to be used for complaints:

When you [X],   I/we feel [Y],   because [Z].
    1   2   3

As in:

"When you yell at the secretary, I feel distressed, because she becomes upset and can't do the typing."

"When you take the files home for the weekend, we feel angry, because none of the rest of us can do any work involving those accounts."

"When you take money from petty cash for personal use, we feel angry, because the petty cash fund isn't available for office emergencies."

The three-part message is easy to understand and to put together. It just takes a little practice in using it instead of the more typical complaint structures.

Begin with "When you [X]," filling X with the specific behavior you want changed—which must be something verifiable in the real world. It can't be anything like "When you act as if you were the only salesperson on the staff" or "When you throw your weight around" or "When you behave with no consideration for other people . . ." It has to be a specific item of behavior that everybody can observe and about which there can be no argument. Joe can argue about whether he's a bully or not, because that's a matter of personal opinion. If he yells at the secretaries, however, he can't argue about that, since it's a concrete event that everyone can perceive and agree on.

Go on by stating the emotion you feel in response to the behavior—"I feel distressed," "We feel frustrated," "Everyone feels annoyed." This emotion is also directly observable in the real world, in the words used (and, when spoken, in the body language), and because it is appropriate in the situation. Don't substitute "you make us angry" or "you frustrate us" or anything of that kind; to do that is to make an additional complaint. It's important to make only one complaint at a time. Don't substitute anything for the emotion; that is, don't write "I feel like a second-class citizen" or "We feel as if you have no consideration for anybody but yourself." Just write down the emotion that is provoked by the behavior.

Finish with "because [Y]," filling Y with a <u>consequence</u> of the undesirable behavior that is again verifiable and directly observable. This third part of the message is very important. It tells the reader what happens, in the real world, that justifies your making the complaint. Don't tamper with the pattern, don't insert any moral judgments or homilies, and be sure you don't add an additional and separate complaint. Not "because no decent person mistreats people he outranks" or "because nobody should have to put up with behavior like yours" or anything of that kind. Such sequences may be accurate and justified, but they are open to argument. A three-part message properly written contains nothing that the reader can argue about and offers none of the opportunities for a row beginning with "Whaddaya MEAN, I'm not considerate of other people?"

The second paragraph of Letter 47 is structured as a three-part message. It tells Joe exactly what behavior his colleagues want changed, exactly what emotion they feel in response to it, and exactly what real-world consequence justifies the request. In this format, you have a very good chance of getting past the "Who do you think you ARE?" reaction, so that the message in the complaint itself will be understood. And if the behavior changes in response to the letter, you can wait a month and send another letter that takes up one more of Joe's unsavory communication habits in the office. This strategy actually works a great deal of the time, and it avoids many otherwise inevitable unpleasant scenes.

I need to say one more thing about this pattern. WHEN YOU CAN'T FILL IN ONE OF THE PARTS, YOU DON'T HAVE A COM-

PLAINT. If someone bothers you, but you can't identify any specific behavior that is the cause of your annoyance, you don't have a complaint. If you know what behavior you want changed, but you don't know how you feel about it—or you can't identify any real-world consequence of the behavior that explains why it should be changed—you don't have a complaint and you shouldn't try to write one. A letter saying "The way you act is driving everybody at Brand & Brand crazy, and you've got to cut it out" is a waste of everybody's time and energy, and is guaranteed to fail as a way of changing somebody's behavior. When you can't construct a three-part message, stop right there. Don't write the letter until you <u>can</u> construct one.

SUPPLEMENTARY LETTERS

LETTER 48
Frailty: His Speech Was Full of Errors—and You Have to Tell Him

Dear Jason:

Writing this letter is harder for me than I can say; the only thing I can think of that would be worse would be giving you its message face to face. You have been the pride of our department for more than fifteen years; you've been the model toward which everyone else was striving. Nobody ever thought the day would come when we'd have to tell you that you'd made a grave error. We were wrong, Jason; that day has arrived.

Suppose that you had gone to a conference and heard a speech by a senior colleague for whom you had the highest regard and respect. Suppose that, to your horror, the speech contained flaws so serious that they might well have misled the students present, as well as the members of the general public. We know what *you* would have done in that situation. You would have gone straight to your colleague no later than the following day, explained your perceptions of the speech and its possible consequences, and done your best to set matters straight. That's what we should have done after we heard your talk on March 11th; cowards that we are, we've waited all this time without a word. I want you to know that we're sorry about that, and that we apologize.

I'm not going to even pretend this won't happen again. I'm sure it will, because telling a respected associate that you think the speech he's just given was completely in error isn't ever going to be easy. I can only promise you that in future we will <u>try</u> to have a bit more courage in a difficult situation. In the meantime, it's our good fortune to know that we can count on you to accept this letter with your usual graciousness and good sense. If you'd like to talk to me about this, just let me know; I'd be happy to meet with you at any time and explain the source of the difficulty.[1]

Cordially,

LETTER 49
Frailty: She Can't Sing the Solo Any More—and You Have to Tell Her

Dear Mrs. Smith:

I write this letter with great reluctance, and considerable sorrow. For nearly fifteen years, the solos that you have sung in our Easter services have been an inspiration to every member of the congregation, as well as a source of tremendous pleasure. The idea that the time would come when we'd have to suggest to you that someone else should do the solos never crossed our mind. Unfortunately, that time has come.

We've put off writing you about this far too long, and we readily admit that. It's not easy to tell someone for whom we have the highest regard and respect, and someone on whom we have relied for so long, that she is going to be replaced. On the other hand, we know very well that if <u>you</u> had noticed that a soloist's voice was growing less strong with the years you wouldn't have hesitated

---

[1] You would of course like to tell him what the errors were. But you must wait for him to ask you for that information; and if he doesn't ask, you must let it pass.

for a moment to point it out—and without all the beating around the bush that I am doing. I only wish I had your communication skills, and your courage.

We've learned a lesson from this, and in future, when we have an unpleasant message to transmit we will try to do it more promptly. In the meantime, we know how lucky we are that you are a person who puts the welfare of the choir and the congregation first, ahead of personal vanity. We know we can count on you to continue to help us offer the finest music possible, as one of the most valuable members of our choir.

Sincerely,

LETTER 50
Flub and Frailty: You Said "I Love You," But You Don't

Dear . . . . .,

It would be easier to write a novel, or a history of the world, than to write this letter. It's not going to even come close to the letter it ought to be, the letter you deserve. It's just the very best I can manage to write, trying with my whole heart.

I haven't forgotten what I said to you last night, and I didn't need the note that was on my desk this morning to remind me. I remember very well. Dearest friend, I told you last night that I <u>loved</u> you—but it's not true. It was true for me when I said it. At that moment, and for all the time that I was with you, I meant it. The problem is that when I'm not with you, it's true no longer. And that tells me what we both need to know: that it's not love, but <u>enchantment</u>. You are that rare person who makes the air golden around you, who brings with you your own perfect weather, who makes time pass sweetly and swiftly, who turns the most ordinary day into a celebration. All those things are wonderful and beyond price; they can serve, if you are willing, as the foundation for a friendship that will last both our lifetimes. But they're not <u>love</u>. Love doesn't go away when the beloved is beyond sight and hearing and touch, you see.

I cannot promise you I'll never again think that I'm in love with you . . . you are the source of enchantment, and I am only human. (If you want me to remain always in a sober frame of mind, you must find a way to be boring and ordinary, and I doubt that that's possible.) But I can promise you that I will never <u>say</u> so again and risk misleading and hurting you. You will always be dear to me, even if you decide it would be best for us not to meet again other than when outside circumstances throw us briefly and unavoidably together; and I will always be sorry that I was so clumsy as to cause you pain.

Regretfully,

Chapter Fifteen

Beyond the Small Appliance: The Letter As Gift

Bonus Chapter

*T*his chapter is a bonus . . . something different. After an entire book full of flubs, flounderings, and frailties, you deserve at least one letter with a <u>positive</u> focus.

Our subject here is the letter that you send, not to repair some dreadful damage, but as a gift, to family or very close friends, to be <u>treasured</u>. The letter you send instead of sending another tie, another pair of socks, another kitchen gadget, another useless present for someone who already has one of everything and two of lots of things. Many people don't have the time or the skill to send a quilt or woodcarving or a watercolor crafted by their own hands—but <u>everyone</u> can handcraft a letter. If you can do it in longhand, so much the better, but you don't have to. When your handwriting is so bad that people can't read it without struggling, it's best to type it instead, and then add a handwritten <u>postscript</u> to demonstrate why you typed the rest.

The model letter below is intended as a Christmas gift, and comes from my own experience; it will serve as an example. You can tailor your own to any occasion.

LETTER 51
The Gentle Art of Crafting a Gift

Dear Tracy,

I know you don't need another pair of socks, or any more golf clubs, or another sweater; I'm sure you don't want (or have any room for) yet one more kitchen gadget. Something you <u>don't</u> have, however, and something that only I can give you, is the story of the first Christmas that I myself can remember. Here it is.

* * *

I am lying on the mohair sofa in my grandmother's parlor . . . a real parlor, where almost nobody ever sat. I'm wrapped in a soft, red blanket to keep the prickly mohair from giving me a rash. And to keep me from getting pneumonia, because I am a very sick child. It's 1939, I am three years old, and I have influenza. From where I lie, without lifting my head, I can see the Christmas tree. It's an artificial one (yes, they did exist in 1939!), all white, with blue ornaments; at the top is a small blue light in the shape of a star. It's a small tree, and it sits in the parlor on the table that ordinarily holds the big red glass lamp my grandmother bought from a Watkins man when she was a little girl, for fifty cents. For me, the lights are unbelievably beautiful . . . great <u>halos</u> of light, with rays that stream out in all directions around them, like you see in medieval Christmas paintings. I have no way of knowing that that's not how lights look to people with normal eyes, and nobody knows yet that my eyes aren't normal; they have no idea I'm seeing a miracle of light.

I can hear the grownups talking in the front room (the room next to the parlor, where people ordinarily sit and talk.) I can't really hear what they're saying, except once in awhile when someone raises their voice and speaks directly to me. My mother says, "Don't you even want to look at your <u>toys</u>?" I don't want to; I don't answer her. I am much too little to know how worrisome that is. I never do look at my toys that day; I am too weak and too feverish to be willing to lift my head.

* * *

It sounds like a sad story, perhaps. But I assure you it's not. What I remember from that Christmas isn't sadness, or sickness. I remember the beauty of the blue lights, that I could see just by opening my eyes, with the star twinkling at the top. I remember the soft steady murmur of the voices of people that I knew loved me dearly, in the next room. And I remember feeling (as I always felt in my grandmother's house) absolutely <u>safe</u>. Absolutely, without-any-question-whatsoever, safe and sheltered and beloved. It was a wonderful Christmas! I'm not sure any Christmas after that, joyful as they have been, has ever topped it.

> Merry Christmas to you all,
> and the happiest of New Years,

PS: I've also sent you a scrapbook to go with this letter. I suspect that if you asked you could get a "first Christmas I remember" letter from everyone in the family and fill the scrapbook full.

PSS: The first time I ever saw a Christmas tree after they got me glasses, I was shocked. I took the glasses off immediately, to see how the tree <u>really</u> looked.

A letter like this is a personal letter, certainly, but it is one that can be shared. Your readers will treasure it because it comes from you, and because its contents are meaningful to them in a way they could not be to outsiders. That doesn't mean that it won't bear analysis; when I said that everyone can "handcraft" a letter, I was serious. Let's take a brief look at how it is put together.

ANALYSIS OF LETTER 51

Paragraph One

I know you don't need another pair of socks, or any more golf clubs, or another sweater; I'm sure you don't want (or have any room for) yet one more kitchen gadget. Something you <u>don't</u> have, however, and something that only I can give you, is the story of the first Christmas that I myself can remember. Here it is.

You can easily adapt this paragraph to your own experience. You begin with "I know you don't need . . . ," followed by the list of things you know personally aren't needed by your reader. Then you write, "Something you <u>don't</u> have, however, and something that only I can give you, is . . . ," followed by a memory of your own that you know will be of interest to your reader. The story of the first Hanukkah or Kwaanza or Thanksgiving or Fourth of July you remember. The story of your first hunting or fishing or camping trip. The story of your first day at school. The story of the day you first came to this country, or first left it. The story of your wedding day or the day your child was born. A story of a day that, though horrible at the time, is hilarious when you look back on it from the safe distance of years. (Like the time I was traveling alone with three tiny children, and they all came down with chicken pox on the train; anything of that kind will do nicely.)

Paragraphs Two and Three

* * *

I am lying on the mohair sofa in my grandmother's parlor . . . a real parlor, where almost nobody ever sat. I'm wrapped in a soft, red blanket to keep the prickly mohair from giving me a rash. And to keep me from getting pneumonia, because I am a very sick child. It's

1939, I am three years old, and I have influenza. From where I lie, without lifting my head, I can see the Christmas tree. It's an artificial one (yes, they did exist in 1939!), all white, with blue ornaments; at the top is a small blue light in the shape of a star. It's a small tree, and it sits in the parlor on the table that ordinarily holds the big red glass lamp my grandmother bought from a Watkins man when she was a little girl, for fifty cents. For me, the lights are unbelievably beautiful . . . great <u>halos</u> of light, with rays that stream out in all directions around them, like you see in medieval Christmas paintings. I have no way of knowing that that's not how lights look to people with normal eyes, and nobody knows yet that my eyes aren't normal; they have no idea I'm seeing a miracle of light.

I can hear the grownups talking in the front room (the room next to the parlor, where people ordinarily sit and talk.) I can't really hear what they're saying, except once in awhile when someone raises their voice and speaks directly to me. My mother says, "Don't you even want to look at your <u>toys</u>?" I don't want to; I don't answer her. I am much too little to know how worrisome that is. I never do look at my toys that day; I am too weak and too feverish to be willing to lift my head.

* * *

The three asterisks (before Paragraph Two and after Paragraph Three) are just a way of setting off the story being told from the letter that frames it. You could substitute a title for the asterisks, like this: "The First Christmas That I Remember." I used asterisks because they are a bit less formal.

I shifted in these narrative paragraphs to what is called "historical present tense." The purpose of the shift is to bring the reader in closer and make the scene and events more vivid, and it's entirely appropriate as a way of making the letter different from ordinary non-gift correspondence. If you don't feel comfortable doing this, however, just write as you would in telling any other story from the past.

Nothing <u>happens</u> in the story I'm telling, but that's all right. It wouldn't interest a general audience, but it is exceedingly interesting to my children and grandchildren. In the same way, you should not be held back by the fact that your own story contains no murders, no glorious battles, no illicit love affairs, no overthrow

of the government. What interests your family are the small details—like the fact that my grandmother's wonderful ruby-red glass
lamp cost her only fifty cents and was bought from a Watkins man.
Those details make the past real to your readers and tell them things
they didn't know, and couldn't know without your gift. If you <u>do</u>
have vivid memories of an important historical occasion—the day
World War II ended, the day of the first moon landing, something
of that kind—a gift-letter about that day would be wonderful. But
it will <u>still</u> be the small personal details you include in your letter
that are most important, rather than the basic facts that can be found
in any history text.

Paragraph Four

It sounds like a sad story, perhaps. But I assure you it's not.
What I remember from that Christmas isn't sadness, or sickness. I remember the beauty of the blue lights, that I could
see just by opening my eyes, with the star twinkling at the
top. I remember the soft steady murmur of the voices of
people that I knew loved me dearly, in the next room. And
I remember feeling (as I always felt in my grandmother's
house) absolutely <u>safe</u>. Absolutely, without-any- question-
whatsoever, safe and sheltered and beloved. It was a wonderful Christmas! I'm not sure any Christmas after that,
joyful as they have been, has ever topped it.

> Merry Christmas to you all,
> and the happiest of New Years,

In this paragraph I've shifted back to <u>commenting</u> on the story
I told. You would tailor this paragraph to your own story. Suppose
you'd written of your first hunting trip; your concluding paragraph
might be something like this:

It sounds like a boring story, perhaps. But I assure you
it's not. What I remember from that hunting trip isn't the
endless hours spent sitting and waiting, or the long drive
to get there and to go home. It isn't going home without
a deer (in fact, I think I was glad about that.) I remember
the incredible blue sky, and the big white clouds blowing
by high up in that blue. I remember the color of the
autumn leaves on the trees—the most amazing red and
yellow and gold and burgundy I ever saw, almost stained

glass colors. I remember how the wind sounded, rustling those leaves, and how your Grandfather Thomas kept grinning about my useless attempts to move around without making more noise than the wind. And I remember being sure that this was unquestionably the most perfect October day that had ever come along in the history of the world. It was a wonderful trip! I'm not sure that any hunting trip since, much as I've enjoyed them all, has ever topped it.

Analysis of Letter 51, Continued: Postscripts

PS: I've also sent you a scrapbook to go with this letter. I suspect that if you asked you could get a "first Christmas I remember" letter from everyone in the family and fill the scrapbook full.

PSS: The first time I ever saw a Christmas tree after they got me glasses, I was shocked. I took the glasses off immediately, to see how the tree <u>really</u> looked.

There's much research indicating that people like postscripts and give them lots of attention; this is a good place to put something you want to stress. It's also the best place for something that might make the letter itself less special. You wouldn't want to clutter a gift-letter with instructions for starting a family collection of similar letters, or with part of a different story about a different Christmas. The postscripts gave me an alternative spot for those two items. If you were enclosing a gift check instead of sending a scrapbook, you probably wouldn't want to talk about the check in the letter; again, the postscript would serve. If, on the other hand, you were sending an old photograph or other piece of family memorabilia with the letter, you might prefer to mention that inside the letter proper. (And you could certainly write a gift-letter with a family photograph or similar item as its <u>subject</u>.)

What matters most about a letter like the model gift-letter is that it should sound like a <u>letter from you</u>. Don't let yourself become self-conscious; don't try to write Great Literature. When you want to give great literature, send a volume of the classics. A letter from you, sharing your memories, will be important to the reader because it comes from you and sounds like you. Your feeling that you are writing for history shouldn't be allowed to make you sound pompous and affected—unless you really <u>are</u> pompous and affected, in which case that's exactly how you should sound.

Appendixes

Appendix A

More Than One Hundred Routine Letters

I NTRODUCTION

The model letters that follow this introduction are intended to supplement the Triple-F model letters for roughly one hundred common letter-writing situations. They are not, however, intended to take the place of a full-scale, traditional letters book. If you want to be sure that you have a model available for every conceivable business situation, I recommend the following two books:

> *Lifetime Encyclopedia of Letters: Revised and Expanded*, by H.E. Meyer. (Prentice Hall 1992; Englewood Cliffs NJ 07632.)

> This book contains 850 model letters for both business and personal correspondence, covering 500 different categories. It includes 57 collection letters, 35 sales letters, 21 job application letters, 18 charity fund-raising letters . . . everything you're likely to need, for the rest of your life.

> *Personal Letters that Mean Business*, by L. B. Sturgeon and A. R. Hagler. (Prentice Hall 1991; Englewood Cliffs NJ 07632.)

> This book contains 370 model letters for handling personal business, including health care, real estate, senior services, travel, insurance, taxes, and many other categories. Plus an extraordinarily detailed and complete directory of federal, state, and national addresses, such as banking au-

thorities, broadcast networks, government offices at every level, and utility commissions.

THE GENERIC BUSINESS LETTER PATTERN

We can begin by excluding items that are often referred to as letters but are in fact types of legal documents, like contracts, letters of agreement, permissions, etc. Most business letters are then of three kinds: letters that tell the reader something (positive or negative); letters that ask the reader to do something; and letters that respond to a letter (or other contact) from the reader. Their parts, which can be assembled and reassembled like a Tinkertoy™ set, are outlined for you below.

I—Openers:

A. (Positive)

I am/We are happy to tell you that

1. our new store is now open.
2. our new product is now available.
3. we are hiring you for the job.
4. we are giving you the contract.
5. you have won our contest.
6. (and so on)

B. (Negative)

I am/We are sorry to tell you that

1. you have been fired.
2. your premium has gone up.
3. we are closing our store.
4. I cannot give a speech at your meeting.
5. your product is defective.
6. (and so on)

C. I am/We are writing you to ask you

1. to send information about your quantity discount.
2. to come to our grand opening.

3. to write an article for our newsletter.

4. to grant a job interview.

5. to set up an account for us with your firm.

6. (and so on)

D. In response to your letter of [DATE],

1. the application forms you requested are enclosed.

2. the price of our Upsydaisy Doll is $34.95.

3. an interview has been scheduled for you at [TIME/DATE].

4. no positions are open at this time.

5. we are not able to attend.

6. (and so on)

II—Closings:

A. Thank you for

1. your interest in our product/firm/organization.

2. your attention to this matter.

3. your consideration.

B. I/We look forward to hearing from you

1. (as is).

2. at your earliest convenience.

3. by [DEADLINE].

Much letter-writing advice today suggests that you should drop the old standard phrases and sentences and replace them with alternatives that are more state of the art. I'm not so sure that this is a good idea. I agree that beginning with "I take my pen in hand" is absurd, as is "Your obedient servant" for the complimentary close. No one would consider using such expressions today. But many of the items being recommended for the discard heap are more like single words in a Basic Business Letter Vocabulary. Their presence is reassuring to the reader. It carries, as a metamessage: "We come from roughly the same business culture and we speak roughly the same business language." And although what you have written might seem overly traditional to some of your readers, it will always seem "correct." This is an advantage that is not trivial and should not be given up lightly.

LETTER FORMAT

Two letter styles are used in business today: the "block" format and the "indented" format. Either is correct, although the block format is slightly more formal, and which one you use is a matter of personal choice. An example of each is provided for you below. Business letters are ordinarily single-spaced, but it's all right to double-space a very brief letter to make it look less lonely on the page.

BLOCK FORMAT (ON LETTERHEAD PAPER)

OZARK CENTER FOR LANGUAGE STUDIES
PO Box 1137
Huntsville AR 72740

December 20, 1991

Mr. J. W. Smith
104 Main Street
Anytown MO 72222

Dear Mr. Smith:

Thank you for your letter of December 9th asking for information about the Ozark Center for Language Studies. We appreciate your interest.

An information packet that should answer all of your questions is enclosed with this letter, together with a catalog of our products and services in verbal self-defense. If you need any additional information, just let us know. We will be happy to help in any way we can.

We look forward to hearing from you.

Sincerely,

Suzette Haden Elgin, Ph.D.
Director

Indented Format (on plain paper)

OZARK CENTER FOR LANGUAGE STUDIES
PO Box 1137
Huntsville AR 72740–1137

December 20, 1991

Mr. J. W. Smith
104 Main Street
Anytown MO 72222

Dear Mr. Smith:

Thank you for your letter of December 9th asking for information about the Ozark Center for Language Studies. We appreciate your interest.

An information packet that should answer all of your questions is enclosed with this letter, together with a catalog of our products and services in verbal self-defense. If you need any additional information, just let us know. We will be happy to help in any way we can.

We look forward to hearing from you.

Sincerely,

Suzette Haden Elgin, Ph.D.
Director

Model Letters

Asking For . . .

Assistance

In the past two months I have made three separate attempts to obtain a set of birth certificates and related documents for my children. The originals were lost during our recent move from Los Angeles to Miami, and my children cannot enroll in school here without replacement copies.

Each time I have attempted to obtain the documents through our local agencies I have been told that they would be forthcoming in the next week or ten days. Each time, this has proved to be false. The explanations given have not been helpful, and I am now genuinely alarmed. Unless this matter can be resolved promptly, my children will face serious difficulties when school begins in September. I am therefore writing to ask you for your help.

I enclose a detailed description of the documents that were lost, for your reference. If you need any additional information, please call me collect at [PHONE NUMBER] or write to me at the above address. Needless to say, it's important that I hear from you promptly. If I can do anything at all to speed up this process, please let me know and I will act on your requests immediately.

Thank you for your assistance in this matter. I look forward to hearing from you at your earliest convenience.

A Contribution or Donation

As you know, our organization is the only charity in this area able to respond immediately to the emergency needs of local residents, without requiring them to wait until some official form or other has been processed. We are the only local source when a family needs money for the next meal, or an urgent prescription, or a pair of shoes, or gasoline to drive a sick child to the doctor.

We depend upon local businesses and individuals for our total funding, and we hope we can count on your firm to join the circle of our supporters. For every dollar you donate to [NAME OF YOUR GROUP], you can be sure that eighty-three cents goes directly to taking care of these small—but truly serious—emergencies.

A brochure describing our operations is enclosed with this letter, together with a return envelope for your convenience in replying. If you need any additional information, please write or call; we will be happy to provide it. We look forward to hearing from you.

Forms or Documents

I would like to apply for a personal charge account with your firm, and I am writing to request the necessary application forms. I enclose a self-addressed stamped envelope for your convenience in responding to this request. Your prompt attention to this matter will be greatly appreciated.

Information

Sometime in the coming year I will be opening a new business in the St. Louis area and moving there with my family. We need to decide which of the small towns within easy commuting distance of St. Louis would be our best choice as a permanent residence. Because we have three children under nine years of age, we will be basing our decision primarily on the availability of good schools. I am therefore writing to you to request information about the schools in Anytown, as well as more general information that would be helpful.

Thank you for your assistance in this matter. I look forward to hearing from you.

A Loan

I'm sure you know that in the current economic situation it's hard to collect accounts receivable. We've had an especially hard time in this state, where the unemployment rate is almost twice as high as the national average, but we've been managing to keep our head above water. And then yesterday our biggest account called to tell us that they had just had a devastating fire at their main plant. It doesn't affect their business status, because they were fully insured, but until they can get set up for business in new quarters everything they do—including the routine payment of bills like ours—will be delayed.

This is a temporary situation, but it puts me in a serious bind. I was counting on receiving their check before Friday, and waiting a week or two will cause grave problems here. What I need is a loan of five thousand dollars for about thirty days, and I'd prefer not to take that much reserve from my credit line at this time. Would you be willing to loan me the money, [NAME]? I'd be very grateful.

You can reach me here at the office every day this week, or you can call me at home any night except Wednesday the 19th, when I'll be out of town. I hope all is well with you, and I send my regards, as always.

A Product (to Buy)

I enclose my check in the amount of $32.00 for two of your Bitty Baby dolls, as advertised in the current issue of *Young Woman News*. My check includes $2.50 to cover the cost of priority mail. Please send the order to the following address:

[ADDRESS]

Thank you for your prompt attention to this matter.

A Reference or Recommendation

When I was a student in your anthropology class (AN-THRO 103) you were kind enough to tell me that you'd be happy to give me a letter of recommendation for graduate school. I am now applying for admission to the ethnology and musicology department at Glendrake University, and I am writing you to ask for the letter.

Glendrake is interested in my academic ability, my character, my skill in personal interaction, and—above all—whether I am <u>tough</u> enough to survive in their high-pressure academic environment.

The letter should be sent to the following address before August 1st, in the enclosed, stamped envelope.

> Jane Doe, Ph.D., Chairman
> Department of Ethnology
> and Musicology
> Glendrake University

[ADDRESS]

If you need any additional information, please call me (collect) at [PHONE NUMBER]; I am almost always there after five o'clock.

Thank you for your help, which is very much appreciated.

A Speaker, Panelist, Performer, or Presenter

On February 11th of this year our Kiwanis Club will be holding its seventh annual WINNING IDEAS conference at the Civic Center from 8:30 A.M. until 5:00 P.M., followed by a reception and banquet. As you know, this event has become a tradition here in Anytown, and we try each year to make it more successful than ever before. This year, we're hoping you will help us achieve that goal.

We would like to invite you to present the keynote speech, from 9:00 to about 9:30. Many of our members had the privilege of hearing you speak at last spring's graduation ceremonies; we would like to extend that privilege to the rest of the members and to the rest of the participants at the conference.

If you're willing to be our speaker, we are prepared to offer you an honorarium of $250.00. (And of course we hope you will join us for the reception and banquet as our guest, as well as for as many of the day's events as you would like to attend.) Our conference chairman, Walter Field, will be calling you next week to ask for your decision, and you can discuss the other arrangements with him at that time.

[NAME], I hope that you will say yes; your speech would be a high point of the conference.

A Trade or Barter

An acquaintance tells me that you have a very fine used motorhome that you would like to sell. He also tells me that you spend a good deal of your leisure time at Lake of the Moon. I am contacting you because I am looking for a used motorhome, and because I am trying to sell my 1986 Blue Dickens houseboat. It occurred to me that you might want to trade the motorhome for the boat.

If you'd be willing to discuss this, please give me a call at [NUMBER] so that we can talk about details.

I look forward to hearing from you.

ANNOUNCING . . .

An Award

It gives me great pleasure to announce that our company will be offering an award this year to the local student who writes the best essay on the subject of "What America Means to Me." The award will be a handsome certificate framed for hanging, and a crisp new one hundred dollar bill.

We are sure you will want your students to participate in this competition. You'll find a brochure explaining the details—length of essay, deadline, and so on—enclosed with this letter.

A Birth

I'm sure you will be happy to know that the baby is here and that both mother and child are doing splendidly. We had a little boy, weighing 7 pounds and 3 ounces, with brown hair and blue eyes. We've named him Frank Edward, after his mother's younger brother.

An Opening

It gives me great pleasure to announce that our company, Blue Sky Pharmaceuticals, will be opening a new plant in your area in early July at the Clepper Industrial Park on Highway 412. We know we will be able to offer you an even higher level of performance and service than we have in the past, and we anticipate an ongoing and mutually profitable relationship.

Let me take this opportunity to invite you to attend our Grand Opening on July 9th, from noon to 7:00 P.M. Feel free to bring your family; there'll be refreshments and activities for all ages. We look forward to seeing you there.

A Death

It is with great sorrow that we are obliged to tell you of the sudden death of our friend and colleague, William Jones. Bill died peacefully at his home Sunday evening after a brief illness. He will be sorely missed by everyone who had the privilege of knowing him and working with him.

The family has asked that no flowers be sent to the private funeral services which are scheduled for tomorrow afternoon. Instead of flowers, please send a small donation in his memory to the Childlight Foundation, which was Bill's favorite local charity.

A Divorce

This letter is to let you know, with much regret, that our divorce is now final. We don't expect to write joint communications in the future, but we did want to tell you, together, how much we have appreciated your concern and your good wishes during this very difficult period of our lives.

We know it's hard to maintain relationships under these circumstances. We thank you for your past friendship; perhaps we will all be lucky enough to find a way to continue as friends.

An Event

We are delighted to be able to announce that September 19th is Metamega's fiftieth anniversary as a company. It's been a wonderful fifty years. Please come help us celebrate.

We'll be expecting you from noon until four P.M., in our executive lounge (9th Floor, Bidwell Building, 400 Main Street). Feel free to bring your spouse, or a friend.

A Marriage

It gives us great pleasure to announce that we were married on April 11th in Cassopolis, Michigan. The secret has been hard to keep; now that it's no secret, will you help us celebrate?

We'll look for you on June 10th at the Fayetteville Hilton, in Suite 500. Please don't bring us any presents; we have everything we need and a good deal more.

A Move to Another Location

We're just writing to let you know that after May 11th you'll find us at our new location: Suite 35, 111 15th Avenue Northwest, in the Palmer Building. We're all looking forward to the move. If you'd like to drop by and look over our new quarters, we'll have coffee, cookies, and conversation ready and waiting.

A New Employee or Executive or Member

This letter will introduce you to the newest member of our state consortium of Hospitality Clubs, Andrew Jones. Andy brings us many valuable skills and much practical experience; he has been a meetings coordinator for more than fifteen years, and has just retired to our state.

Please make Andy welcome there in Blankville, and let him help you plan the Spring Festival. You'll quickly find him indispensable.

I look forward to seeing you at the coordinating meeting in February.

A New Product

[COMPANY NAME] is proud to announce that our new software package, TULIP 8-9-10, is now ready for shipping. We know you've been waiting for this product for a long time, and we've been as frustrated by the delay as you have. Let's put it behind us and concentrate on enjoying the best database program that's ever been written!

Let us know how many copies you need, and we'll get them right out to you.

A Transfer

We're writing to let you know that your sales representative here at Metamega, Joe Smith, is being transferred to the Detroit office. This is a transfer Joe's been asking for since 1975, and we are all happy for him; on the other hand, it will be hard to get along without him. Our loss is Detroit's gain!

Your new representative will be Doris Wills. I'm sure you know Doris, who has filled in for Joe on many occasions in the past few years. You can count on her to give you the same excellent service and cooperation you always received from Joe.

If you have any questions, just give me a call at [NUMBER].

APPLYING FOR . . .

College Admission

I am writing to apply for admission to [NAME OF COLLEGE] for the fall quarter of [YEAR]. I enclose the following:

1. Completed application forms.
2. A check for your $10.00 processing fee.
3. Three letters of recommendation.
4. Report of my SAT scores.
5. My high school transcript.

6. A black and white photograph.

7. A one-page essay explaining why I wish to attend [NAME OF COLLEGE.]

If you need any additional information or documents, I can be reached at [PHONE NUMBER] or at the above address.

Thank you for your consideration of my application. I look forward to hearing from you at your earliest convenience.

An Account

I am writing to apply for an account with your firm. As requested, I am enclosing my check for $10.00 to cover your processing fee, my completed application forms, and a stamped self-addressed envelope for your convenience in replying.

If you need any additional information, I can be reached at [PHONE NUMBER] or at the above address. I look forward to hearing from you at your earliest convenience.

Credit or a Loan

I am writing to apply for a line of credit with /A LOAN FROM/ your bank. As requested, I am enclosing the completed credit /LOAN/ application and two letters of recommendation from current business references.

If you need any additional information, or if I can do anything to help with the speedy processing of this application, please call me at [NUMBER] or write me at the above address. As you know, I am hoping to open my new business before July 15th. I therefore look forward to hearing from you at your earliest convenience.

A Grant

I am writing to apply for one of the Research Incentive Grants awarded annually by your agency. I enclose the following:

1. Completed application forms
2. Three letters of recommendation
3. My resume
4. Resumes for my two co-investigators and for our clerical assistant

If you need any additional information, please let me know and I will provide it immediately. As you know, the startup procedure for our project is time-consuming, and we cannot begin until we have your decision. We would therefore be grateful for anything that can be done to expedite this application process.

Thank you for your consideration. I look forward to hearing from you.

A Job

In response to your ad in this morning's newspaper, I am writing to apply for the position of manager trainee with your firm. For the past three years I have been employed as manager of a small office staff, and I have completed all but one of the courses required for an Associate Degree in Business Management. The position you describe appears to be exactly what I have been looking for, and I would very much like to schedule an interview.

My resume is enclosed with this letter. If you need additional information, I can be reached at [PHONE NUMBER] or at the above address. I have enclosed a stamped, self-addressed envelope for your convenience in replying.

I look forward to hearing from you.

Membership

I am writing to apply for a membership in [NAME OF ORGANIZATION]. I enclose the following:

1. Completed membership application form
2. Letter of recommendation from a current member
3. My resume
4. A stamped, self-addressed envelope for your reply

I understand that a personal interview is required before a final decision is made, and I would like to schedule it as quickly as possible. I can be reached at [NUMBER] during business hours, or at [NUMBER] after 6 P.M.

Thank you for your consideration. I look forward to hearing from you.

C ELEBRATING . . .

An Anniversary

On behalf of everyone here at [NAME], I am writing to offer our warmest congratulations on your twenty-fifth anniversary. May the two of you enjoy another—even more wonderful—quarter of a century together!

A Birthday

On behalf of the entire staff of [NAME], I am writing to offer our warmest wishes for a very happy sixtieth birthday. May all the years to come be as wonderful as these sixty have been.

A Holiday

On behalf of everyone here at [NAME], I am writing to send you our warmest best wishes, for the holiday season and for the New Year to come.

C OLLECTING . . .

ACCOUNTS RECEIVABLE (series of five letters)

1. Notice of Check Returned

We're sure you are unaware that the check you recently sent us for $67.45 was returned to us stamped "insufficient funds." This sort of thing happens to most of us now and then, even though we do our best to be careful with our pluses and minuses.

We'd be most grateful if you would send us the money owed so that we can mark your account "Paid In Full."

Thank you for your prompt attention to this matter.

2. Notice of Past Due Account

As you know, it has been two weeks since we wrote to advise you that your check for $67.45 had failed to clear, and to ask you to set that right by sending another check immediately. We are not at all sure why we haven't heard from you—perhaps you have been out of town. In any case, we now must ask that you send your certified check or a money order for the full amount due, without any further delay.

If there is a problem in paying this account, please contact us so that we can discuss it. And of course, if your check is already in the mail, please accept our thanks—and our apologies for this followup letter.

3. Third Notice of Past Due Account

Mr. [NAME], we have now notified you twice of your past due account and your bad check. We have now asked you twice, courteously, to set matters right by sending us the money you owe. We have asked you to contact us if there was a problem we could help you with.

You have not yet responded to any of our messages, and we are beginning to be seriously concerned. We have advised our Credit Department to allow you no further credit until this problem has been corrected. We would be sorry to lose you as a customer, but we cannot afford to keep a customer who refuses to pay his bills.

We look forward to receiving your certified check or money order in the amount of $67.45 by return mail.

4. Final Notice

It is clear to us now that you are unwilling to pay your past due account in the amount of $67.45, and that you have no objection to being known as someone who writes bad checks. Our patience is exhausted, and your account with us has now been closed.

We are forwarding your file to our collection agency for further attention. We have notified your credit bureau of your actions and of your unwillingness even to show the minimal courtesy of contacting us to discuss this problem. We regret that this has been necessary; we have made every effort to avoid it.

If we are in error, or if there is some simple explanation for this situation that you would like to discuss with our collection agency, please contact [NAME] at [ADDRESS, PHONE].

5. Dues

As you know, your dues in the amount of $60.00 for membership in the Science Fiction Writers Guild were due on June 1st of this year, and it is now almost July. We would be most grateful to have your check for the amount due (plus the $5.00 late fee) by return mail.

If there is a problem that makes it difficult for you to pay your dues at this time, we would be happy to try to work out a payment arrangement with you. Just call us at [NUMBER] and we will do our best to help.

We look forward to hearing from you.

C OMPLAINING ABOUT . . .

Accommodations

My husband and I were guests at your hotel on the night of November 9th, during a recent business trip. We were looking forward to our stay, since we have been watching your television commercials. We were deeply disappointed, and it is our opinion that the commercials are either misleading or deliberately deceptive.

Our room was cramped, dirty, and poorly heated. Although there was a thermostat on the wall, adjusting it had no effect on the room's temperature. Two of the light bulbs in the room were burned out on our arrival, and those that were functioning were so dim that it was almost impossible for us to read by them. To top it off, the noise from your atrium lounge—which does not close until 3 A.M.—kept us awake most of the night.

We did of course attempt to complain at the time. In response to each of our phone calls we were advised that "someone will take of it as quickly as possible." Someone did arrive around 9 P.M. to replace the two burned-out light bulbs; other than that, we received nothing but promises.

Under no circumstances will we stay at any [HOTEL NAME] again, and we will do our best to spread the word to our friends and our business associates that your television commercials can only be referred to as science fiction. We are sending a copy of this letter to the Better Business Bureau for their information.

Behavior

We have tried very hard to be good neighbors, Mr. [NAME]. And we have gone out of our way to avoid interfering with you or with your family, despite numerous inconveniences. We have no desire to be on bad terms with you.

However, in the past month your teenage son has begun playing his stereo system at full volume not only during the day but often until as late as two o'clock in the morning. We cannot imagine how you and your family are able to tolerate this noise, much less how you are able to sleep.

We would be very grateful if you would see to it that your son plays his stereo at a volume that does not force the entire neighborhood to share his musical tastes.

Performance

On February 13th of this year, I arranged with your company to have an air conditioning unit installed at my home at [ADDRESS]. I did this in February specifically to be sure that the work would not be scheduled during your rush season—and to be sure that it would be completed before the summer's heat began.

It is now May 1st, and your technicians have not yet begun the work promised. I have called your office repeatedly, and have been told each time that [COMPANY NAME] was sorry for the delay and that work would begin promptly. Needless to say, these statements have yet to be followed by action.

It is much too late in the year for me to cancel my arrangement with you and hire another air conditioning firm. Under the circumstances, therefore, I have no choice but to give you an ultimatum. Either you will install the air conditioning unit I ordered from you in February before May 15th, or I will turn the matter over to my attorney.

Product

Two weeks ago I ordered an electric mixer from your company. I chose it specifically because I was looking for a product that would not wear out in its first few months of use and because one of the claims you make in your advertising is that the [NAME] mixer outlasts all other brands.

I am sorry to report that the unit you sold to me performed badly the first time I used it. The identical unit I exchanged it for was no improvement—and now it has broken down completely.

I am not interested in another exchange. Your product is clearly not reliable. Will you please, therefore, send me a prompt refund for its $78.95 purchase price and the $4.95 shipping and handling charge.

Published Material

I am writing to object in the strongest terms to the story you recently published in your magazine titled [NAME OF STORY], by [NAME OF WRITER]. It's bad enough to have to read about serial murders in the newspaper and hear about them on radio and television—perhaps a case can be made that the public needs to know about these terrible events. But there is <u>no</u> justification for including a story like the one in your recent issue in a magazine that claims to be intended for young teenagers.

I am thoroughly disgusted by this situation. I am canceling my son's subscription and requesting a full refund; I am also canceling all my family's subscriptions to magazines published by your company. And I will go out of my way to persuade my friends and my business associates to do the same.

A Requirement

The purpose of this letter is to make my objection to your residency requirement a matter of record, and to request once again that you consider removing it from the list.

In the past nine months, during a period when it has been extremely difficult to find competent personnel, our office has had to turn down more than a dozen applications from otherwise eligible individuals who lived outside the city limits. This complicates the hiring process and makes it impossible to maintain adequate staff levels. It is an unreasonable requirement. There is no connection between residency within the city limits and qualification to fulfill the duties of the various positions.

Please give this matter your attention and get back to me as quickly as possible. If you would like to schedule a meeting to discuss the problem, I will be happy to attend. I look forward to hearing from you before March 10th.

Service

I am writing to let you know that I will no longer eat at your restaurant until the quality of service provided by your staff is radically improved.

Twice in the past month I have entertained business guests at the [NAME OF RESTAURANT] and have had to apologize to them for the surliness of your waiters. The food you serve is excellent, and the atmosphere is exactly what is needed for business lunches. But neither of those things makes up for the embarrassment your staff causes to your customers.

I have reservations with you on the 19th of April, and will once again be entertaining clients. If there is no change in the service on that occasion, I will take my business elsewhere in the future.

Thank you for your attention to this matter.

FIRING . . .

A Recently Hired Employee

When you joined us here at [COMPANY NAME], we all were confident that it would be for a long and mutually productive stay. You seemed to be precisely the sort of employee we needed.

However, although you've been with us only a few months, that has been long enough to make it clear that this is not an appropriate place of employment for you. We are sure you would be happier in a position where your hours would be more flexible and where you would not have to interact constantly with the public.

We regret the necessity to terminate your employment, but we know you will agree with us that it is for the best. Please be advised, therefore, that Friday the 11th will be your last day with this company. If you have any questions, please see the Personnel office.

We wish you the best of luck in the future.

A Long-term Employee

Few business tasks are more difficult than that of terminating an employee who has been with a company for many years. When it must be done, however, no purpose is served by delay.

As you know, over the past six months your sales have steadily declined. We have made every effort to help you reverse this trend, but you have been unwilling to participate in any of the training programs we have suggested for you. Your position has consistently been that your deteriorating performance is due only to the economy and that you did not need to make any effort to improve it, and you have refused to consider any other possibility. Obviously, this is a situation that cannot be allowed to continue.

Please be advised, therefore, that your employment with [NAME OF COMPANY] will end on the 27th of this month. You should set up an appointment with [NAME OF EMPLOYEE] to discuss arrangements regarding your health insurance, retirement account, stock options, and so on, as soon as possible.

We can say honestly that we deeply regret losing you, and that we wish this termination could have been avoided.

A Firm

This letter will notify you that as of April 20th we will no longer require the services of your law firm. As you know, our association over the past six months has been marred by frequent disagreements and differences of opinion. Our meetings with you in an attempt to solve the problem have been uniformly a waste of time both for you and for us. We have therefore retained another firm to handle our legal affairs.

We will expect to receive all documents and files needed to effect this change no later than the 15th of April. If you have any questions, please write or call.

HIRING . . .

A Consultant

It gives me great pleasure to advise you that at the Friday meeting of our committee you were selected as research consultant for [NAME OF FIRM], effective October 1st. Our personnel office will answer all your questions about parking and work space, provide you with the necessary forms to be filled out, and so on. Please make an appointment with them by calling [NUMBER] at your earliest convenience.

We look forward to a long and mutually beneficial association.

A Firm

As I told you in our telephone conversation yesterday morning, we have decided to retain your firm to handle our publicity and public relations, beginning on September 9th. After one year we will review the association, and if it has worked out as well as we now are confident that it will, a more permanent arrangement will be considered.

Please call [NAME] at [PHONE NUMBER] to set up a meeting in the near future, so that you can begin giving our account the expert attention we are counting on you to provide.

We look forward to a long and mutually beneficial association.

A Professional

I am delighted to be able to inform you that at the Friday meeting of our search committee, after a lengthy review of all candidates, you were chosen by unanimous vote to fill the position of [TITLE OR DESCRIPTION] here at [NAME].

If you have any questions, please feel free to call me or one of my staff at any time. (Routine questions about parking, office space, and the like should of course be taken up with the Personnel Office, which is the authority on such matters.)

We look forward to having you with us, and we are sure that our association will be a long and mutually rewarding one.

A Service

I am writing to notify you that we wish to hire your service for all cleaning and custodial duties in our building at [ADDRESS], beginning on May 1st. Two copies of our contract are enclosed; please sign both and return them to us so that we may provide you with a signed copy for your files. If you have any questions, please call [NAME] at [NUMBER].

NVITING TO . . .

Join a Group

As you know, the Huntsville Friendship Club has been one of the most active civic organizations in this area for more than thirty years. Our record is outstanding, and I know you will agree that the community has benefited greatly from our projects.

We would like very much to have you with us as a member. If you would be interested, just give me a call at [NUMBER] anytime in the next week or two and we can talk about details. Or you could simply come to our next meeting and talk there. We meet on the second Monday of every month from 2:30 to 4:30 at [ADDRESS]. We'd be delighted to have you as our guest and to answer any questions you might have.

I look forward to hearing from you and to having you with us in the Friendship Club.

Breakfast, Lunch, Dinner, Etc.

I'm writing to invite you to join us at the Country Club on May 13th for an informal lunch to celebrate, [EVENT, OCCASION, ETC.]. We know you will want to be with us for the occasion, and we can promise an excellent meal and an interesting speaker. Dress casually, and be prepared to enjoy yourself.

If you can't join us, would you call [NAME] at [NUMBER] as soon as possible? If we don't hear from you, we'll look forward with great pleasure to seeing you at 1 P.M. on the 13th.

A Ceremony

On June 4th, at 11:00 A.M., our family and friends will be gathering at [LOCATION] to attend the christening of our first grandchild, [NAME OF CHILD]. We would be so pleased if you would join us on this very special occasion, and at the reception afterward.

Please RSVP by returning the card enclosed.

A Party

We've all been working too hard for too long—it's time for a party! [NAME OF HOSTS] have endorsed the idea by offering us their home at [ADDRESS] from 7 P.M. till midnight on June 17th. Join us there and help us show them our appreciation by bringing a covered dish or a dessert and having a wonderful time. Feel free to bring your children; a corps of expert teenagers will be providing child care. Directions for getting to the house are enclosed.

Please call [NAME] at [PHONE NUMBER] if you can't attend, or if you have any questions. We are looking forward to seeing you for a spectacular evening!

O FFERING . . .

Assistance

We were very distressed when we heard about your recent loss. We know how long you waited and planned for your lovely home; it doesn't seem possible that a fire could have taken it away from you so quickly.

No amount of sympathy will bring back your home or the possessions it contained. But you must have many problems with which we <u>could</u> help. Please don't hesitate to call us and tell us frankly what you need! If we can't manage it, we'll tell you so at once; otherwise, it would be our pleasure to help.

An Award or Prize

It gives us great pleasure to offer you three of our finest miniature rosebushes (already blooming in porcelain flowerpots) to be used as prizes at your Spring Fundraising Festival.

Tell us where and to whom we should deliver the roses and we'll see to it immediately. We are one hundred percent behind this event, which is so important for our community, and we wish you the best of luck.

Information

In response to your letter requesting information about our ballet school, I am sending you a complete information packet. It contains answers to all the questions parents ordinarily ask us. If you have questions it <u>doesn't</u> answer, please feel free to call me at [PHONE NUMBER], or make an appointment to stop by and talk to me here at the school.

Thank you for your query. I look forward to hearing from you.

A Product for Sale

Your name has been given to us by a mutual friend as someone with a sincere interest in the neglected art of lacemaking. We have a lacemaking kit that is available nowhere else. It is modestly priced at only $29.95, and contains everything you need to get started in lacemaking, including materials and instructions for three complete projects. A brochure is enclosed with this letter.

If you would be interested in this unusual kit, or in any of our other lacemaking products, just fill in the information on the order blank inside the brochure.

We would be very pleased to have you as a customer.

A Service

For a long time there has been a need in this area for convenient, reliable, affordable childcare. That need is now being filled. Beginning October 1st, the staff of [NAME OF COMPANY] will be ready to welcome you and your children to our new facility at [ADDRESS].

Because your children are so important to you, we know you will have many questions. We have tried to anticipate and answer them in the brochure enclosed with this letter—but there are sure to be some that didn't occur to us. We'll be delighted to talk with you at any time; just call us at [PHONE NUMBER] during regular business hours or any Saturday morning.

We look forward to serving you.

P RAISING . . .

With a Compliment

As you know, when you first joined us here at [NAME] we were all a little worried about how you would deal with the problem of communicating with our Spanish-speaking customers. Because you were so well qualified in every other way, and because we were so impressed by you, we took a chance. We hired you, because we were convinced that you would find a way.

Well, we were right. But you surprised us. It's a rare employee who would be willing to give us a 100 percent effort all day long and then go straight from work to a course in Conversational Spanish!

We just wanted you to know that we appreciate your willingness to go the extra mile.

* * *

As you know, when you first joined us here at [NAME] we were all a little worried about [DESCRIPTION OF PROBLEM]. Because you were so well qualified in every other way, and because we were so impressed by you, we took a chance. We hired you, because we were convinced that you would find a way.

Well, we were right. But you surprised us. It's a rare employee who [DESCRIPTION OF EMPLOYEE'S EFFORT TO DEAL WITH THE PROBLEM].

We just wanted you to know that we appreciate your willingness to go the extra mile.

With Encouragement

We know that it's been hard for you here at [NAME OF COMPANY] recently, because the change from typewriters to computers was made with so little notice and so little time to prepare.

We just want you to know that everyone in management is aware of the difficulties you are facing. We want you to know that we are absolutely certain you will be able to get past this performance barrier. And we want you to know that we are willing to give you as much time and support as you need. We are confident that in another few months you'll be wondering how you ever managed with a machine as primitive as a typewriter.

Keep up the good work!

With Congratulations

You can't imagine how happy everyone here at [NAME OF COMPANY] is about your recent appointment to the Board of Governors. We all know how long and hard you've worked for that appointment, and we know how much you deserve it. We're proud to have you on our team.

Congratulations!

REFUSING TO . . .

Accept a Job Offer

Thank you for your kind letter offering me a position as administrative assistant at [NAME OF COMPANY]. I am sorry to have to tell you that I cannot accept your offer because I have already found a position with another firm.

Attend

Thank you for your kind letter inviting me to attend the upcoming [NAME OF CONFERENCE]; I am most grateful to be asked. Unfortunately, however, the conference is scheduled on a weekend when I am already committed to present a workshop. Maybe next year!

I wish you the best of luck with your conference, and I am sorry that I will not be with you.

Buy a Product

Thank you for your recent letter offering us an opportunity to purchase your latest software product. It sounds like a real advance over existing products of the same kind, and we congratulate you on it. However, although we see the advantages that undoubtedly come with [NAME OF PROGRAM], we are happy with the program we're now using and we don't anticipate changing to any other system in the near future.

Best of luck with [NAME OF PROGRAM].

Contribute or Donate

Thank you for your very interesting letter describing your organization's efforts to renovate our downtown area. Certainly this is a commendable project, and you are to be congratulated on the design.

However, our company has decided that for the immediate future our charitable activities will be confined to those that address emergency needs, such as the famine in Africa. Downtown renovation, although desirable, does not meet this criterion, and will not, therefore, be receiving our support.

We wish you the best of luck with your project.

Help

Your letter of March 15th describing your recent loss arrived in our office today. It is clear that the fire at your plant caused you tremendous damage, and you have our sympathy.

However, because we are at the present time short-staffed and facing a discouraging economic climate, we will not be able to give you the temporary increased discount that you requested. We are sorry to refuse your request, and we wish that our own situation allowed us to respond differently.

We wish you the best of luck and a speedy rebuilding.

Hire

We have received your letter applying for the position of Manager Trainee here at [NAME OF FIRM] and enclosing your résumé. You appear to have all the necessary qualifications for the job, and we appreciate your interest. However, we regret to tell you that the job had been filled before your letter reached us.

Thank you for your interest in [NAME OF FIRM]. We wish you the best of luck in your search for employment.

Join a Group

Thank you for your kind letter of [DATE] inviting me to become a member of the Huntsville Friendship Club. I have always been greatly impressed with the work your organization does for Huntsville, and I consider it an honor to have been asked to join.

Unfortunately, I have just lost my administrative assistant and am facing the task of finding and training a replacement (as well as taking on many extra duties until that task is finished.) Under the circumstances, I don't feel that I could be a useful member of HFC; I just will not have enough time available.

Thank you again for asking me. I send my best wishes to you and to all the members.

Sell a Product or Property

Your letter asking me if I would be interested in selling my stamp collection to your firm arrived yesterday. The offer you make is very fair. However, at the present time I am not interested in selling my stamps. They are my only leisure-time activity and I would be most reluctant to give them up.

Thank you again for your offer.

Speak (Give a Talk) or Write (for Publication)

I was delighted to receive your recent letter asking me if I would be willing to speak to your class on the subject of growth stocks;/WRITE A BRIEF ARTICLE FOR YOUR NEWSLETTER ON THE SUBJECT OF GROWTH STOCKS; thank you for asking me. Unfortunately, my current schedule is so full that adding even one more task is impossible. You would be far better served by a speaker/WRITER who could give the preparation for the talk/PREPARATION OF THE ARTICLE the time and attention it deserves.

You might consider asking John Smith, at [NAME OF FIRM], who is well known in this area as an expert on growth stocks. Please feel free to tell him that I suggested his name if you wish.

RESIGNING FROM . . .

A Board, Committee, Task Force, Etc.

It is with much regret that I write to advise you of my resignation from [NAME], effective immediately. I have enjoyed being a member of the group and I feel that I have learned a great deal from the experience; I will certainly miss our meetings.

Unfortunately, my duties during the construction of our new headquarters building will require me to be available on site almost twenty-four hours a day. This will make it impossible for me to give adequate attention to anything else for many months, and you would be badly served if I tried to remain a member.

Please pass along my regards and my regrets to all the other members, with my best wishes for the future.

A Job

It is with much regret that I write to advise you of my resignation from [NAME OF COMPANY], effective March 25th. As you know, when I joined this firm I fully expected to remain here until retirement. But the recent bad news from my doctor has forced me to change my mind. He tells me that I must find a position that does not require me to travel, and I respect his judgment.

I have enjoyed my years here very much, and I hate to leave. I'm sure you know that. In the meantime, if I can do anything to help with the tiresome task of finding and training a replacement, just let me know.

An Organization

It is with much regret that I write to let you know that I must resign from [NAME OF GROUP] at the end of this month. When I became a member, the group's goals were <u>my</u> goals, and I felt that I could be an effective member. The direction of the group has changed over the years, however, and I am no longer able to participate with whole-hearted enthusiasm. In fact, I have recently found myself obliged to work for objectives to which I was actually opposed. Under the circumstances, it's best that I not continue as a member.

I have enjoyed being part of [NAME OF GROUP]. I wish you the best of luck in the future.

RECOMMENDING . . .

A Person

I am writing to recommend [NAME], who is applying for a position with your firm as Technical Supervisor. I have known [NAME] for more than ten years, both as a colleague and as a friend, and I can recommend him to you without reservation. He is capable and efficient and conscientious. In addition, he has the ability to maintain strong friendships even with those who may not see eye to eye with him at all times; in my experience, this is a rare and valuable skill.

If I can provide you with any additional information, or answer any questions you may have, please do not hesitate to write me at the above address or to call me at [PHONE NUMBER].

A Place

Our mutual friend, [NAME], tells me that you have been trying unsuccessfully to find a summer camp for your children that would meet all your needs without costing a small fortune. I know what this search is like; I've been there. Perhaps I can be of assistance.

My own children have been spending a month or more of every summer at [NAME OF CAMP], near [LOCA-TION]. The counselors and the program there are superb, the facilities are much better than average, the fees are reasonable, and our children look forward to their stay each year with real eagerness. So far as I know, the only negative feature is food that my kids describe as "boring"; that hasn't kept them from wanting to return year after year.

If you'd like to look into [NAME OF CAMP], you can call the owners at [PHONE NUMBER] almost any time. Please feel free to tell them I recommended the camp to you if you wish.

A Procedure

It has recently come to my attention that your division is having trouble with [NAME OF EQUIPMENT]. The problems described are ones I am familiar with, since we struggled with them here for a number of years.

I strongly recommend that you remove [NAME OF PART] and replace it with [NAME OF PART]. We did that, and the results were amazing; all the problems we'd been having with the equipment came to an end after we made that one change.

CHARLOTTE,

FEW THINGS IN LIFE ARE MORE DIFFICULT ~~REQUIRE~~ to ENDURE THAN THE LOSS OF A LOVED ONE. I HOPE ~~YOU ARE SOME GOOD AND~~ ~~TAKE SOME COMFORT~~ YOUR EFFORTS to DO SO ARE SOMEHOW ENHANCED BY THE KNOWLEDGE THAT YOUR FRIENDS & COWORKERS SUPPORT YOU & WOULD APPRECIATE ANY OPPTY TO HELP. ~~IF ANY OF US CAN DO~~ ANYTHING TO HELP, PLEASE ~~DON'T HESITATE~~ TO ASK. PLS ACCEPT MY SINCEREST CONDOLENCES. TJ

977-6163

If I can give you any additional information or help in any way, feel free to call me at [PHONE NUMBER].

A Product

I don't ordinarily take it upon myself to suggest to other people what they should buy; I don't feel that that's my role in this world. However, on a rare occasion like this one, when I've come across a product that I feel would be genuinely helpful to a colleague, keeping the information to myself seems like selfishness.

[NAME], I strongly recommend the new padded envelopes that [NAME OF COMPANY] has just come out with. We tried them here when the brand we'd been using was discontinued, and we were amazed. They not only look good and stand up to the most brutal mailing conditions, they actually do both those things at substantially less cost. I know how much product you ship, and I know what the prices for shipping supplies are like. I think you'd find these envelopes as much of an improvement over everything else available as we do.

SYMPATHIZING ABOUT . . .

A Death

Nothing anyone can say will ease the sorrow that you feel at this moment. I won't try to come up with any magic words, because there aren't any. I only want you to know that everyone here sends you their deepest sympathy. Don was a wonderful man, and much loved; we will miss him more than I can say.

If we can do anything to help, please don't hesitate to ask.

A Disaster

We all know what terrible damage tornadoes can do; we see it on the news and hear about it on the radio. But when it happens to someone we know, it somehow seems unbelievable—we take it for granted that disasters happen only to strangers.

[NAME], there's nothing we can do to bring back the home you've lost, or the possessions it contained. There's nothing we can do to remove the memory of the terror you must have felt as the storm approached. We just wanted to let you know that our hearts go out to you, and that we are thinking of you. Please let us know if there is anything we can do to help.

A Failure or Lost Job

Failure hurts. <u>Any</u> failure hurts. When it's the loss of a business that has been your life's work, the pain can be almost too much to bear. When we heard about the trouble you were having, we felt that we had to write and offer our sympathy. We know you'll come out of this and go on to even greater things, but that's not a heck of a lot of comfort to you right now. Right now, I'm sure things look very black.

Let us know, [NAME], if there is anything we can do to help.

* * *

Losing a job hurts. Losing <u>any</u> job hurts. When it's a job you've waited for for years and have always wanted, losing it can seem like an almost unbearable setback. [BALANCE OF LETTER AS ABOVE.]

An Illness

Few things are more frustrating than an illness that just seems to come along out of nowhere, and of course no illness ever comes at a convenient time. I know that for you this is one of the worst possible times, because you were just beginning to see real progress in [DESCRIPTION OF PROJECT] and this hit you with no warning and no time to prepare.

If I can help, please don't hesitate to ask. Like everyone who knows and loves you, I send my sympathy and my warmest best wishes. Please take care of yourself and get well as quickly as you can.

THANKING FOR . . .

Assistance

I don't know how we could possibly have gotten through this past month if we hadn't had your generous help. First there was the fire, then the hassle with the insurance and the government, and then there was the task of moving to a new location. At every stage, you were there with the one thing we needed most: your experience with the same problems. Your patience has been remarkable; I know there have been times when our lack of that quality has made us seem ungrateful. You were right every time!

There's no way we can repay you for your help. The last thing we want is for you to need our help. But we can tell you how much it has meant to us to have you right there for us through this difficult time. And we can tell you that if, God forbid, you should ever find yourself facing serious trouble, you can count on us to be there for you.

Contribution or Donation

I am writing to thank you for your recent generous donation of [AMOUNT OR DESCRIPTION]. Without people like you, we could not even begin to accomplish our goals. We thank you from the bottom of our hearts.

A Gift

You can't imagine how surprised I was to come back to my desk today and find your wonderful gift! How did you know that I have always wanted [DESCRIPTION OF GIFT]? You are a dear friend, and I cannot thank you enough.

An Invitation

Your letter asking me to the dinner on January 9th arrived this morning, just in time to brighten an otherwise gloomy day. Of course I'll come; I'd love to. Thank you for asking me.

A Job Offer

Thank you for your kind letter offering me a position as [NAME OF POSITION] at [NAME OF COMPANY]. I accept with pleasure, and I will get in touch with your personnel department immediately to take care of all the details.

I look forward to working with you/working at [NAME OF COMPANY].

A Speech or Presentation, or Something Written for Publication

It gives me great pleasure to write and tell you how much everyone here enjoyed your speech on retirement investment strategies./the article you wrote for us on retirement investment strategies. I can honestly say that I remember no previous speaker/writer who had such an enthusiastic response from our people.

Thank you very much for sharing your ideas with us and for being so effective and compelling. I hope you will allow us to call on you again at a later date.

A Suggestion

I am writing to thank you for your suggestion about the mailing envelopes. We've tried fifteen different kinds, each seemingly more annoying and more expensive than the one before. You are absolutely right—the [NAME OF PRODUCT] is what we've been looking for all along.

If you have any more suggestions like this up your sleeve, [NAME], please send them along. You'll find us most appreciative.

WELCOMING . . .

A Colleague

We are delighted to know that you are going to join our department. Welcome aboard!

If we can do anything to help you settle in, don't hesitate to ask. We look forward to a long and mutually enjoyable association.

An Employee

It gives me great pleasure to welcome you to [NAME OF COMPANY]. I know that you are going to enjoy working here as much as we will enjoy having you on our team.

Let us know if there is anything we can do to help you settle in.

A Member

On behalf of all the members of [NAME OF ORGANIZATION], I am writing to extend to you our warmest and most enthusiastic welcome. We are delighted to have you join us.

We look forward to seeing you at the next meeting, which will be on [DATE] at [TIME], in the usual place. In the meantime, if there is any information we can give you or any question we can answer about the group, please don't hesitate to call.

A Visitor

On behalf of the entire company, I want to welcome you to [NAME OF COMPANY]. We've been looking forward to having you here and to showing you around our facility for a very long time. It's great that you're here at last.

Please don't hesitate to let us know if there is anything at all we can do to make your stay more pleasant or more informative. [NAME] will be your official liaison person, but anyone at [NAME OF COMPANY] would be more than happy to lend a hand.

Thank you for accepting our invitation and sharing your limited time with us; we appreciate it.

Appendix B

A Brief Guide
to Punctuation

*S*ome languages (French, for example) use punctuation partly to indicate how words are pronounced or to provide historical information. For English, however, almost all punctuation marks serve just one purpose: They are used to *write down body language*, including the intonation of the voice. (The exception is the *apostrophe*.) As you might expect, this leads to confusion, because different people have different body language dialects and because the set of punctuation marks is too small to transmit the information needed. Nevertheless, it's helpful to keep the basic principle in mind when you select punctuation. Remembering a list of seemingly arbitrary rules is difficult for everyone; remembering that the rules are based on the goal of writing down body language is easy, and adds a significant amount of clarification.

THE MOST FREQUENTLY NEEDED PUNCTUATION MARKS

Apostrophe

The apostrophe doesn't reflect body language. It has three functions. It's used to mean "Something has been left out at this point," as in contractions, and to indicate the English possessive.

- "I'm"—The apostrophe marks the "a" left out from "I am."

- "John's"—The apostrophe means that whatever follows belongs to John.

When using a typewriter or computer, it's also the symbol used for a quotation inside another quotation.

Comma

A comma is a picture of a short pause inside a sentence.

- *To indicate your approval, please initial the memo.*

Colon

A colon is a picture of a very formal pause that is inside a sentence and is followed by an example, a quotation, or a list.

- *This contract has a single purpose: to repair the shortfall in engine maintenance.*
- *As the president said: "No one can predict the future."*
- *This document has three parts: a brief introduction; a main text, which is divided into several subsections; and a concluding section that incorporates a budget.*

Dash

A dash is a picture of a long and usually informal pause inside a sentence; it is used sparingly in business letters. (Use two hyphens together if you don't have a dash character on your typewriter or in your software.)

- *People arriving at our plant—which, given its isolated location, may be difficult to find—should go directly to the conference room.*

Dots

A series of four or more dots is a picture of a long and *dramatic* pause inside or at the end of a sentence; this almost never is found in business letters.

- *The fire was a catastrophe . . . . . there is no other way to describe it.*

A series of exactly three dots (called an *ellipsis*) means "I have left out part of this quotation at this point."

- *According to the CEO, "Anyone who was sufficiently motivated to follow through would have . . . discovered the error."*

Exclamation Point

An exclamation point means, "If these words were being spoken, they would sound excited, angry, surprised, or alarmed."

- *These delays in customer service will not be tolerated!*

Parentheses

Parentheses mean "This information is something I could leave out; I'm including it just in case you might find it useful."

- *At the end of the sales period (which is sometimes cut by three days to allow for in-service training) all ledgers are closed.*

Period

A period is a picture of a pause at the end of a sentence; it means "This sentence is finished." It usually indicates a drop in the pitch of the voice.

- *We have fulfilled our contract with your firm.*

Periods are also used to signal the end of an abbreviation.

- *"Mr."*

Question Mark

A question mark means "I am requesting information from you." (If the information requested is only "yes" or "no," a question mark is a picture of a voice rising in pitch.)

- *What was the date of your most recent order?*

Quotation Marks

Quotation marks usually mean "These words were not spoken by me, I am only reporting them."

- *Phil said, "There was no one in the office when I arrived."*

Quotation marks are also used to mean that the words inside them should be considered "so-called" or "alleged," or to mark a sequence as an <u>example</u>.

- *We are told that he is the "director" of a "conglomerate."*

Quotation marks <u>never</u> mean "What's inside these marks is important, and I want to call it to your attention!"

- *Order now and get your "free" issue!* (This would mean that the issue was only allegedly free.)

<u>Single</u> quotation marks mean "This is a quotation inside another quotation." You will very rarely need them in a business letter.

- *According to R&D's assistant manager, "Nobody heard Tutwiler say 'Don't put medical waste in the red bins!' at Thursday's meeting."*

Semicolon

A semicolon is a picture of a pause between two or more sequences that could stand alone as independent sentences. It means "These sentences are so closely related that I'm treating them like just one sentence."

- *We have run into significant delays on this project; we have had to listen to many complaints; we intend to complete it on time, nevertheless.*

A semicolon also signals the brief pauses after items in a list that follows a colon.

- *There are six divisions here at Brand & Brand: two for sales; two for maintenance; an engineering division; and a legal department.*

Appendix C

Glossary

ADJECTIVE.   An adjective is a word that <u>describes</u> another word or group of words; "blue, little, interesting, obvious, expensive" are all adjectives.

AWKWARD (when used to describe a sentence).   A sentence is awkward when one or more of its parts exceeds the limits of the short-term memory. For example: "That John would insist on going fishing over the weekend in spite of the fact that he hasn't yet written his speech for Monday night is difficult to understand." In this sentence a twenty-five word subject has to be held in the short-term memory until the predicate "is difficult to understand" is reached. The capacity of the short-term memory is only seven, plus or minus two.

COMPLIMENTARY CLOSE.   The complimentary close is the word or words used after the final sentence of a letter, such as "Sincerely" or "Very truly yours."

CONTINUUM.   A continuum is a <u>range</u> of items or values, from one extreme, such as "least complicated," to the other, such as "most complicated."

DOMINANCE DISPLAY.   Dominance displays are actions carried out to demonstrate power over a particular territory, product, object, etc.

EMBEDDED SENTENCE.   An embedded sentence is a sentence inside a larger sentence; it may or may not be a sentence that could stand alone. In "The idea that Janet had cancelled the order was absurd," the embedded sentence is "Janet had cancelled the order."

EMPHATIC STRESS. Emphatic stress is extra emphasis given to words or parts of words by a speaker; it is <u>perceived</u> as slightly higher pitch, a bit more volume (loudness), and perhaps longer duration. It's signaled in written English by underlining or italics.

FACTIVES. Factives are words or phrases (most often verbs or adjectives) which, when an embedded sentence follows them, presuppose that the embedded sentence is true. In both "We regret that all the tickets have been sold" and "We do not regret that all the tickets have been sold" the factive is "regret," and the embedded sentence "all the tickets have been sold" is presupposed to be true.

FLUB. A flub is an error made when you think you know what to do, you do it, and it turns out that you <u>shouldn't</u> have done it.

FLOUNDER. A flounder is an error made when you don't know what to do but you feel that you have to do <u>something</u>, and you do it—and it turns out that you shouldn't have done it.

FOCUS (of a sentence). The focus of a sentence is that part of the sentence that the speaker wants to give the most importance to. In "It was the <u>warehouse</u> that lost the order" the focus is on the warehouse; in "The order was lost by the warehouse" the focus is on the order.

FRAILTY. A frailty is an error that is made through no fault of your own, as a result of circumstances beyond your control, including the fact that you are a human being with the normal flaws of a human being.

GRAMMAR. A grammar is the set of rules that a speaker of a language uses to produce or understand that language.

HEDGES. Hedges are an irritating linguistic device that allows speakers to say something they know will provoke a negative response and at the same time state that negative response for the listener in advance. For example: "I know this is a stupid question, but what's a leveraged buyout?"

ILLUSION OF CHOICE. Illusion of choice (from the work of Gregory Bateson and his associates) is a strategy for offering someone a choice as part of a larger utterance about which there is no choice. For example: "While you are in Detroit closing the Hartwelle account, would you rather stay at the airport Hilton or go into town to the Hyatt?" The question presupposes that the listener will go to Detroit and close the account, offering no choice; the illusion of choice is provided by letting the listener choose between the two hotels.

INDEFINITES.   Indefinites are words or phrases referring to some entity that is identified only in general terms; "someone, something, everybody, everything," are indefinites.

INTERNALIZE.   When you learn something so completely that you do not have to use the information or rehearse it in order to remember it, you have internalized that information. Your native language is an example.

INTONATION.   The intonation of a sentence or language sequence is the tune to which the words it contains are set—its melodic pattern.

LANGUAGE INTERACTION.   A language interaction is any situation in which two or more human beings attempt to communicate by language, such as a conversation, an interview, an argument, etc.

LANGUAGE PROCESSING.   Language processing is the set of acts carried out by human beings in order to speak, listen to, understand, remember, read, write, and sign language.

METAMESSAGE.   A metamessage is a message about some other message or messages. When you say "Close that sale!" the metamessages include I ORDER YOU TO DO THIS, and I HAVE THE RIGHT TO GIVE YOU THIS ORDER.

METASTRATEGY.   A metastrategy is a strategy for dealing with another strategy or strategies. A strategy used to decide which of a set of three other strategies to use would be a metastrategy.

NOMINALIZATION.   Nominalization is a process by which something that is not a nominal is turned into one. "Abandon" is a verb; to nominalize it so that it can be used the way a noun or noun phrase is used, you add the ending "-ment" ("abandonment of a patient is illegal") or "-ing" ("abandoning a patient is illegal.")

NOMINAL. A nominal is a word or group of words that can be used as the subject of a sentence or can fill any other role in a sentence that a noun could fill.

PARALLELISM. Parallelism is a language device that matches words or sequences of language in their structure as closely as possible. "We are here to find the problem, to locate its cause, and to solve it once and for all" uses parallelism. "We are here to find the problem, and then we'll locate the cause and a final solution will be put in place" does not use parallelism.

PLAGIARISM. When speakers or writers use someone else's words and behave as if the words are their own, that is called plagiarism. Oddly enough, the term is not used when a professional speechwriter or ghostwriter has been hired to produce the language.

POSSESSIVES. Possessives are the set of forms used to indicate that something is owned by, or belongs to, or is part of, an individual or entity. They include the possessive pronouns "his, her, its, my, etc." the apostrophe plus "s" as in "Jack's" and "the company's," and the word "of" followed by the possessor, as in "the color of the envelope."

PREDICATE. The word "predicate" has two common meanings. (1) A predicate is everything in a sentence except its subject. In "John left one of our most important files in a subway station," the predicate is "left one of our most important files in subway station." (2) A predicate is one of the set of items that can follow the subject of a sentence. This includes verbs ("John resigned"), adjectives ("John is tired"), noun phrases of location in time or place ("The meeting is in Los Angeles" or "The meeting is on June 10th"), and noun phrases that identify the subject ("John is an engineer.")

PREPOSITION. Prepositions are the set of words English uses to indicate what role a nominal is filling in a sentence. In "We wrote the book with a word processor," the preposition "with" tells you that "a word processor" fills the role of INSTRUMENT (what is used to carry out the action.)

PRESUPPOSITION. A presupposition, in the *Gentle Art of Verbal Self-Defense* system, is anything that a native speaker of a language knows is part of the meaning of a sequence of that language even when it does not appear on the surface of the sequence. "We stopped producing implants" presupposes that you <u>started</u> producing them.

SALUTATION. The salutation is the opening words of a letter, before its first sentence, addressed to the reader. For example: "Dear Mr. Jones:"

SHORT-TERM MEMORY. The short-term (also called "working") memory is the part of memory you use to hold information while you process it for storage. For example, to remember a phone number from the time you look it up until you dial it, you use your short-term memory. The rest of your memory is called your <u>long-term</u> memory.

SPEECH ACT. A speech act is the action that is represented by a word or group of words. Speech acts include commands, questions, threats, etc.

UTTERANCE. An utterance is any word or sequence of words said by a speaker.

VAPs (VERBAL ATTACK PATTERNS). The English VAPs are sentence patterns used to hold the attention of a listener, demonstrate power over the listener, and carry hostile messages. They always contain unusually strong emphatic stress on words or parts of words. "If you REALLY wanted to make that sale, YOU wouldn't dress like a THUG!" is an example.

VERBS. A verb is one of the possible predicate types. In English, any word you can add "–ing" to is a verb.

WORKING MEMORY. See "short-term memory."

Appendix D

The Gentle Art
of Verbal Self-Defense—
an Overview

*J*ust as there is a grammar of English for such things as verb endings and the order of words in sentences, there is a grammar of English for verbal violence and verbal self-defense. All native speakers of English know this grammar flawlessly, although many factors—such as stress, nervousness, illness, lack of time, and the like—interfere with their demonstration of that flawless knowledge. The problem is that the information is not available at a level of conscious awareness, and people cannot therefore conveniently make use of it. The *Gentle Art* system is designed to correct this problem.

When you use this system, you won't be restricted to sarcastic comebacks and counterattacks when you're involved in verbal confrontations. Instead, you will be able to create for yourself a language environment in which such confrontations will be very <u>rare</u>. And when they do occur you will be able to deal with them quickly and competently, with no sacrifice of your own self-respect, and no loss of face on either side of the interaction.

This is a brief overview of the basic concepts of the system, together with three examples of techniques for putting it to use. (For complete information about these and other techniques, please refer to the books in the *Gentle Art of Verbal Self-Defense* series.)

REFERENCE ITEMS

The Four Basic Principles

ONE: *KNOW THAT YOU ARE UNDER ATTACK*
TWO: *KNOW WHAT KIND OF ATTACK YOU ARE FACING*
THREE: *KNOW HOW TO MAKE YOUR DEFENSE FIT THE ATTACK*
FOUR: *KNOW HOW TO FOLLOW THROUGH*

The first principle is important—because most verbal victims are not aware that they are victims. Typically, they feel miserable but they don't know why, and they tend to blame not those who abuse them but themselves.

The second and third principles work together, to help you tailor your responses. When you learn to recognize language modes (like the Sensory and Satir Modes described below) and to construct responses based on rules for their use, you are applying these two principles.

The fourth principle is often the hardest. There are two barriers to its implementation: (1) The idea that if you don't participate in the power game of verbal abuse you are letting the abuser "get away with it"; and (2) the problem of feeling guilty about defending yourself (especially common among women.)

Miller's Law

"In order to understand what another person is saying, you must assume that it is true and try to imagine what it could be true of." (George Miller, 1980)

Elgin's Corollary

In order for other people to understand what you are saying, you must make it possible for them to apply Miller's Law to your language.

Syntonics

Syntonics, in the *Gentle Art* system, is the science of language harmony. The name is taken from the term "syntonic," used in radio telegraphy to describe two radio sets sufficiently well tuned to one another to allow the efficient and effective transmission of information. When people attempt to communicate with each other, they need to try for a similar syntonic state.

Presupposition

A presupposition is anything that a native speaker of a language knows is part of the meaning of a sequence of that language even when it does not appear on the surface of the sequence. For example: Every native speaker of English knows that the meaning of the sentence "EVen JOHN could pass THAT course!" includes two more propositions saying that the class is somehow second-rate and so is John. The sentence means: "Even John (who, as everybody knows, is no great shakes as a student) could pass that course (which, as everybody knows, is a really trivial class.)" But the negative comments about John and the course are not there in the surface structure of the sentence; they are presupposed.

Most verbal attacks, with the exception of the very crudest ones, are at least partly hidden away in presuppositions.

First Technique—Using the Sensory Modes

Human beings can't survive without information. We need data from the outside environment and from our bodies; we need data from other human beings and living creatures. And we need a system for managing all this data, or it would be impossible to deal with. Information that's coming in has to be processed. It must be selected, and understood, and then either discarded or indexed for storage in memory. Information going out has to be processed also, so that it can be expressed for other people to understand. Our primary tool for this processing is the set of sensory systems—sight and hearing and touch, taste and smell, etc.

Each of us has a preferred sensory system that we find easiest to use, and that helps us the most in understanding and remembering. And when we express ourselves, we often demonstrate that preference by using one of the language behavior modes called Sensory Modes. Like this—

SIGHT: "I really like the way this looks."

HEARING: "This just sounds great to me."

TOUCH: "I don't feel right about this."

SMELL: "This whole plan smells fishy to me."

TASTE: "This leaves an awful taste in my mouth."

People who hear you matching their preferred Sensory Modes are more likely to trust you and to listen to what you say. They think of you as someone who speaks their language and shares their perceptions. This is the easiest of all the *Gentle Art* techniques, and it is one that you can put to use immediately.

Under normal circumstances, people can switch from one Sensory Mode to another without any difficulty. But when they're under stress they tend to get locked in to their preferred mode. The more upset they are, the more trouble they will have understanding communication in other Sensory Modes, and the more trouble they will have using other Sensory Modes to express themselves. In such situations, you will improve communication drastically if you <u>match</u> the Sensory Mode the other person is using.

You'll have no trouble identifying the Sensory Mode coming at you. Because you are a fluent speaker of English, you'll do this automatically. You can then tailor your own response for maximum efficiency and effectiveness by following two simple rules.

RULE ONE: *MATCH THE SENSORY MODE COMING AT YOU.*

RULE TWO: *IF YOU CAN'T FOLLOW RULE ONE, USE NO SENSORY MODE LANGUAGE AT ALL.*

SECOND TECHNIQUE—USING THE SATIR MODES

Dr. Virginia Satir was a world-famous family therapist. As she worked with clients, she noticed that the language behavior of people under stress tends to fall into one of the following five categories, which we call the <u>Satir Modes</u>.

Blaming

"WHY don't you ever think about anybody ELSE's feelings? DON'T you even CARE ABOUT OTHER PEOPLE?"

Placating

"Oh, YOU know how I am! Shoot—whatever YOU want to do is okay with ME!"

Computing

"There is undoubtedly a good reason for this delay. No sensible person would be upset."

Distracting

"WHAT IS THE MATTER with you, ANYway? Not that I care! YOU know me—I can put up with ANYthing! However, common sense would indicate that the original agreement should be followed."

Leveling

"I like you. But I don't like your methods."

Each of the Satir Modes has a characteristic style of body language. Blamers shake their fists or their index fingers; they scowl and frown and loom over people. Placaters cling and fidget and lean on others. Computers are stiff and rigid, moving as little as possible. Distracters cycle through the other Modes with their bodies just as they do with their words. The body language of Levelers is distinguished by the absence of these other patterns, and by the fact that it's not in conflict with their words.

The first four Satir Modes are examples of the lack of a personal syntonic state. People use Blamer Mode because they are insecure and afraid that nobody will respect or obey them. They use Placater Mode—saying that they don't care—because they care so very much. They use Computer Mode—saying "I have no emotions"—because they are aware of an emotion they actually feel and are unwilling to let it show. Distracter Mode cycles through all of these states of mismatch and expresses panic. Only with Leveler Mode (or with Computer Mode used deliberately for strategic reasons) do you have a syntonic state. To the extent that they are capable of accurately judging their own feelings, people using Leveler Mode use words and body language that match those feelings.

As with the Sensory Modes, people can ordinarily switch from one Satir Mode to the other, but they tend to become locked in to preferred Satir Modes in situations of tension and stress.

The rules for using the Satir Modes are based on the same metaprinciple as those for using Sensory Modes: ANYTHING YOU

FEED WILL GROW. When you match a language pattern coming at you, you feed it and it escalates. The difference between the two techniques is that it's always a good thing to match another person's Sensory Mode—because increasing the level of trust and rapport is always a good thing—but you should only match a Satir Mode if you want the behavior it produces to grow. Here are the results you can expect from feeding the Satir Modes.

BLAMING AT A BLAMER causes fights and scenes.

PLACATING AT A PLACATER causes undignified delay.

COMPUTING AT A COMPUTER causes dignified delay.

DISTRACTING AT A DISTRACTER is panic feeding panic.

LEVELING AT A LEVELER means an exchange of the simple truth, going both ways.

In any language interaction, once you've recognized the Satir Mode coming at you, you have to choose your response. You make your choice based on the situation, on what you know about the other person, and on your own communication goals. Here are the two rules you need.

RULE ONE: *IF YOU DON'T KNOW WHAT TO DO, USE COMPUTER MODE.*

RULE TWO: *IF IT WOULD BE DESIRABLE TO HAVE THE SATIR MODE COMING AT YOU ESCALATE, MATCH THAT MODE.*

THIRD TECHNIQUE: RECOGNIZING AND RESPONDING TO THE VERBAL ATTACK PATTERNS OF ENGLISH

Many people don't realize that they are verbal victims because the verbal abuse they're subjected to isn't <u>openly</u> abusive. Most verbal abusers don't just spit out curses and insults. Instead, they use verbal attack patterns (VAPs) that are part of the grammar of English verbal violence. These patterns are just as dangerous as shouted obscenities, but much more subtle.

The attack patterns discussed below have two parts. There is the BAIT, which the attacker expects you to respond to. It's easy to recognize, because it's the part that <u>hurts</u>. And then there is the attack that matters, which is usually hidden away in the form of one or more presuppositions. Here's an example.

"If you REALLY loved me, YOU wouldn't waste MONEY the way you do!"

The bait is the part about wasting money; it's what your attacker expects you to respond to. You're expected to take the bait and say, "What do you MEAN, I waste money! I DO NOT!" And then you're off to a flaming row, which is a poor way to handle the situation.

The important part of the attack is not the bait, but the pre-supposition at the beginning—"YOU DON'T REALLY LOVE ME." Instead of taking the bait, respond directly to that presupposed attack. Say "When did you start thinking that I don't really love you?" or "Of course I love you!" This is not what the attacker expects, and it will short-circuit the confrontation.

Here are some other examples of English VAPs. For complete information about these attacks, and suggested responses, please refer to the books in the series.

"If you REALLY wanted me to get good grades, YOU'D buy me a comPUTer like all the OTHER kids have got!"

"A person who REALLY cared about his health wouldn't WANT to smoke!"

"DON'T you even CARE if the neighbors are all LAUGH-ING AT US?"

"EVen a woman YOUR age should be able to cook LUNCH!"

"EVerybody underSTANDS why you're so TOUCHY, dear!"

"WHY don't you ever LISTEN to me when I talk to you?"

"YOU'RE not the ONly person with PROBlems, you know!"

"You could at LEAST get to WORK on time!"

"EVEN if you DO forget my birthday, I'LL still love you!"

It's important to realize that what makes these examples attacks is not the words they contain. For English, more than half of the information is not in the words but in the body language, including the intonation of the voice. To recognize a verbal attack, you have to pay attention to the intonation—the melody of the voice—that goes with the words. Any time you hear a lot of extra stresses and emphasis on words or parts of words, you should be on the alert.

THERE IS NO MORE IMPORTANT CUE TO RECOGNIZING VERBAL ATTACKS THAN ABNORMAL STRESS PATTERNS

The sentence, "Why do you eat so much junk food?" may be very rude and unkind, but it's not a verbal attack. The attack that goes with those words sounds like this: "WHY do you eat SO MUCH JUNK food?"

In dealing with verbal attack patterns, you have three rules to follow. Here they are:

RULE ONE: **IGNORE THE BAIT**

RULE TWO: **RESPOND DIRECTLY TO THE ATTACK HIDDEN IN THE PRESUPPOSITION(S)**

RULE THREE: **NO MATTER WHAT ELSE YOU DO, SAY SOMETHING THAT TRANSMITS THIS MESSAGE: "DON'T TRY THAT WITH ME—I WON'T PLAY THAT GAME."**

Nobody can carry on a verbal attack alone. It takes two people—one to be the attacker, and one to be the victim.

People who use verbal abuse do so because they want the fight or the scene—they want your <u>attention</u>—and they enjoy the havoc they create. When you take the bait in their attacks and go along with their plans, you aren't showing them how strong and assertive you are, you are giving them exactly what they want. And the more you do that, the worse the situation will get.

EVERY TIME YOU TAKE THE BAIT IN A VERBAL ATTACK, YOU ARE PARTICIPATING IN A SELF-REINFORCING FEEDBACK LOOP.

Instead of doing that, use this third technique and break out of the loop. That's not "letting them get away with it." Letting them sucker you into an ugly row, giving them your attention on demand, playing verbal victim for them: <u>That</u> is letting them get away with it.

For more techniques in the *Gentle Art* system, see any of the books and audio programs in the series; for additional information, write to Dr. Elgin at the Ozark Center for Language Studies (OCLS), P.O. Box 1137, Huntsville, AR 72740-1137.

Index

A

Abusive language. *See* Verbal attack patterns
Accommodations, complaints about, 222–223
Account, application for, 218
Accounts receivable
    notice of check returned, 220–221
    notices of past due account, 221
Adjective, use of, 249
Anecdotes, use of, 136–137
Anniversary
    announcement of, 216
    congratulations on, 220
Announcement, letters of, 214–217
Apostrophe, use of, 245
Application, letters of, 217–220
Assistance
    offering of, 230
    refusal of, 234–235
    request for, 209–210
    thank you for, 241
As you know strategy, 33
Attendance, refusal of, 233–234
Awards
    announcement of, 214
    offering of, 231
Awkward sentences, 125–126, 249

B

Barter of goods, letter for, 214
Bateson, Gregory, 81
Behavior, complaints about, 223
Birth, announcement of, 214
Birthday, congratulations on, 220
Blaming, nature of, 45, 48, 256, 257
Block format, business letters, 208
Board, resignation from, 236
Body language, Satir Modes, 258
Business letters

block format, 208
closers, 207–208
generic business letter pattern, 206–208
indented format, 209
openers, 206–208
types of, 206

C

Celebration, letters of, 220
Ceremony, invitation to, 230
Check returned, notice of, 220–221
Choice, illusion of, 81–84
Code, writing in, 103–105
Colleague, welcome to, 243
Collection letters, 220–222
College admission, application for, 217–218
Colon, 187
    use of, 246
Comma, use of, 246
Committee, resignation from, 236
Complaints
    letters of, 222–226
    triple–F message pattern for, 191–193
Compliments
    group compliment, 137
    praise with, 232–233
Computing
    basic principle of, 50–53
    examples of, 44, 59, 175–176
    nature of, 46–47, 50–51, 258
Congratulations, letter of, 233
Consultant, hiring of, 227–228
Contribution
    refusal of, 234
    request for, 210–211
    thank you for, 24
Cover letters, 28–90

Credit, application for, 218

D

Dash, use of, 246
Death
   announcement of, 215
   sympathy letter, 239
Disaster, sympathy about, 239–240
Disclaimers, writing of, 162–163
Distracting, nature of, 45–46, 258
Divorce, announcement of, 215
Documents, letter asking for, 211
Dominance displays, 153, 249
   reasons for use, 80
   writing with, 80–81
Donation
   refusal of, 234
   request for, 210–211
   thank you for, 241
Dots, *See* Ellipsis
Dues, past due, 222

E

Elgin's Corollary, 255
Ellipsis, use of, 246
Embedded sentence, 123
   nature of, 249–250
Emotional distance, creation of, 51–53
Emphatic stress, nature of, 250
Employee
   firing, 226–227
   welcome to, 243
Encouragement, letter of, 233
Exceptions, making exceptions in
      speech, 49
Exclamation point, use of, 246–247

F

Factives
   nature of, 250
   and presuppositions, 17–18
Failure, sympathy letter for, 240
Firing
   letters for, 226–227
   long–term employee, 226–227
   recently hired employee, 226
Firm
   discontinuing service of, 227

hiring of, 228
Flounder, nature of, 250
Flub, nature of, 250
Focus
   marking focus, 28
   meaning of, 250
   shifting focus, 28–33, 51–52
   See also Shifting focus
Formality, 108–110
   continuum for, 108–109
   example of, 109, 120–121
   and sentence structure, 122–125
   word choices related to, 110, 122
Forms, letter asking for, 211
Frailty, definition of, 250

G

Gender and communication, 176–177
   genderlects, existence of, 177
   and written language, 177
Generics, to create emotional distance,
   53
Gift, thank you for, 241
Gift letters
   analysis of, 201–204
   examples of, 198–199
Gordon, Dr. Thomas, 191
Grammar, nature of, 250
Grant, application for, 218–219
Group compliment, 137

H

Hearing mode, 63
   example of, 63, 68
Hedges, 75, 116
   examples of, 27
   nature of, 27, 250
   revision of, 27–28
Help, refusal to give, 234–235
Hiring, letters for, 227–229
Holiday, best wishes for, 220

I

If/then construction
   examples of, 149, 152
   and presupposition, 149
Illness, sympathy about, 240–241
Illusion of choice, 81–84

example of, 82–84
nature of, 81, 250–251
I–message, 191
Indefinites
    to create emotional distance, 53
    nature of, 251
Indented format, business letters, 209
Information
    letter asking for, 211
    offering of, 231
Intonation, 251
Invitations
    letters of, 229–230
    thank you for, 241–242

J

Job
    application for, 219
    refusal of offer, 233
    refusal to hire, 235
    resignation from, 237
    sympathy about lost job, 240
    thank you for offer, 242

K

Keidel, Robert, 108

L

Language
    interaction, 251
    processing, 251
    Satir Modes, 257–259
        blaming, 45, 48, 257, 259
        computing, 46–47, 50–51, 258, 259
        distracting, 45–46, 258, 259
        leveling, 46, 47, 48, 258, 259
        placating, 257, 259
        results from, 259
Letter writing
    advantages of, 3–4
    business letters, formats for, 208–209
    customizing letters, 36–38
    format, *See* Business letters
    and nonstandard situations, 5–7
    sources for model letters, 205–206
    triple–F letter pattern, 34–36

Leveling
    examples of, 52, 53, 59, 92, 147, 171–172
    nature of, 46, 47, 48, 258
Loan
    application for, 218
    letter asking for, 211–212
Lost job, sympathy letter for, 240
Lunch, invitation to, 229
Lying
    social lies, 118
    writing carefully crafted truths, 117–119

M

Male/female communication, 176-77
Marriage, announcement of, 216
Membership
    application for, 219–220
    invitation to join organization, 229
    refusal of, 235
    resignation of, 237
    welcome to new member, 243
Metamessages, 76, 148, 187
    meaning of, 251
Metaphors, 93–95
    familiar metaphors, 94
    forms of, 93
    new metaphors, creation of, 94–95
    reasons for use of, 93, 95
    sports metaphors, use of, 106–108
Metastrategy, meaning of, 251
Miller, George, 64
Miller's Law, 255
    use of, 64
Moving to another location, announcement of, 216

N

New employee, announcement of, 216
New product, announcement of, 217
Nominal, nature of, 252
Nominalization
    meaning of, 251
    moving nominals to shift focus, 28–31
    and presuppositions, 15–17

O

Offering, letters of, 230–232
Opening of company, announcement of, 215
Organization
  invitation to join, 229
  resignation from, 239

P

Paper trail, laying paper trail letters, 150–153
Parallelism, 77–81, 103, 183
  advantages of, 79
  examples without deliberate parallelism, 78
  example with deliberate parallelism, 78–79
  nature of, 252
  purpose of, 77
Parentheses, use of, 247
Party, invitation to, 230
Past due account, notices of, 221
Performance, complaints about, 223–224
Period, use of, 247
Person, recommendation for, 237–238
Personal anecdote, using, 136–137
Placating, nature of, 257, 258
Place, recommendation about, 238
Plagiarism, nature of, 252
Possessives
  nature of, 252
  and presuppositions, 14–15
Postscripts
  favorable attitude towards, 203
  use of, 203
Praise, letters of, 232–233
Predicate, nature of, 252
Prepositions
  nature of, 152
  position of and formality of sentence, 124
Presuppositions, 13–18, 116
  and factives, 17–18
  and if/then construction, 149
  nature of, 252–253, 256
  negative presuppositions, 149
  and nominalization, 15–17
  positive presuppositions, 149

and possessives, 14–15
power of, 13–14
and time words, 149–150
Prize, offering of, 231
Procedure, recommendation for, 238–239
Products
  complaints about, 224
  new, announcement of, 217
  offering of, 231
  purchase of, 212
  recommendation for, 239
  refusal to buy, 234
  refusal to sell, 235–236
Professional, hiring of, 228
Property, refusal to sell, 235–236
Published material, complaints about, 224–225
Punctuation
  apostrophe, 245
  colon, 246
  comma, 246
  dash, 246
  for effects, 186–187
  ellipsis, 246
  exclamation point, 246–247
  parentheses, 247
  period, 247
  question mark, 247
  quotation marks, 247–248
  semicolon, 248
Purchase of product, letter for, 212

Q

Question mark, use of, 247
Quotation marks, use of, 247–248
Quotations, 96–99
  letters related to, 88–89, 97–99
  references for, 97
  sources for, 96–97

R

Recommendation
  letter asking for, 212–213
  letters of, 237–239
Reference, letter asking for, 212–213
Refusal, letters of, 233–236